REACH EVERYONE, TEACH EVERYONE

TEACHING AND LEARNING IN HIGHER EDUCATION
James M. Lang, Series Editor

Other titles in the series:

Teaching the Literature Survey Course: New Strategies
for College Faculty
Gwynn Dujardin, James M. Lang, and John A. Staunton

The Spark of Learning: Energizing the College Classroom
with the Science of Emotion
Sarah Rose Cavanagh

Reach Everyone, Teach Everyone

Universal Design for Learning in Higher Education

Thomas J. Tobin and Kirsten T. Behling

WEST VIRGINIA UNIVERSITY PRESS · MORGANTOWN 2018

Copyright © 2018 by West Virginia University Press
All rights reserved
First edition published 2018 by West Virginia University Press
Printed in the United States of America

ISBN:
Cloth 978-1-946684-59-2
Paper 978-1-946684-60-8
Ebook 978-1-946684-61-5

Library of Congress Cataloging-in-Publication Data is available
from the Library of Congress

Book and cover design by Than Saffel / WVU Press
Cover image by Foxy burrow / Shutterstock

One thing about systems, especially systems as old as American higher education, is that people grow unconscious of them. The system gets internalized. It becomes a mind-set. It is just "the way things are," and it can be hard to recover the reasons *why* it is the way things are. When academic problems appear intractable, it is often because an underlying systemic element is responsible, but no one quite sees what or where. People who work in the academy, like people in any institution or profession, are socialized to operate in certain ways, and when they are called upon to alter their practices, they sometimes find that they lack a compass to guide them.

—L. Menand, *The Marketplace of Ideas: Reform and Resistance in the American University*

CONTENTS

Acknowledgments ix
Introduction 1

Part 1 Where We Are Now

1. How Universal Design for Learning
   Got to Higher Education 19
2. It's the Law . . . Except When It Isn't 44

Part 2 Reframing UDL

3. Meet the Mobile Learners 73
4. Engage Digital Learners 98
5. Adopt the Plus-One Approach 128
6. Coach the Coaches and the Players 141

Part 3 Adopt UDL on Your Campus

7. Expand One Assignment 175
8. Enhance One Program: UDL across the Curriculum ... 203
9. Extend to One Modality: The Online Environment 219
10. Embrace One Mind-Set: Campuswide UDL 244
11. Engage! The UDL Life Cycle 270

Coda 285
References 287
Index 305
About the Authors 324

ACKNOWLEDGMENTS

This book would not have been possible without the generosity and support of colleagues throughout the United States and Canada. The authors wish to thank the myriad of people at colleges, universities, advocacy organizations, vendors, and in government who made time to talk with us, share their stories, and explain their research. Because this book provides a combination of evidence-based practices, case studies, and theoretical advice, we are indebted to the hard work of our colleagues who are proving the effectiveness of the UDL framework in their rubrics, courses, programs, products, theories, standards, and laws.

We could not fit all of their stories into this book. Their ideas nonetheless inform our writing and our conclusions. Of course, any infelicities in the text are our own, and we are especially grateful to the following people for their willingness to share their work and ideas with us over the past four years: Kimber Andrews, Eileen Bellmore, Ken Berchenbreiter, Fair Berg, Lisa Bibeau, Lily Bond, Christina Bosch, Roy Bowery, Wendy Brasuell-Fisher, Cynthia Brown-Laveist, Sheryl Burgstahler, Jordan Cameron, Andrew Cioffi, Rachael Cobb, Matt Crowley, Luciano da Rosa Dos Santos, Erin DeSilva, Karen Edwards, Richard Gorrie, Felicity Grandjean, Emily Griffin, Aisha Haines, Marcia Ham, Carey Hamburger, Beth Harrison, Carin Hedrick, Colin Hesse, Lance Hidy, Leonia Houston, Angela Jackson, Dennis James, Darin Jerke, Sam Johnston, Sara Kacin, Bruce Kelley, Jonathan Kulp, Doug Lawson, Elke Leeds, Andrew Lessman, Katie Linder, Patrick Loftus, Shaun Longstreet, Ryan Los, Laura Lubin, Trey Martindale, Julie McElherny, Lindsey Mercer, Art Morgan, Jessica Dzyak Morrison, Eric Mosterd, Anne de Laire Mulgrew, Adam Nemeroff, Bryan Ollendyke, Mathew Ouellett, Heidi Pettyjohn, Jessica Phillips, John Raible, Whitney Rapp, Scott Ready, Karen Rubinstein, Adam Schultz, Kate Sonka, Aaron Spector, Nancy Swenson, Roberta Thomson, Philip Voorhees, Sean Yo, and Todd Zakrajsek.

INTRODUCTION

Access and Accessibility

Access. That's what this book is really all about.

For a long time, when designers and theorists have talked about broadening people's access to learning opportunities, we in higher education often heard that in narrow and specific ways: accessibility for people with disabilities, alternative media formats to comply with legal and policy requirements, and accommodations to serve the needs of learners with physical barriers who use wheelchairs, hearing aids, or service animals. This thinking is incorrect—or at least incomplete, and this is no accident. The purpose of this book is to explore how this mind-set came into being, to describe the effects it has produced, and to advocate for a new way of framing our interactions with our learners across all of their experiences at our institutions.

When we change our mind-set—when we chop off the end of the word *accessibility* and think only about access—we free ourselves to create colleges and universities that truly serve the needs of an increasingly diverse population of learners. In addition to respecting the ethnic, gender, socioeconomic, and ability-based diversity on our campuses, we can design courses, services, and interactions that expand the reach and efficacy of higher education. In doing so, we also make it easier for our learners to achieve their goals, with a significant side benefit of making it easier for us to teach courses and deliver student- and faculty-facing services as well.

Because our interactions with our learners go well beyond the classroom, this book is intended for a broad higher education audience especially in the United States and Canada:

- faculty members of all descriptions (e.g., tenure-line professors, adjunct faculty members, graduate students, teaching assistants),

- staff members who serve students directly (e.g., those in the disability services, registrar, counseling, tutoring, and financial aid offices),
- administrators who support faculty efforts (e.g., teaching center staff, media services people, information technology offices), and
- campus leaders who are concerned with increasing student persistence, retention, and satisfaction (e.g., department chairs, deans, provosts, presidents, and chancellors).

In our conversations with two-year and technical colleges through Research-1 state systems, we hear stories about the need to balance our responsibility to provide access against the limitations of our human, financial, and time resources. *Reach Everyone, Teach Everyone* is a practical solutions–focused book for anyone who interacts with students and those who support them.

Universal Design for Learning

In this book, we will advocate that you adopt the conceptual framework known as Universal Design for Learning (UDL), which was first formalized in the 1990s by the neuroscientists at the Center for Applied Special Technology (CAST) in Boston. First adopted widely in the U.S. K–12 education world, UDL has recently gained attention in higher education (we will examine why this is so later on). UDL is an approach to the creation of learning experiences and interactions that incorporates multiple means of

- engaging with content and people,
- representing information, and
- expressing skills and knowledge (CAST, 2014b).

UDL has its roots in the concept of Universal Design (UD) in the built environment, an advocacy effort for the access rights of people with physical challenges. In the United States, the Architectural Barriers Act of 1968 mandated access for "physically handicapped persons" to buildings created or modified with federal funds (U.S. Access Board,

2016). After many years of protests by people with disabilities, the Americans with Disabilities Act (ADA) was passed in 1990 to mandate even broader access to the built environment (U.S. Department of Justice, 2016).

These days, more than twenty-five years since the ADA, we seldom think twice about the universal design that surrounds us. Curb cuts accommodate not just wheelchairs but bicycles, shopping carts, and rolling luggage. Wider doorways accommodate baby strollers, wheelchairs, and the kind friends helping you move your couch.

The fight for equal access rights to the built environment may seem to be largely won, thanks to the advocacy of people with disabilities and their allies. The end result has been to make the physical world more accessible for everyone—not just for people with disabilities.

Emotional Valence and Accommodations

Most of us have received accommodation requests from students with disabilities. Our emotional response to UDL gets inflected with the valence from our experiences making disability accommodations. Valence refers to our emotional coloring for "events, objects, and situations. . . . They may possess positive or negative valence; that is, they may possess intrinsic attractiveness or aversiveness" (Frijda, 1986, 207).

We all know how faculty members and staff members *should* respond when students come to them with disability accommodation forms at the end of the second week of class (because the paperwork never seems to be done on time), saying, "I need time and a half on tests." Of course, the answer should be "Sure, I'll set that up." This, thankfully, is how most people do respond. But how do a lot of us actually feel about accommodation requests?

Researchers have been studying for decades how we in higher education respond to students with learning challenges. In a dozen large research studies (Fonosch and Schwab, 1981; Fichten, 1986; Nelson et al., 1990; Houck et al., 1992; Bento, 1996; Benham, 1997; Bigaj et al., 1999; Cook et al., 2009; Murray et al., 2009, 2011; Zhang et al., 2010; Lombardi and Murray, 2011), the emotional valence associated with accommodations is almost uniformly negative.

In many faculty members' minds, the fact that one must accommodate learners with disabilities brings up feelings of uncertainty, confusion, annoyance, and even anger. These emotions came to the surface in one 2017 instance, when Michael Schlesinger, a professor of atmospheric sciences at the University of Illinois at Urbana-Champaign, was placed on paid administrative leave because he refused to provide electronic copies of lecture slides in advance of class sessions for a student who had a documented disability accommodation. Schlesinger argued that "based on my experience of providing all my students my lecture slides after each lecture for most if not all of the 16 times I have taught this course, I knew that one-third of my class would cease coming to my lectures if I provided them my lecture slides electronically. And their ceasing to attend my lectures would lower their course grades" (Flaherty, 2017). The professor derided the disability services staff member who notified him about the student's accommodation, writing, "although you have a doctorate, I doubt that you teach. Although you have a doctorate, I doubt that you do research," and saying that he would "fight for a more balanced approach to assisting disabled students, an approach that does not disadvantage non-disabled students" (Flaherty, 2017).

Most of us do not react to such an extreme, thankfully. Whether we act consciously on negative emotions or not, they ground our approach to learners with disabilities. In the research literature and in interviews with faculty members and staffers throughout North America, we hear similar feedback:

- "I don't have time to do all that work if it benefits just a few students with disabilities."
- "My institution doesn't have a captioning service. I'd have to do it all myself, and I have a lot of videos."
- "I think at least a few of my students are trying to game the system by claiming to have disabilities."
- "I know I should follow the law, but no one at my institution is enforcing it."
- "I haven't had a student with a disability for years. I will just wait until I get an accommodation request."

In all of these scenarios, the contrary is actually so. Sam Johnston, a research scientist at CAST, says that "we want a situation that is good for everybody. Part of it is thinking about what has to happen at the level of design that makes accommodation less necessary" (personal communication, November 15, 2013). Johnston means that by adopting UDL principles in our course design, we greatly reduce the need for specific accommodation requests. This message is weakened by the same fundamental misperception that makes the atmospheric scientist's story such a preventable one: UDL isn't about accommodations.

So, What Do We Do Next?

Most of our existing college and university training programs and advocacy for adopting UDL stand poor chances of being effective due to the negative emotional valence associated with making disability accommodations—even though UDL is not a means of granting individual disability accommodations (making one change, one time, to help one person). Despite this, our collective experience of making accommodations colors our response to a term we think is associated with the same subject: learners with disabilities. We react.

We react for many reasons. Applying UDL can be expensive and resource intensive. It takes design-level thinking, often beyond our current scope of subject expertise. UDL is not perceived as being for everyone—just for people with disabilities. The work we put into UDL is perceived as benefiting a small slice of our learners, so why not just wait until we get accommodation requests?

We must first uncouple UDL from the negative emotional valence of people's experiences with accommodation requests. For that, we propose two reframing statements; these form the core principles of the book you are about to read.

- Our students today aren't like our students fifteen years ago.
- Our faculty members aren't like their counterparts from the past, either.

Oh, Wait, I Was Looking at My Phone

First, we should reframe UDL beyond a narrow disability services mind-set and situate it in an emotionally neutral narrative with which we're all familiar: mobile learning. This helps us address some key challenges in higher education. For example, in comparison with learners just fifteen years ago, college students today are

- more likely to require remediation (Adams, 2015),
- more likely to have poor study and time-management skills (College Board, 2015), and
- less likely to have significant time for study outside of the classroom (College Board, 2015).

Many college students are adult learners with families and jobs—and little time for studying: "Adult learners are juggling family, work, and educational responsibilities. They don't do optional" (Mason, 2014). Even our eighteen- to twenty-two-year-old students are often juggling work and study responsibilities. Today, the young, single college student who lives at home, takes a full load of courses, and focuses solely on his or her studies is, with few exceptions, a mythical creature.

On the other hand, a recent EDUCAUSE study shows that 86 percent of college students in North America own smartphones (Chen et al., 2015). Couple this with busy lifestyles, and adopting a mobile-friendly design framework like UDL fosters anytime, anywhere learning: "As an integral part of students' daily lives, mobile technology has changed how they communicate, gather information, allocate time and attention, and potentially how they learn. . . . Learners are no longer limited to the classroom's geographical boundaries; for example, they can now record raw observations and analyze data on location. Furthermore, mobile technology platforms let individuals discuss issues with their colleagues or classmates in the field. The ever-growing mobile landscape thus represents new opportunities for learners both inside and outside the classroom" (Chen et al., 2015). The argument for adopting UDL has always been based on its benefits for all learners, but for years we haven't had a simple case that demonstrates those benefits. Now we have one: UDL reaches out to learners on mobile devices and gives them more time for studying (Tobin, 2014, 20–24). Giving learners with family, work, and service obligations just twenty more minutes in their busy days for learning and interacting can be the difference between struggling and keeping up with their studies.

UDL Is Not Just Faculty Members' Job

Next, we should move the focus away from training only faculty members about UDL. Let's train the people who support them: information technology (IT) departments, teaching-and-learning centers, media services areas, academic department staff, and the help desk.

There is near consensus among academics that institutions are responsible for providing education to the broadest audience of learners (Rapp and Arndt, 2012). Too often, though, we leave inclusion to the office of disability services or to individual faculty members. UDL training courses increase faculty members' confidence in working with students across the ability spectrum (Murray, Lombardi, and Wren, 2011), but the higher education UDL adoption rate hovers around 10 percent of faculty members (cf. Murray et al., 2009). Why? Faculty members don't do what they used to.

Over the past three decades, the role of faculty members has become increasingly atomized. Included in their primary duties, faculty members in 1985 were expected to

- design their course structure,
- create individual syllabi,
- pull together ancillary materials (e.g., prof packs, transparencies, and vendor-produced VHS tapes),
- teach course sessions,
- grade student work, and
- hold office hours.

Today, faculty members are still responsible for content expertise. However, much of what used to be an individual faculty member's job is now the responsibility of the whole faculty (e.g., agreeing on common syllabi, reading lists, and texts) or support staff (e.g., creating videos, multimedia, and learning management system [LMS] content). Often course content and interactions are designed by a team made up of the faculty members, an instructional designer, a media specialist, an IT coder, and others throughout the institution. UDL training should focus on the people who actually put together the interactions for learners, and here we're referring not only to designing courses but also to designing the interactions that students have with our application processes, registrar's offices, tutoring services, and other touchpoints common to the higher education experience. For all types of interactions, we can apply UDL principles to make it easier for everyone to engage with them. Implementing UDL principles across an institution requires leadership support and resources. As Candyce Rennegarbe at Tacoma Community College reports, the investment is worth it:

> By far, strong administrative support is the most important element. Our Vice President of Academic and Student Affairs has supported this project with funding and personal support since we started. He has used Achieving the Dream [program] funds and reserve funds; no major grant funding has been accessed to fund this project. We give release time to a faculty member to be the project manager in an affordable way to make sure there is sustained leadership. . . . We have also secured stipends for faculty members and mentors and have involved the instructional research department from the beginning. We have a strong cross-disciplinary advisory team (Dean/VP of Instruction, Access Services, E-Learning, Developmental Studies, Professional Development, Student Services, Faculty), and strong support for building technology resources on campus. (Quoted in Meyer, Rose, and Gordon, 2014, 169)

This approach—training those who actually do the development work on materials and interactions on which UDL touches—results in greater levels of adoption of UDL across the institution (Meyer, Rose, and Gordon, 2014, 172–73).

The College STAR (Supporting Transition, Access, and Retention) consortium, for example, is a UDL success story. Colleges and universities across North Carolina used a federal grant to create a curriculum shared across campuses (College STAR, 2015). All participating campuses sent their support and design staff to UDL training sessions; now all courses are created with UDL principles in mind.

This is the goal of UDL, after all: to reduce barriers to learning for everyone. While we should always keep learners with disabilities in mind, we serve the broadest audience by situating UDL as a way to reach mobile learners through anytime, anywhere interactions, and we should train our support staff in UDL so faculty members who want to innovate are automatically presented with UDL as simply being the way things are done at our institutions.

Looking Ahead

With this book, we want to accomplish three interconnected tasks. First, we want to provide an alternative way of perceiving UDL, to reframe it so that we can move the conversation beyond the narrower confines of disability service advocacy. Second, we want to show you how to actually do some specific tasks that help to establish UDL principles throughout the design of interactions in your institution's courses and student services. Finally, we want to offer concrete ways to talk with senior campus leaders in order to demonstrate that UDL is not only a way to comply with accessibility laws but also a sound educational and business practice that has been demonstrated again and again to move the needle on issues dear to campus leaders: student persistence, retention, and satisfaction.

Part 1 of the book is called "Where We Are Now." It provides a general overview of what UDL is, where it came from, and how it functions in higher education.

In chapter 1, we offer a brief history of how UDL came to the attention of colleges and universities across North America. What started as an offshoot of the physical access movement was first called UDL and adopted in the K–12 education system in the United States. We will show how a field that was originally focused on the use of assistive technology (AT) to help students with disabilities expanded exponentially as the technology in everyone's pockets became advanced enough to support UDL on an anywhere, anytime basis. In recent years, UDL has rapidly gone from being an advocacy topic put forward by our college and university disability services offices to a comprehensive access-as-a-civil-right program adopted by whole institutions. Chapter 1 is a solid overview for those who are teaching, those supporting faculty members, disability- and student-service professionals, and campus leaders.

Chapter 2 examines the legal requirements with which UDL helps institutions to comply, and also shows how legal compliance—unless it is forced on you—is seldom the best place from which to start your campus UDL adoption program. You'll hear why disability access advocacy organizations filed high-profile lawsuits against colleges and universities, and we will share some takeaway lessons for the rest of us, based on how those institutions have responded. Chapter 2 is most useful for disability service providers, administrators who support faculty members, and campus leaders.

In part 2 of the book, "Reframing UDL," we discuss why the right time for adopting UDL is now. Social, technological, and resource circumstances are different today than they were just fifteen years ago, and we share ways that you can talk to your colleagues and institutional leaders about why it is now possible to adopt UDL as an approach for broad, general benefits to faculty members, institutional staff, and the students they serve.

Chapter 3 is a deeper dive into a trend many years in the making: now that nearly everyone has an Internet-capable phone, we've turned into a society of information-browsing consumers. We will show you how to turn questions like "Google, where is the nearest Mexican restaurant?" into a research-supported rationale for expanding access to learning interactions beyond the classroom, office walls, and support staffers. Chapter 3 is most useful for faculty members and the administrators who support them.

Chapter 4 focuses on how technology, although not essential for inclusive design, really enhances our ability to create interactions that can take place at anytime, anywhere. Our learners are already using technology in their lives. The work that we do as educators to reach out proactively through design and provide students with just twenty more minutes for studying in their already busy day pays us back many times over. The biggest challenge to adopting UDL has been, for decades, answering why we would do a significant amount of work to benefit what some colleagues perceive as a very small number of students—those with disabilities. We provide practical arguments for why faculty members and staffers should start using UDL principles in the first place. In this way, your institution can grow beyond the typical 10 percent of faculty members who adopt inclusive-design practices. Chapter 4 is most useful for faculty members and the administrators who support them.

In chapter 5, we continue the reframing conversation by demystifying the neuroscience behind the concept of UDL in a simple, easy-to-remember and easy-to-implement mental model of plus-one thinking. By situating the project of adopting UDL principles less in a scientific argument and more in a conceptual one, you will see greater adoption and more creativity in how UDL gets expressed. We share the stories and research data to help you increase the usefulness of UDL across campus. Chapter 5 gives faculty members and the administrators who support them a solid approach to responding to the needs of diverse learners.

In chapter 6 we make a radical argument for reframing UDL. If faculty members are the only ones who are trained in UDL and who are expected to implement it, your institutional UDL program will likely never get off the ground. UDL is, by its very nature, a reflective and painstaking process, and the surest way to success is to train not just faculty members but the people who support faculty and student populations, as well, in UDL principles. We will show you real-world examples of colleges and universities that have adopted just such an it's-just-the-way-we-do-business approach to UDL and inclusive design. Chapter 6 is most useful for disability and student service providers, administrators who support faculty members, and campus leaders.

Part 3, "Adopt UDL on Your Campus," is where we get practical. We share the specific projects, programs, and plans that you can use in order to help your entire campus adopt inclusive design. We share the research about why it's effective, not just in an it's-the-right-thing-to-do sort of way but also where institutional leaders want to see positive change: in student retention, persistence, and satisfaction.

The structure of part 3 starts out small, in chapter 7, where we share how to look at one assignment or one interaction with an eye toward applying UDL to offer participants more freedom, more choices, and to make things generally easier and smoother—for the institution, faculty, and staff, as well as for the students. The success stories in this chapter are compelling models from across the curriculum and across the institution, and we show you how to get the maximum impact for the work you will put into the design of one interaction (hint: ask where learners always have questions or get things wrong, and you'll likely find a starting point for applying UDL). Chapter 7 is most useful for faculty members and the administrators who support them by providing practical examples around UDL and assignments.

Once you've shown your colleagues that UDL helps to save them time and energy, increases their end-of-course student ratings, and reduces the number of students who need special accommodations, it's time to scale up your UDL program to the department or college level. Chapter 8 contains the project-based elements that go into a successful UDL program for an entire department, including the roles that team members play, how to keep momentum going, and where to focus resources in order to reap the greatest benefits. Chapter 8 is most useful for faculty members and the administrators who support them, while also offering resources for disability- and student-service providers.

In chapter 9, we expand our focus again by examining the online and technology tools and interactions that support most learners' face-to-face, blended, and online interactions with colleges and universities. Although technology is not necessary for good UDL to take place, the inclusion of common technologies in our UDL tool kit offers faculty members and support staff a simple and easy-to-grasp reason to begin using UDL principles. Chapter 9 is most useful for faculty members who teach with technology, the administrators who support them, and disability service professionals who support students in technology-enhanced courses.

The final stage of UDL adoption is at the institutional level, where UDL becomes just part of what we do and is embedded into the cultural practices of the institution itself. The University of Cincinnati followed a process like the one we outline in chapter 10. In a 2016 interview, Heidi Pettyjohn and Kimber Andrews told us how the University of Cincinnati moved from compliance to commitment to culture:

- **Compliance.** The university applies an audit tool to its publicly available web content in order to identify gaps in accessibility, builds awareness across campus about access challenges for all types of learners, and provides training in good interaction design techniques for faculty members and support staff.
- **Commitment.** The university gears up for making needed changes. All areas of the institution identify the resources they will need in order to equip their staff to remedy challenges as they are found.
- **Culture.** The university adopts UDL principles in the design of all interactions between learners and materials, each other, instructors, support staff, and the wider world. UDL becomes just a part of what we do here. (Andrews and Pettyjohn, 2016)

We share a similar broad-based approach, including how to measure success and reinvest resources once the basic work of UDL is in place. Chapter 10 is most useful for disability and student service providers, administrators who support faculty members, and campus leaders.

This book ends where it begins by bringing new voices into the mix. In chapter 11, we offer strategic techniques for moving UDL out of the realm of projects (things that have a defined beginning and ending) and into the realm of operations, where UDL becomes baked into the everyday running of your college or university. The UDL life cycle guides you through the entire UDL process and offers real-world advice about hiring new faculty members, staff, and leaders who can move the campus forward with inclusive practices, and how best to sustain gains and good practices at your institution. Chapter 11 is useful for all audiences, as it brings the concept of UDL from its infancy full circle to the impact it can have in higher education.

Multiple Paths through This Book

UDL is all about offering learners choices in how they move through the interactions that we design for them, and our book is no different. Although we hope that the entire book will be useful for every reader, we have created a suggested first-read chart (see table 1), based on the role that you play in your college or university. Chapters with check marks are first-read recommendations.

The Requisite Disclaimer

In this book, we will talk about a number of U.S. and Canadian laws related to accessibility, inclusive design, and UDL. We are obliged to mention that the information contained in this book is provided for educational purposes only, is not a substitute for legal advice, and should not be construed as the rendering of a legal opinion. The authors are also not lawyers (we don't even play them on TV). The ideas and materials herein are based on more than twenty-five years of our practice as educators, faculty developers, disability services advocates, and all-around accessibility nerds.

So, Why UDL, and Why Now?

This book is all about the types of thought processes and the mindsets that UDL encourages. Today, many college and university professionals are "doing inclusion" or "doing diversity" from a limited, deficiencies-based, or savior point of view. We invite you and your colleagues to adopt a broader and more practically oriented way of doing inclusive design: UDL.

In 1979, the Florida Orange Growers Association ran television ads proclaiming that orange juice was a drink for any time of day; their slogan was "it isn't just for breakfast anymore." We want to do the same thing for UDL and show you how to spread the word that it's an anytime strategy. After all, UDL isn't just for people with disabilities anymore.

Table 1. Suggested first-read chart

	Campus leaders (e.g., department chairs, deans, provosts, presidents, and chancellors)	Faculty services staff (e.g., teaching center, media services, information technology)	Student services staff (e.g., disability services, registrar, counseling, tutoring, financial aid)	Faculty members (e.g., tenure-line professors, adjunct faculty members, graduate students, teaching assistants, instructors)
Chapter 1: How UDL Got to Higher Education	✓	✓	✓	✓
Chapter 2: It's the Law . . . Except When It Isn't		✓	✓	✓
Chapter 3: Meet the Mobile Learners	✓		✓	✓
Chapter 4: Engage Digital Learners	✓		✓	
Chapter 5: Adopt the Plus-One Approach	✓		✓	
Chapter 6: Coach the Coaches and the Players		✓	✓	✓
Chapter 7: Expand One Assignment	✓		✓	
Chapter 8: Enhance One Program	✓	✓	✓	
Chapter 9: Extend to One Modality	✓	✓	✓	
Chapter 10: Embrace One Mind-Set		✓	✓	✓
Chapter 11: Engage! The UDL Life Cycle	✓	✓	✓	✓

PART 1

Where We Are Now

CHAPTER 1

How Universal Design for Learning Got to Higher Education

Meet Kate

Kate Sonka is the academic specialist for the Academic Technology Office in the College of Arts and Letters at Michigan State University, and she is the driving force behind their annual Accessible Learning Conference. We spoke with Sonka in 2017 about how Michigan State created space for accessibility, generally, and for Universal Design for Learning (UDL), in particular. "I came on board with MSU to work on a large project: just reviewing accessibility, understanding what that is for a higher education audience of students, faculty members, and administrators. Up until a few years ago, we talked about accommodations for people with disabilities when we did onboarding for new faculty members, but we didn't have a good way of talking with faculty members about how to be inclusive as a broad practice" (Sonka, 2017).

In our conversation, Sonka revealed that the key to adopting UDL came when she and her colleagues started talking to faculty members, support staffers, and campus leaders in terms of student needs and benefits: "I worked with an undergraduate student who had gotten grant funding to create a series of tutorials about accessibility, and I came to see the value of the student perspective." That student graduated and then joined the MSU team in their central information technology (IT) area. The president and provost soon signed an update to the university's 2009 accessibility policy, explicitly adopting both technical standards for multimedia and a UDL framework for the design of interactions (Michigan State University, 2015). The policy also, importantly, adopts unit-level five-year plans and a purchasing workflow for assessing third-party tools for accessibility. We will explore these ideas in chapters 9 and 10.

For Sonka, UDL principles (which we'll explore in this chapter) served as the framework that allowed everyone on campus to approach accessibility without limiting their perspective solely to disability services. "MSU is all about experiential learning: studying abroad, working in internships. No matter what kind of teaching and research we engage in, there is a place for students in all of that work" (Sonka, 2017). Sonka conceived of a conference to bring together everyone on campus to talk about UDL and accessibility.

Because UDL had been widely adopted in the K–12 world but not yet in higher education, having students themselves advocate for broader access to learning was a winning strategy with the university's senior leaders. "Once we got beyond the echo chamber" of her team, the disability services coordinators, and the central IT staff, Sonka says that "our students helped us to make the case to our president and provost for a one-year experiment to put very different 'buckets' of people together via the conference." The first accessible learning conference (see Michigan State University, 2017) was a response to feedback from students and faculty members about a felt need within the university community, with many people "feeling as though they were floating out there on their own." The conference provided forums for asking questions and resource-sharing opportunities for faculty members and staff members; Sonka's aim was for the conference "to be a way for people to see each other as resources."

Sonka's team has seen precisely the kind of networking and conversations that they envisioned: "we had hoped that UDL would help us to demonstrate the value of students being part of solutions. We value their voices, and they are learning about skills and theories. Other units on campus are asking how they can get involved."

Sonka's story is one of bringing a new frame—UDL—to an existing challenge: How do colleges and universities improve student persistence, retention, and satisfaction? How do we do better at keeping the students we already have, and how do we reach out to new populations of potential students whom we have traditionally served poorly or not at all? UDL is an especially practical response to these questions, but higher education has been relatively late to the UDL game. To understand why, we have to start back in the 1960s, with the architectural concept of Universal Design (UD).

From UD to UDL

In architecture, Universal Design is "the design of products, environments, and communication to be usable by all people, to the greatest extent possible, without adaptation or specialized design" (Institute for Human Centered Design, 2016). Imagine that you are moving into a new house. The three steps leading to the front door will present a barrier to your elderly neighbor visiting with a welcome-to-the-neighborhood gift, to your daughter bringing your grandson over in his stroller, and to you when you are carrying in your couch. Design the house to be universally accessible from the beginning, however, and you create a welcoming space for all.

We can trace the formal concept of UD back to architect Ron Mace (Schwab, 2015). Mace had polio as a child and used a wheelchair to get around. He recognized in the 1950s that the U.S. population was aging. He foresaw that people who were no longer able to navigate stairs or small bathrooms would have to move out of their unusable homes and into nursing facilities or the homes of relatives. Mace believed that if architects designed homes to be "usable by everyone to the greatest extent possible" from the beginning, then more people could continue to stay at home as they aged (Gaylord et al., 2004). The fundamental idea of extending such barrier-free environments to everyone was introduced in the United States partly through the 1968 Architectural Barriers Act.

The concept of Universal Design makes intuitive sense. Designing supermarkets to have sliding doors with electronic sensors allows more people to enter and exit the store with ease: people pushing shopping carts as well as people in wheelchairs. By adding audio signals to traffic intersections, more people can cross safely: those who are guided by the visual walk signals and those paying attention to the audio chirp. By adding closed-captioning to television programs, more people can enjoy them: viewers who are learning the language, who want to keep up with unfamiliar accents, or who have hearing impairments. All of these design elements in the built environment are simple, unobtrusive, and make our lives easier. We may not even think of them as originating to support a certain group of people— people with physical disabilities.

And yet, if you ask scholars where these affordances come from, most will point to Universal Design, specifically as it applies to barrier-free living. The 1950s saw the beginning of the deinstitutionalization movement. People with disabilities were removed from institutional settings and placed into inclusive community-based settings. Architects and city planners began examining how to make such transitions more successful for people with physical disabilities. This movement also coincided with the U.S. civil rights movement, also motivated by equality. The civil rights of people with disabilities then became an action item for lawmakers, who, with Section 504 of the Rehabilitation Act of 1973, included physical access to public spaces as a condition for receiving federal financial assistance.

This civil rights movement was extended in 1988 with the Fair Housing Act, which requires builders to ensure that people with disabilities can get physical access to multifamily housing. The Americans with Disability Act (ADA) of 1990 took the initiative further when it required both public and private entities to ensure equal access to their physical space, regardless of whether they received federal funding. Suddenly, this meant that any public places people went (restaurants, shops, libraries, parks, theaters, museums) must be accessible.

As the United States progressed in its efforts to ensure equal access to the built environment, disability rights advocates began raising awareness that telecommunication was also not accessible. Shortly after the ADA was signed into law, Congress amended Section 508 of the Rehabilitation Act to include all communication and information technology. This meant that phone lines, television shows, movies, the Internet, and information kiosks must be accessible. This extension of UD principles from the physical environment to the digital one was a major step toward the eventual creation of UDL.

Table 2. Seven principles for Universal Design (Connell et al., 1997)

Principle	Definition
Equitable use	The design is useful and marketable to people with diverse abilities.
Flexibility in use	The design accommodates a wide range of individual preferences and abilities.
Simple and intuitive	Use of the design is easy to understand, regardless of the user's experience, knowledge, language skills, or current concentration level.
Perceptible information	The design communicates necessary information effectively to the user, regardless of ambient conditions or the user's sensory abilities.
Tolerance for error	The design minimizes hazards and the adverse consequences of accidental or unintended actions.
Low physical effort	The design can be used efficiently and comfortably and with a minimum of fatigue.
Size and space for approach and use	Appropriate size and space is provided for approach, reach, manipulation, and use regardless of user's body size, posture, or mobility.

In short, Universal Design became a conceptual framework that supports the civil rights of all American citizens. It reduces the need for people with disabilities to have to ask for special treatment through accommodations (making one change, one time, for one person), instead promoting a more holistic existence through UD that is aimed at making life easier for everyone.

The work that Mace initiated continues today at the Center for Universal Design at North Carolina State University. The Center for UD developed seven principles to guide the designs of environments, products, and communications (see table 2). Over the years, these principles have guided designers in the work they do, while also uniting people with various needs through equal access.

UDL in Elementary and Secondary Education

The transition from UD in the built world to UDL in the sphere of educational interactions was a gradual one that started in the K–12 world. If students cannot get access to school buildings, then they are at a disadvantage compared to their peers. Likewise, if students cannot participate in the curriculum or methods of instruction, then they are also at a disadvantage. UDL examines what happens once students get through those school doors. How can we remove the barriers in the learning environment?

David Rose and his colleagues at the Center for Applied Special Technology (CAST) argue that UDL "puts the tag 'disabled' where it belongs—on the curriculum, not the learner. The curriculum is disabled when it does not meet the needs of diverse learners" (Council for Exceptional Children, 2011). The scientists at CAST incorporated neuroscience into the mind-set of UDL because UD principles that were created to guide the design of things (e.g., buildings, products) were not adequate for the design of social interactions (e.g., human learning environments).

In the 1990s, CAST began by examining the diversity and academic success of students in U.S. public elementary and secondary schools. Was it an indication of students' ability when some seemed unable to pay attention to their teachers after fifteen minutes of lecturing? Were students whose first language was not English being punished unfairly because they couldn't take notes fast enough? Why were students who did not have access to computers weaker than their peers on writing concepts? CAST looked holistically at student demographics, methods of instruction, and curriculum design, initially seeking a frame that would fit all of these differences into one instructional method. Their finding, however, was that variability is the norm: no two students learn alike, regardless of ability. Curriculum design at the time was largely monolithic, forcing all students to receive information and demonstrate skills in only one way. David Gordon writes about the need to recognize and design for learner variability: "Options are essential to learning, because no single way of presenting information, no single way of responding to information, and no single way of

Table 3. Universal Design for Learning (CAST, 2016b)

Brain Network	Question	Solution
Recognition	The what of learning. How do we gather information?	Present information in multiple ways.
Strategic	The how of learning. How do we express our ideas?	Differentiate the ways that students can express what they know.
Affective	The why of learning. How do we motivate learners?	Find a way to connect with student interests. Provide multiple methods of engaging with the material.

engaging students will work across the diversity of students that populate our classrooms. Alternatives reduce barriers to learning for students with disabilities while enhancing learning opportunities for everyone" (Council for Exceptional Children, 2011). CAST set about translating Mace's principles of Universal Design for the built environment into a design for interactions in the elementary and secondary education systems. Their resulting framework is called Universal Design for Learning (UDL; see table 3), and it maps the seven principles of UD into three principles specific to learning and neurological processing, focused on three brain-based information networks.

It is important to note that, in the UDL framework, there is no requirement that information be presented in all of its different possible permutations, or in one unique way per student, as in the theory of Differentiated Instruction (DI), which asks teachers to identify the strengths of their learners and then customize instruction to play to those strengths. Rather, UDL posits that designing for learner variability ahead of time—before instructors even know their students—is the most effective way to reduce individual accommodation needs. In other words, offering students choices in how to recognize, engage with, and report back the information that they learned increases the chances that instructors can connect with their students and their learning needs.

UDL has been successfully adopted by many elementary and secondary schools since the 1990s. For example, an elementary school science teacher in Massachusetts whom Kirsten Behling knows saw UDL as an opportunity to support students from various cultural backgrounds in her classroom. After a class activity went poorly, the teacher asked her students to engage actively in a class discussion in which they could push back against her, but she met quite a bit of reluctance from some students. When she reflected on why this happened with some learners, she suggested that in some cultures it is considered rude to contradict or challenge authority figures like teachers.

In addition, for some students, speaking up in class causes paralyzing fear. Recognizing this, the science teacher used UDL to foster a sense of collaboration and community among her students by encouraging the students to be active members of the teacher/student process through means that worked for them. She gave her students opportunities to reflect on how the lessons were going, choosing from journal writing, class discussions, and anonymous surveys. The reflective assignments provided students with a comfortable outlet for sharing their thoughts and provided the teacher with feedback on what was working in the class. By creating multifaceted ways for students to share their opinions and then using those opinions, she created an environment that optimized learning.

Another example of a UDL success story comes from a grade 10 English teacher in Ontario whom Tom Tobin knows. The teacher was considering whether to ask his class to read *To Kill a Mockingbird*. Some students were high achievers who would benefit from the traditional read-out-loud-and-discuss model. Others were visibly unengaged, and a few had Individualized Education Programs (IEPs) that required audiobooks and guided prompts throughout the content. The teacher wondered whether taking on a novel as complex as *To Kill a Mockingbird* was really wise, given the diversity of learners in his class. After speaking with a UDL facilitator, he decided to give it a try. The first thing he did was to make sure that all of the students had access to the audio version of the book, not just the students with disabilities. This immediately gave his students a choice of how to experience the book. He also started off the lesson by showing them scenes from the 1962 Robert Mulligan film.

Some of his colleagues questioned this decision, claiming that the students wouldn't read the book if they had access to the audio version or had seen the film. The English teacher argued that it was more important for students to have a general knowledge of the story and cultural milieu, which the movie would provide, and the book itself would serve to fill in the details. Indeed, knowledge construction and analysis were the stated learning objectives for the unit that the teacher had prepared. His UDL approach tied the choices given to learners directly to the goals, objectives, and targets of the interactions, and that is why the approach was effective.

The teacher asked the students to research a historical occurrence that happened during the book's time frame that was interesting to them, and to teach the class about it. The students worked in groups and researched everything from the music of the civil rights era to well-known leaders and the laws referred to in the story. Giving the students choices about how they responded to the common text increased their engagement with the subject. The English teacher believes that if he had not added the principles of UDL to his first foray into *To Kill a Mockingbird* it would not have been so successful.

UDL in Higher Education

In the United States and Canada, higher education has not been as quick to adopt UDL as it has been in the elementary and secondary settings. UDL in higher education began in earnest in the early 2000s, when the Office of Postsecondary Education (OPE) in the U.S. Department of Education created grants for colleges and universities seeking to bring the concept to higher education. The OPE saw the positive effects of inclusive-design efforts in elementary and secondary education and recognized that as students in those schools graduated and transitioned to college, they would expect the same breadth of learning opportunities they had previously enjoyed. Many of those who applied for and received federal grants were members of disability services offices in colleges and universities. In the early 2000s, campus disability services offices were most likely to be part of conversations about inclusive education and were the campus areas most likely to know about the work of CAST. They also saw UDL as a built-in service to improve the educational experiences of both their students with disabilities as well as of those who chose not to disclose disabilities or who had yet to come to their office.

The success of the OPE grants was enormous. These grants worked to figure out how to bring inclusive design to college and university campuses, given the differences among elementary, secondary, and higher education. Grant-funded researchers recognized the difficulty in mandating any particular training or implementation scheme in college and university settings. For this reason, most grantees created implementation frameworks not through a disability services lens but, rather, through the diversity lens that Mace had established years before for UD.

The goal of the OPE grants was to increase awareness about inclusive design in higher education. Different OPE-grant institutions created or adopted different definitions and approaches to accessibility, all based on UD. Each of these definitions, approaches, and strategies differs slightly in its approach and scope.

Some institutions simply adopted the core principles of Universal Design (UD) as-is from the Center for UD. The University of Wisconsin system used the UD architectural principles to increase access for students with disabilities. They focused on using UD to increase the accessibility and usability of the educational technology that the university was using at the time.

Other institutions focused on crafting education-specific offshoots from UD. Universal Course Design (UCD) includes curriculum design, instruction techniques, assessment methods, and learning environment design. The University of New Hampshire and the University of Massachusetts Boston collaborated to create UCD core teams: in-house support teams that helped small groups of faculty members to modify their course designs during the course of a semester.

Universal Design for Instruction (UDI) and Universal Design in Education (UDE) are closely linked in that they both apply the seven architectural UD principles to higher education spaces. OPE grantees who adopted UDI and UDE tended to focus on making physical environments more accessible and flexible. Longwood University developed a training curriculum to support new, part-time, and temporary foreign-language instructors in inclusive classroom techniques. The University of Connecticut crafted three phased projects intent on including students with learning disabilities in college courses. The Disabilities, Opportunities, Internetworking, and Technology (DO-IT) Center at the University of Washington established a national reputation for collecting and developing resources to support instructors in applying UDE tenets, and later adopted the UDL framework for its materials and approach.

The focus of this book is UDL, which follows the three principles of multiple means of engagement, representation, and action established by CAST. At Temple University, the OPE-grant project included UDL in the orientations for new faculty and staff members, who were then asked to incorporate the principles in their courses and student interactions. The University of Iowa conducted a campus UDL needs assessment and developed a university-wide policy focusing on the goal of giving universal access to learning interactions. The University of Hawaii combined UDL with multiculturalism and mentoring in an effort to get campus staffers and faculty members to better support diverse learners. Colorado State University's twice-funded project focused on supporting faculty members in adding UDL strategies to the materials they created for their courses.

The OPE grants resulted in a diverse group of researchers trying to figure out how best to introduce the concept of inclusive design into the college environment. Each project branched out on its own to create its own sense of how inclusive design could be integrated into the higher education landscape. Despite the varying acronyms and strategies, UD, UCD, UDI, UDE, and UDL all try to answer the same question. How do colleges and universities adopt a set of design principles for learners' interactions with materials, each other, their instructors, and the wider world that positively affects the greatest number of students from the start?

This book focuses on the UDL framework as the most easily adopted in colleges and universities. CAST's theory that learner variability is best addressed by inclusive design is supported by brain-based science and decades of evidence from the K–12 world. UDL is rapidly gaining recognition and adoption in higher education, but it still has not been adopted by colleges and universities to the same extent as in the K–12 world: hence, this book. Many higher education faculty and staff members are using UDL strategies in their work. Colleges and universities are increasingly broadening the scope of their efforts to address student diversity across an increasing number of identity spaces, including ethnicity, socioeconomic status, gender and sexual identity, and, now, the ability spectrum.

For example, Lyman Dukes at the University of South Florida at St. Petersburg worked with his accessibility committee to study the impact of captioning on all students in a law and business course. He recorded his lectures and gathered all of the multimedia materials that he used throughout the semester. He then captioned all of his videos and posted them online for his students to access. At the end of the semester, he surveyed his students about their attitudes toward captioning. Ninety-four percent of his students reported that the ability to turn on the captions while watching his videos was helpful, and 92 percent of them actively used the captions. Only 1 percent of his students reported working with the university's disability services office, although 13 percent said that they identified as having a disability and had not yet registered. Dukes's small-scale study is an example of the individual approach many faculty members have taken toward implementing UDL principles in their courses (Dukes, 2014).

Some institutions have entire departments that have embraced UDL. In Boston, Suffolk University's Mathematics Department faculty members have rethought the way that they offer instruction to their students. After dealing with inaccessible textbooks and an increase in the number of students who struggled to pass first-level math courses, the department got together and focused on addressing learner variability. They now offer a math course designed for students who don't love math, where learners apply math concepts to real-life situations. The student feedback has been phenomenal.

At the University of New Hampshire, the Occupational Therapy (OT) Department ran a small study a few years ago implementing UDL strategies (specifically sharing videos of OT movements) into one section of a core course, using another section as a control group. After seeing the grade improvement and increase in overall student understanding of OT, the department decided to adopt UDL as a group and infuse those strategies into all of their courses. They try to add at least one new strategy each time a course is taught, evaluating its effectiveness as a department at the end of the semester.

Few institutions have adopted the concept of UDL as an entire institution. Rather, while many agree that it is a good idea and actively support grassroots efforts on the part of their instructors, institutions tend to devote their resources elsewhere. Our aim in this book is to provide reasons, research, tools, and arguments for moving beyond the individual adoption stage and moving toward campuswide UDL implementation.

Bringing UDL to Higher Education

Ideally, the combination of disability service offices, faculty developers, and interested faculty members would be the trifecta that catapults UDL into wide adoption across college and university campuses. A 2014 study of disability service providers and faculty development offices found that these two offices often do not work together on this initiative as much as they could or should (Behling and Linder, 2017). Rather, the most collaboration these two offices tend to have is around new faculty orientation, in which disability service staff members give a short overview of what they do and how they serve students. The possibility is there, but typical barriers—time and resources—continue to work against active collaboration around an agreed-upon best practice.

The most common advocates of UDL on college and university campuses are the staff and faculty members with roles in the disability services offices. UDL presentations at local and national conferences for higher education disability service providers date back to the early 2000s. The national average of students with disabilities seeking services from their higher educational institution is about 10 percent of the undergraduate population (Trammell and Hathway, 2007). But the graduating high school population of students with identified disabilities is much higher. Some students with disabilities are not going to college. Of the rest who do go on to higher education, many choose not to seek disability services and choose not to disclose a disability status formally.

There are a number of reasons: some college students are unaware of services, choose to not use services, do not know that they must seek out services, or were never diagnosed in K–12 education and are effectively new to their disability and unaware that they qualify for services. Disability service providers are well aware of these reasons and are used to seeing a flurry of new students right before final exams or after they have done poorly for a semester. To disability services providers, adopting UDL allows them to push support resources and structures to students who choose not to use their services or who do not know they might need the disability support office at all. A further benefit is that UDL happens in the classroom environment, unobtrusively, and early on in students' academic careers. If students can successfully navigate their courses without specific accommodations (making one change, one time, for one person), then they have a better chance of continuing on with their college education.

Implementing UDL in the design of course interactions also reduces the number of individual accommodations that disability service providers must implement. This is very attractive to those one-person disability service offices with few resources. For example, if faculty members allowed extended time on all exams for all students, then the number of individual proctoring sessions for time accommodations could be cut dramatically.

Faculty development offices have also had success in bringing UDL to higher education. With the mission of supporting faculty members in their efforts to improve their teaching as a whole, the hundreds of faculty development centers on college and university campuses in the United States and Canada (Center for Teaching Excellence, 2012) are well placed to advocate for UDL as an inclusive-design framework. The size of faculty development offices varies according to the size and resources of the institutions they are designed to serve. Recent research indicates an institutional shift over the last ten years, from a model of re-allocating one faculty member to dedicate part of his or her professional time to one supporting the teaching of colleagues to a model faculty development office that is more formalized, complete with staff members and a programming budget. This signals a shift in the value of varying instructional strategies to reflect the needs of an increasingly diverse student body (Beach et al., 2016).

UDL resonates with faculty development offices because it supports faculty members in their efforts to reach diverse learners. As learner variability increases across college campuses, faculty developers work with faculty colleagues to design interactions that increase student persistence, retention, and satisfaction. UDL streamlines previous instructional concepts like differentiated instruction (DI) and other inclusive practices under one umbrella framework that is fairly easy to understand and implement. Faculty developers also tend to offer their services through multiple modalities such as in-person consultations, phone conversations, e-mail exchanges, and self-paced training—a very UDL practice in itself.

Faculty development offices are often seen as successful campus change agents, getting faculty members to embrace best teaching practices, thus improving student ratings and retention. In the early 2000s, a few college and university developers began referring faculty colleagues to resource articles on UDL, including Dave Edyburn's seminal "Would You Recognize Universal Design for Learning If You Saw It?" Early higher education adopters of UDL began providing workshops and hands-on suggestions for how to address learner variability in college courses. Their message was effective to the extent that its audience of faculty members wanted to learn how to be better teachers, which often was composed of a relatively small number of actively involved colleagues. In the United States, the 2008 reauthorization of the Higher Education Opportunity Act (Public Law 110-315, 2008) boosted the cachet of UDL for faculty development by requiring any college or university receiving federal aid to report on the outcomes of UDL training offered to students pursuing education majors and minors.

Finally, outside of institutional efforts, some individual faculty members and course designers have applied the framework of UDL to their courses, as we saw with Dukes. When we have shown colleagues what UDL is, many people deduce that they have already unknowingly incorporated some interactions that support UDL principles and claim to be doing UDL by accident. This is a common misperception. There is no such thing as accidental UDL. If interactions are not explicitly designed to tie directly to goals, objectives, and desired outcomes, that's not UDL. We will argue in later chapters about why a deliberate and concentrated approach to UDL yields the most consistent, measurable, and effective outcomes for learners of all stripes.

Barriers to Adopting UDL in Higher Education

In elementary and secondary schools in the United States and Canada, teachers must complete a required number of college credits in education courses, and many programs require that inclusive-education theories—like UDL—be part of that curriculum. In many states and provinces, there are likewise requirements that teachers craft their curricula in order to be as inclusive as possible. Not all K–12 teachers are experts in UDL, but the majority of them know what it is and have been trained in how to apply its principles to their lesson planning, and the 2015 Every Student Succeeds Act (ESSA) in the United States now explicitly includes UDL as a standard for assessing curriculum design and technology plans (CAST, 2016b).

Conversely, higher education instructors are hired primarily for their experience, research, and publication in their subject areas; few are vetted for evidence of readiness to teach. For the most part, instructors at higher education institutions are not trained to teach. Few have taken formal education courses, and even fewer are certified teachers. Many college instructors tend to teach in the way that they were taught or in a manner with which they are most comfortable. This is partly why faculty development centers proliferated, starting in the early 2000s: to address higher education faculty members' general lack of formal education about teaching and instructional design. For faculty members and developers who understand learner variability, the UDL framework is easy to accept and implement. For the large number of faculty members who fall back on the assumption that all students should learn the way they were themselves taught, there is little incentive to change or add to their instructional repertoire. UDL seems like extra work, at best, and disruptive and a way to slow down the class period, at worst. This mind-set makes bringing UDL to college a bit more challenging.

Likewise, some colleagues perceive UDL not as a way to increase access to interactions; rather, they feel that offering learners choices for access to information and demonstrating their skills dumbs down the course, reducing the academic rigor. College is supposed to be hard, the argument goes, so why would we coddle students by making it easier to get access to the content or provide ways for them to listen to a book instead of reading it? Further, aren't college students supposed to write long, detailed essays and take hundred-question multiple-choice exams? The suffering inherent in the student experience supposedly validates the rigor of the process: in such a rite-of-passage mind-set, not everyone will (or should) succeed. People who believe in the guarding-the-ivory-tower model are often resistant to UDL, especially in terms of allowing for multiple ways to assess learner skills.

The other side of the coin for concerns about diluted rigor is the fear that incorporating UDL strategies is too cumbersome, requires too much time to implement, and will alter the nature of courses already designed. UDL is indeed resource intensive, and this aspect of the framework, if not presented in a context of manageable scope, reduction of other workload, or increased support availability, can become another extra-work to-do item on faculty members' already full list of tasks. For colleagues who are already teaching a full load, serving on several committees, advising doctoral students, and juggling family responsibilities, UDL can seem overwhelming, which prevents them from attempting it at all.

Instructors will seldom adopt new educational concepts without institutional support; in the coming chapters, we will suggest effective ways to put such support in place. Colleagues may get wind of UDL at conferences and buy into it as a good practice, but when they struggle for the first time with new ideas, approaches, and technologies, they will look for campus support resources and policies that require implementation. Without both, instructors will quickly abandon UDL. This is one reason faculty development offices are so critical to the UDL movement.

Disability services offices are also champions of UDL. To them, UDL is about proactive inclusion and supporting students' various learning preferences and needs in a manner that does not call out the differences of individual students. UDL is the foundational step in the inclusive-design staircase that narrows to individual accommodations. UDL supports the needs of students who may not seek out individual services but who benefit from choices nonetheless.

Like faculty members and faculty development offices, disability service providers are short on resources and time. As noted above, the average staff size for college and university disability service offices is usually quite small, fewer than two full-time employees (Kasnitz, 2013). This leaves little time for larger initiatives. The time that disability service providers do have for engaging with faculty members is usually spent educating them about the work that the office does and supporting faculty members in implementing individual accommodations.

Finally, disability service providers are not often high on the totem pole of campus movers and shakers. Most university administrations are grateful for their presence and their work, but few are viewed as proactive change agents. Rather, making UDL change happen requires collaboration across departments, with specific faculty colleagues, and eventually with administrators to really get the attention needed for wide-scale UDL implementation. Well, that or a lawsuit—which we will address in chapter 2.

Two UDL Early-Adopter Schools

Despite the challenges of competing priorities, entrenched mental models of what education should supposedly be like, and a general lack of resources, there are decades of evidence that UDL is effective in increasing learner persistence, retention, and satisfaction (see Roberts et al., 2011). Further, we have seen broad agreement, even among those ill disposed to try it, that inclusive design is a best practice and should be valued. We can look to two schools in Massachusetts as practical examples.

In 2005, a small community college in Massachusetts was struggling with an increase in the portion of incoming students who were not yet ready for college-level courses. Such students struggled with managing their course loads, staying on track with due dates, and writing college-level papers. The community college also saw an increase in the percentage of incoming nontraditional students (see chapter 9 for why the "nontraditional" label now applies to the majority of our students), as more and more people were coming back to school to improve their career options. College leaders noted a decline in their retention of students from semester to semester: students and faculty members were growing increasing frustrated.

At the same time, the University of Massachusetts Boston received another round of funding through the U.S. Department of Education's Office of Postsecondary Education (OPE) to implement UDL in higher education. The university reached out to the community college and offered them a spot in their pilot grant project, which was designed around the researchers' experience that in order for new concepts to gain traction in higher education, they must come from within and be perceived as stable and supported by campus leadership. The two schools agreed to work together.

As a requirement for participation in the grant, the community college had to identify a core group of people who would commit themselves to the adoption of UDL for an entire semester. The college examined which faculty members were most affected by the trends in the composition of the student body, and campus leaders asked someone from each department to participate. The team also included someone from the community college's Learning Accommodation Center, a representative from the Center for Professional Development, and someone from the Center for Instructional Technology.

The group named itself the Universal Course Design (UCD) team and began meeting weekly for a year. They began by acknowledging that their perception of what students needed had changed significantly over the previous ten years. This, they argued, had to be the starting point for getting the rest of the community college on board. There needed to be a broad cultural agreement that the student demographic had shifted in several key ways. In order to show that this was more than a casual observation, the UCD team contacted the admissions office for demographic data. This information became the first three slides of all of their presentations to faculty colleagues. The team realized that in order to get faculty members to buy into UDL, they needed to understand why there was a need.

The UCD team's next step was to figure out how to bring the concept of UDL to their campus effectively. First, they identified potential barriers to adoption. At the community college, the number of contingent instructors far outnumbered the full-time faculty. This meant that the UCD team needed to create an information and training module that was flexible and that could be repeated often. They began by offering faculty workshops that were sparsely attended: only the most curious faculty members came. The team chose not to be disappointed by this and instead invited those faculty members to join the team. The faculty team members brought their instructor perspectives to the team. Their active classroom practices informed them about what was really happening on the ground and what hurdles faculty members were dealing with on a day-to-day basis.

Over the course of the college's involvement in the project, the UCD team met consistently and twice modified their approach to supporting the college's adoption of UDL. During the early stages of the project, the UCD team identified the Center for Instructional Technology as the unit that should lead, promote, and offer all UDL information and training sessions. Of the offices associated with the team, this center had the most existing faculty traffic. However, by the end of the project, the Center for Instructional Technology acknowledged that it did not have the bandwidth to offer faculty members the one-on-one UDL consultations that they were seeking. So the UCD team proposed creating a part-time position, held by a faculty member with a partial course-load release, to do this work.

The community college agreed. The data that the UCD team had been collecting over the course of the project showed the initial need, positive changes in the student demographics, and a desire by faculty members to adopt UDL as a framework for best practices. One of the best parts about the new UDL support position was that it was held by a faculty member who was also a UCD team member. Because he was a faculty member, he garnered more trust from his colleagues than those team members who were administrators or not currently teaching. This model is still in effect today at the community college.

Captioning as a Cultural Shift

Around the same time, at another university across the country, there was an increase in the number of students who needed captioning as an individual accommodation. The disability services office was overwhelmed by this need, both in terms of staying on top of it and trying to get faculty colleagues to be more proactive when they selected their course materials. The disability services office reached out to the IT office looking for help and was met with the responses, "we'd like to but we don't have the bandwidth" and "it's not our office's responsibility." Without a supportive partner on campus, the disability services office continued to pour time, funds, and staff effort into the mounting captioning needs of their students.

Staff morale sank until the director of the disability services office attended the annual Association on Higher Education and Disability (AHEAD) conference. The director attended a session on UDL in which captioning was highlighted as an example. The speaker argued that the benefits of proactive captioning for an entire class were far more productive and inclusive than providing it only as just-in-time accommodations for individual students. Further, the speaker advocated describing the creation of captions as an inclusive teaching tool, and that such an approach is far more effective than referring to captioning within the accommodation narrative of making one change, one time, for one student. The conclusion was that UDL strategies should be the responsibility of the college or university as a whole, not solely the responsibility of the disability services office, as many in the room were used to. This session was the aha moment that the disability services director needed.

The director went back to her campus and quickly convened a meeting with IT officials and those faculty members who would be teaching students with identified captioning needs in the next semester. The meeting had a twofold focus. The first was to make sure the faculty knew the legal ramifications of not captioning the videos and the process and cost of creating captioned videos. The second part of the meeting was to brainstorm how captioned videos might positively affect more than just students with disabilities. For this second part, the director led the group to this idea but did not supply it directly. As the faculty members came to the idea that captioning could benefit many students, they—not the director of the disability services office—pushed the IT office to support them. It was as if, in an instant, UDL was adopted and the long-awaited support of the IT department was in place. The director refers to this as the "UDL miracle."

Over time, this model began to strain. As more and more faculty members bought into it, the resources to caption all of their multimedia grew less and less available. In fear of losing the momentum, the director of the disability services office called the chair of the computer science department with an idea. She asked whether he might agree to create an in-house captioning solution, using some of the computer science students as federally funded work-study students to caption videos for faculty colleagues. This would save thousands of dollars and offer the computer science students training and insight into the importance of captioning. The department chair thought this was a great idea and was willing to work through the details to figure out how to do it.

It took about a year to work the kinks out of this system. They had to decide what software to use, how to track requests, how to rush-caption videos if they could not be completed in one student's shift, and how to release captions back to faculty members, but slowly they developed a process that dramatically reduced the need to send video and audio files off campus for captioning. The system was built and developed with close monitoring by the disability services office, the IT office that owned the process, and the computer science department.

As a result, the chair of the computer science department made a sweeping change to the curriculum in his major. He decided to incorporate lessons on how to caption directly into the core curriculum. After watching the university go through trial and error to set up the in-house system, and seeing the benefits of the multiple learner uses of captions, he argued that in order to be the best computer scientists that they could be, his students needed not only to understand the mechanics of how to caption but also to appreciate the need for captions by a wide group of people. This departmental and institutional adoption of UDL continues today.

Conclusion

In chapter 2, we will explore why legal compliance is often a driver for interest in UDL, at least in the United States. Kate Sonka's approach allowed her and her team to talk about accessibility both from a legal perspective and in a positive way: "There is, of course, a huge concern about whether we could get sued, and that message can come from the office of general counsel and the ADA [Americans with Disabilities Act] coordinator's office. Because we wanted to be proactive, we wanted to actually do something tangible. We had the luxury of framing accessibility when we talked about it. We talk in terms of UDL— why it benefits everyone—and we are very conscious about how we frame the changes in mind-set and practice. It's always 'we know you're here to support your students'" (Sonka, 2017).

Sonka and her colleagues are empathetic to the demands on faculty time. Behind the annual Accessible Learning Conference are policies, tutorials, and checklists that help to scaffold and define incremental stages of work with, for, and by faculty members. The first time faculty members teach using UDL structures, "There's a lot of hand-holding and collaboration. The second time, we hear faculty colleagues saying 'refresh my memory,' and by the third time they teach, they're usually comfortable and experienced with UDL" (Sonka, 2017).

Sonka and her team adopted UDL as a frame for accessibility because it is value-neutral. "For sustained change, tapping into empathy lasts longer than fear" of possible lawsuits. The Michigan State University model uses UDL to move the conversation "away from 'you have to do it because I said so'" (Sonka, 2017) and allows the university to address the common concern that faculty members want to do what is right for their students but don't necessarily know what steps to take in order to broaden access for the greatest number of learners.

Next up for Sonka and her colleagues is to teach access via a campuswide task force that focuses on driving student academic engagement; Sonka is the campus representative for the Teach Access initiative that brings together industry and academic representatives to "think and build inclusively" (Teach Access, 2017). The plan for Michigan State University is to create undergraduate student ambassadors for inclusive-design thinking like UDL who partner with staff members and faculty members to do the work of UDL, implement it in class- and campus-based scenarios, and then present their work at local and national conferences.

UDL has come a long way over the last fifty-plus years. It began with the concept of Universal Design in the field of architecture, concerned with designing the broadest access to physical spaces. Beginning in the 1990s, UDL was formalized by the neuroscientists at CAST and the framework was infused into elementary and secondary education. Now, higher education is beginning to adopt UDL as a way to reach out to address learner variability. The impact on students is amazing. By simply recognizing that no two students learn in the same way and taking that recognition into account when designing, teaching, and assessing interactions, faculty members and designers give students a greater likelihood of coming away from courses having actually learned something. Faculty members using UDL strategies feel empowered for successfully imparting knowledge and providing students with choices in their interactions with materials, each other, their instructors, and the wider world. Disability services staff members feel more confident that "their" students, and those who have not yet sought services, are on an equal playing field. And institutions provide a welcoming environment to a more diverse group of learners; doing so only enhances their reputations.

A THOUGHT EXERCISE

Before you put together a plan for bringing Universal Design for Learning to your institution, it is helpful to better understand your experience with UDL. This activity is a great one to use with faculty and disability service providers when introducing the concept of UDL. Use the guiding questions below to consider how UDL principles have had an impact for you personally.

Think of a learning interaction that currently takes place at your college or university (e.g., a course unit that you or a colleague design or teach, a common conversation that your student support area has with students all the time), and use these reflection questions to identify areas of your course where you might want to incorporate UDL strategies.

Name of the interaction: _____

- What is the format of the texts that you will use throughout the interaction (e.g., textbooks, journal articles, websites, handouts, videos, audio files)?
- What is your primary method of facilitating this interaction (e.g., lecture, seminar, lab, phone call, in-person consultation)?
- How do you plan to assess the performance of the learners (e.g., papers, exams, presentations, fills out forms correctly)?
- What aspect of the interaction are you concerned about (e.g., a particular topic, assignment, lecture, or outcome)?
- What alternatives have you considered or tried to make this particular aspect become successful?

CHAPTER 2

It's the Law . . .
Except When It Isn't

Meet Andrew

Andrew Lessman is the associate director for state authorization in Temple University's Office of Digital Education. In lay terms, he's the lawyer responsible for ensuring that the university's distance-education programs are in compliance with state and federal regulations. In his January 2016 keynote speech at the Alfred State University accessibility conference, he focused on legal accessibility. As a lawyer in the inclusive-education field, Lessman provided an overview of how accessibility was initially envisioned in U.S. laws and how it has been implemented in practice.

Basing his ideas on the requirements found in the Americans with Disabilities Act (ADA) and Sections 504 and 508 of the Rehabilitation Act, Lessman began by talking about how "accommodations are supposed to be for extraordinary circumstances," arguing that it should be very rare for people to need to make specific requests to have circumstances altered just for them. The environments that we provide for people who use our services—and here Lessman called out not only classrooms and course environments but also student housing, tutoring, registration, financial aid, and other student-facing parts of colleges and universities—all of these environments, whether physical or virtual, should be designed so that the broadest segment of the general population will be able to interact successfully with materials and people. Such a situation "would make accommodation requests very rare, indeed" (Lessman, 2016a).

In practice, however, those in higher education often find themselves in nearly the opposite situation. Lessman said of a common approach, "'We will accommodate anyone who comes to us' is not really an acceptable solution" (2016a), since it presumes that people who need special access must make their needs known in order to be accommodated. Lessman noted that recent legal challenges to this wait-for-the-accommodation-request approach have been successful, and these courtroom successes are pushing the scope of the law toward proactively inclusive design—a perfect argument in favor of Universal Design for Learning (UDL). "Reasonable accommodation is no longer considered good enough. You still can be found to be discriminating if all you have is a reasonable-accommodation policy in place" (2016a).

In 2016, Lessman encouraged campuses to adopt the Web Content Accessibility Group (WCAG) accessibility guidelines in order to audit current web content and build new web materials according to industry standards. The WCAG 2.0 guidelines have subsequently been adopted into U.S. law, colloquially referred to as the Information and Communication Technology (ICT) Refresh (U.S. Access Board, 2017a), with the requirements going into effect on January 18, 2018, so it made sense to adopt the standards proactively.

Campuses also should be as proactive as possible. Lessman noted legal cases in which "you don't always need a complaint to have a need" (2016a). He cited the EDUCAUSE *IT Accessibility Risk Statements and Evidence* (EDUCAUSE, 2015) report that lists the major accessibility cases brought against higher education institutions up to 2015.

In his speech, Lessman also mentioned just a few of the recent legal settlements and their implications for higher education:

- The University of Montana at Missoula now must verify during its procurement process the accessibility of third-party software purchased and leased by the university.
- The Pennsylvania State University reached a settlement with the National Federation of the Blind to make its web materials and online courses accessible.

- Harvard and the Massachusetts Institute of Technology (MIT) were in the midst of a suit from the National Association of the Deaf (NAD) seeking captions for media content in their joint-venture edEX MOOC courses.

In all of these settlements and legal actions, Lessman argued that the common thread was how preventable the situations were, and how the institutions involved could have saved themselves the expense and frustration of the lawsuits by following the existing laws and treating accessibility as a civil right.

Accessibility Is a Civil Right

Lessman granted us an interview in February 2016 (Lessman, 2016b) in which he expanded on his focus on accessibility as a civil right, saying that legal compliance can force people to enact changes where they otherwise might not be willing or inclined to change. Lessman mentioned a student in one of his online courses who, he found out only after the course was finished, had multiple sclerosis: "Here's this whole space where people can be what they want to be—to disclose or not." Lessman argues that, as students, faculty members, and staff members, we should all have the right not to disclose aspects of our lives that we would rather not. Applying UDL principles makes it less necessary for people to have to identify their own barriers and then ask for help. By incorporating elements of UDL into course interactions, we provide students who may need accommodations (or who may not yet know that accommodations are a possibility for them) with natural entry points into our courses. If, for example, a course allows extended time on exams for all students, then those who need it as an accommodation are less likely to have to contact the disability services office and ask for it. In this way, UDL definitely creates a climate of greater autonomy and control across all groups of learners.

Lessman advocates that we should build interactions using UDL principles, and we should rely on our library and teaching-center staff to assist in the process. "They are there—there are ways the university can help faculty members. We should focus our support efforts for the faculty members who say 'don't tell me what to do. I have academic freedom to run my courses my own way.' Teaching is probably their least favorite part of the job, and if we understand their mind-set, then the law really does help. We tell such faculty members that these are the rules, and we have to follow the rules." Some faculty colleagues are resistant to inclusive design, Lessman says, "not just because they don't see the helping argument, but because they think it's nonsense." For colleagues who have heard it all before and have closed their ears to the logical arguments for UDL, Lessman says that the law is the only way to reach them: "they say 'if I have to, I will; if I don't, I don't want to,' and the law tells them that they must."

Lessman's goal is to be pragmatic, to find the right message for the people. The law helps because it is there to change behavior: "if people were already doing well and behaving the way they should, the law wouldn't need to exist. The law embodies the values that we cherish." Lessman works with state governments, colleges, and universities on issues of legal compliance, which eats up time and is not as satisfying for him as accessibility work, in which he is able to effect actual changes. "A lot of people care, and there is still work to do to get changes on the ground."

. . . Except When It Isn't

Part of the challenge of adopting Lessman's approach is that UDL is not a set of standards or specific practices. Rather, it is a framework intended to get faculty members and course designers to think proactively about the needs of all of their learners, following the instructional planning process outlined by James Basham of the Universal Design for Learning Implementation and Research Network (UDL-IRN):

> **Step 1: Establish clear outcomes.** Establish a clear understanding of the goals of the lesson or unit.

Step 2: Anticipate learner needs. Prior to planning the instructional experience, teachers should have a clear understanding of the learner needs within their environment.

Step 3: Plan measurable outcomes and assessment. Prior to planning the instructional experience, establish how learning is going to be measured.

Step 4: Instructional experience. Establish the instructional sequence of events.

Step 5: Reflection and new understandings. Establish checkpoints for teacher reflection and new understandings. (Basham, 2017)

Because UDL is a mind-set rather than a set of specific actions, it is useful in meeting legal requirements for accessibility without being subject to the qualification tests of legal requirements: the "learner needs" that Basham talks about are really learner barriers of all kinds. By thinking about the barriers as being in the environment rather than in the learners, we can create interactions that change or expand the learning environment—and that's the point of this entire book.

Federal accessibility laws in the United States (and statutes in some Canadian provinces as well) require that everyone has equal access to educational opportunities, and the way that UDL helps us to stay on the right side of the law is by lowering barriers for everyone ahead of time—in the design stage of curriculum and course development— instead of waiting for complaints or requests to come in. As in Lessman's story, the aim is to progress in making our campus interactions accessible to the broadest range of people, rather than to aim for perfection. In this chapter, we will review the relevant accessibility laws, examine some of the major lawsuits that have been recently brought and settled against colleges and universities, and then talk about why legal compliance is actually a poor way to start a UDL-adoption conversation on your campus.

Accessibility Laws and UDL

In the United States and Canada, no laws explicitly require colleges and universities to use UDL principles, although a definition for UDL is part of several laws. There are some federal grants in the United States, such as the U.S. Department of Labor's Trade Adjustment Assistance Community College and Career Training (TAACCCT) grant program, which requires grantees to demonstrate their application of UDL principles in the design of all grant-funded interactions (U.S. Department of Labor, 2016), but the UDL framework should not yet be construed as being legally required in higher education.

However, federal law in the United States and provincial laws in Canada require that institutions that receive government funding or provide public services make their interactions and materials accessible. The following timeline outlines the relevant U.S. and Canadian laws regarding accessibility and points to ways that UDL helps colleges and universities meet legal accessibility requirements.

Section 504, Rehabilitation Act (29 U.S.C. §701) (1973)

Section 504 of the Rehabilitation Act (commonly shortened to "Section 504") was the first national civil rights legislation in the United States that provided equal access for students with disabilities to higher education institutions receiving federal financial assistance. Both public and private colleges and universities supported by federal grants and funding programs must comply with Section 504. "No otherwise qualified individual with a disability in the United States, as defined in section 705(20) of this title, shall, solely by reason of her or his disability, be excluded from the participation in, be denied the benefits of, or be subjected to discrimination under any program or activity receiving federal financial assistance or under any program or activity conducted by any Executive agency or by the United States Postal Service." In practice, Section 504 establishes the civil rights of people with disabilities to be free from discrimination when interacting with programs and institutions that receive federal funding.

49

Section 508, Rehabilitation Act (29 U.S.C. §794d) (1973)

If Section 504 establishes the civil right, Section 508 of the Rehabilitation Act, especially as amended in 1998, bars the U.S. federal government from procuring information and communication technology (ICT) goods and services that are not fully accessible to those with disabilities.

> Each Federal department or agency . . . shall ensure . . . that the electronic and information technology allows, regardless of the type of medium of the technology . . . individuals with disabilities . . . to have access to and use of information and data that is comparable to the access to and use of the information and data by such members of the public who are not individuals with disabilities.
>
> The Access Board . . . shall issue and publish standards setting forth . . . a definition of electronic and information technology, . . . and the technical and functional performance criteria necessary to implement the requirements set forth [above].

In 1998, this section of the law was amended to include the Internet and authorizes the Architectural and Transportation Barriers Compliance Board (commonly referred to as the Access Board) to create binding, enforceable standards that clearly outline and identify specifically what the federal government means by accessible ICT. See below for the very recent ICT Refresh of the standards by the Access Board as well.

Canadian Human Rights Act (1977)

This is the earliest law in Canada that, like the U.S. Rehabilitation Act, establishes access to higher education interactions as a civil right:

> It is a discriminatory practice in the provision of goods, services, facilities or accommodation customarily available to the general public
>
> • to deny, or to deny access to, any such good, service, facility or accommodation to any individual, or

- to differentiate adversely in relation to any individual, on a prohibited ground of discrimination. (Government of Canada, 1977)

The Canadian Human Rights Act explicitly categorizes (but does not define) disability as a protected category, and covers all interactions that are offered "to the general public."

Americans with Disabilities Act (ADA) (1990, amended 2008)

The ADA provides broad nondiscrimination protection in employment, public services, and public accommodations—including many areas of colleges and universities—for individuals with disabilities. The ADA is enforced by multiple U.S. federal agencies, including the Department of Justice, Department of Labor, and the Equal Employment Opportunity Commission. One of the key provisions in the ADA has to do with the ways organizations can legally refuse to provide accommodation for disability reasons:

Discrimination includes

1) the imposition or application of eligibility criteria that screen out or tend to screen out an individual with a disability or any class of individuals with disabilities from fully and equally enjoying any goods, services, facilities, privileges, advantages, or accommodations, *unless such criteria can be shown to be necessary for the provision of the goods, services, facilities, privileges, advantages, or accommodations being offered*;

2) a failure to make reasonable modifications in policies, practices, or procedures, when such modifications are necessary to afford such goods, services, facilities, privileges, advantages, or accommodations to individuals with disabilities, *unless the entity can demonstrate that making such modifications would fundamentally alter the nature of such goods, services, facilities, privileges, advantages, or accommodations*;

3) a failure to take such steps as may be necessary to ensure that no individual with a disability is excluded, denied

services, segregated or otherwise treated differently than other individuals because of the absence of auxiliary aids and services, *unless the entity can demonstrate that taking such steps would fundamentally alter the nature of the good, service, facility, privilege, advantage, or accommodation being offered or would result in an undue burden.* (Americans with Disabilities Act, 1990; italics added)

Where the Rehabilitation Act covered only entities receiving federal funding, thus exempting many private and religiously affiliated colleges and universities, the ADA applies to all "places of public accommodation" (Americans with Disabilities Act, 1990). The definition of which services and locations at colleges and universities fall within this category was recently expanded (see Higher Education Opportunity Act, below).

Assistive Technology Act (1998)

The Assistive Technology Act, or Tech Act, promotes awareness of and access to assistive technology (AT) devices and services. It defines what AT devices and services are: "any item, piece of equipment, or product system, whether acquired commercially, modified, or customized, that is used to increase, maintain, or improve functional capabilities of individuals with disabilities" (Assistive Technology Act, 1998). The Tech Act also provides federal funding for states to implement programs designed to meet the AT needs of individuals with disabilities. The passage of the Tech Act is often seen as the last legal encoding of separate services for people with disabilities instead of folding accessibility into the design of tools and services for everyone.

Workforce Investment Act (Public Law 105-220) (1998), Workforce Innovation and Opportunity Act (2014)

The Workforce Investment Act (WIA) and its later replacement, the Workforce Innovation and Opportunity Act (WIOA), specifically set aside funds for American Job Centers, colleges, and universities to be used to make access to job training more equal for people with disabilities. The WIA and WIOA also update the Rehabilitation Act of

1973 to require adult education and adult literacy programming (U.S. Department of Labor, 2015).

Ontarians with Disabilities Act (2001), Accessibility for Ontarians with Disabilities Act (2005)

In the absence of a Canada-wide law mandating equal access across the ability spectrum, the Province of Ontario enacted its own far-reaching legislation in 2001, the Ontarians with Disabilities Act (ODA). Often considered the model for how governments should require inclusive practices, the ODA requires governmental bodies to identify barriers and remove them to the extent possible. Updated several times since its initial passing, and superseded by the Accessibility for Ontarians with Disabilities Act (2005), the law now requires the removal of barriers in both private and public spaces, under five general standards:

a) Customer Service Standard
b) Information and Communication Standard
c) Employment Standard
d) Transportation Standard
e) Design of Public Spaces Standard (Accessibility for Ontarians with Disabilities Act, 2005)

Colleges and universities in Ontario are affected by all five of the AODA standards, especially in regard to customer service and information/communication, since admissions, registration, course offerings, and student support services are all included in them.

The Council of Ontario Universities now provides a resource hub of "tools and resources that help university students, educators and administrators identify and remove barriers to accessibility, as well as provide support for mental health issues on their campuses. In particular, these resources support universities in meeting their obligations under the Accessibility for Ontarians with Disabilities Act (AODA)" (Council of Ontario Universities, 2017). The AODA is one of the models for the proposed Canada-wide accessibility law that is before Parliament as this book is going to press. For updates to this legislation see the What We've Heard document from Minister Kent Hehr (Government of Canada, 2017).

Higher Education Opportunity Act (2008)

The Higher Education Opportunity Act marked the first time that UDL was explicitly defined in U.S. law. Section 103.a.24 defines UDL:

> The term "Universal Design for Learning" means a scientifically valid framework for guiding educational practice that
>
> - provides flexibility in the ways information is presented, in the ways students respond or demonstrate knowledge and skills, and in the ways students are engaged; and
> - reduces barriers in instruction, provides appropriate accommodations, supports, and challenges, and maintains high achievement expectations for all students, including students with disabilities and students who are limited English proficient. (Public Law 110-315, 2008)

Moreover, the act directs teacher training programs at U.S. colleges and universities to include UDL as part of their curriculum, which the federal government would support with grants "to pay the Federal share of the costs of projects to . . . assess the effectiveness of departments, schools, and colleges of education at institutions of higher education in preparing teacher candidates for successful implementation of technology-rich teaching and learning environments, including environments consistent with the principles of Universal Design for Learning, that enable kindergarten through grade 12 students to develop learning skills to succeed in higher education and to enter the workforce" (Public Law 110-315, 2008, §231.a.3). This law encodes UDL as a preferred framework for the design of K–12 teacher-training programs at colleges and universities, and paved the way for the Section 508 ICT Refresh, below.

Canada Accessibility Law Consultations (2017–18)

We've mentioned that no countrywide laws govern accessibility in Canada and that legal requirements for accessibility vary from province to province. In 2015 and 2016, the federal government of Canada conducted listening sessions in cities around the country and online to determine the desire for and possible scope of a nationwide accessibility law (Government of Canada, 2016).

In developing this new legislation, the Government of Canada is consulting Canadians both in person and online. The Government of Canada is seeking your ideas to inform the development of this planned new legislation, including:

- feedback on the overall goal and approach;
- whom it should cover;
- what accessibility issues and barriers it should address;
- how it could be monitored and enforced;
- when or how often it should be reviewed;
- how and when to report to Canadians on its implementation; and
- how to raise accessibility awareness more generally and support organizations in improving accessibility. (Government of Canada, 2016)

Especially in the sphere of higher education, several Canadian institutions, including McGill University and the University of Calgary, have taken part in the conversation toward a national set of accessibility laws and proposed making UDL a legally supported framework for creating interactions across colleges and universities (Ostrowski et al., 2017). Access experts from around the world are advising the Canadian government about the scope, language, and enforcement actions that should be included in the new law (Alliance for an Inclusive and Accessible Canada, 2017), which will cover inclusive practices in workplaces, educational institutions, and public spaces throughout Canada.

UDL is beginning to be recognized by lawmakers as a meaningful and effective way to provide broad access to interactions and materials without prescribing specific techniques for doing so. The principles of UDL are part of the proposed Canadian national accessibility law that was being introduced into Parliament at the time this book went to press in summer 2018 (Isai, 2017; Canadian Press, 2017). As a governing framework, UDL is a measured response to accessibility requirements in the law, as the following section demonstrates.

Section 508 ICT Refresh and WCAG Standards (2018)

The Web Content Accessibility Guidelines are the generally accepted worldwide standards for accessibility of Internet-based materials. They cover everything from the use of ALT-text tags in the coding for images to the acceptable levels of color contrast on web pages (W3C, 2013). In 2018, the United States formally adopted the WCAG 2.0 standards as the measurements for web-based content compliance with Section 508 of the Rehabilitation Act (U.S. Access Board, 2017a). Adopting WCAG 2.0 for information and communication technology (ICT) puts specific practices into the law regarding "electronic and information technology procured by the federal government, including computer hardware and software, web sites, multimedia such as video, phone systems, and copiers" (U.S. Access Board, 2017b).

In higher education, this means that all publicly available web pages must comply with the WCAG standards. In practical terms, the ICT Refresh provides specific, measurable design targets for testing the compliance of college and university web resources.

Three Lawsuits

This book is about how to reframe UDL in terms of reaching out to learners on their mobile devices (see chapter 3). The U.S. Department of Justice's Office of Civil Rights (OCR) has been doing some reframing of its own in recent years, joining lawsuits brought by individuals and advocacy groups against colleges and universities in order to highlight the need to make the interactions offered by colleges and universities accessible to the broadest possible range of people. In the cases below, notice three important shifts in the framing of the access argument that differ from how many institutions have historically viewed accessibility.

First, waiting for accommodation requests is no longer enough. In consulting with several colleges and universities across the United States and Canada, the authors have heard variations on the theme of "we know that accessibility is the right thing to do, but we don't have enough people, time, and money to do everything that we should." This leads to a passive institutional stance where accessibility must always be asked for. The OCR, in two of the narratives below, argues that colleges and universities have a positive duty to make their interactions open and accessible, even if people with disabilities are not asking for such services.

Second, offering unequal access is discrimination. In response to the not-enough-resources way of thinking, all of the narratives below confirm that the OCR takes a dim view of such arguments, especially since the law in the United States is pretty clear about the requirement for any institution that receives federal funds to provide equal access to its services. The OCR joins lawsuits in order to ensure that such cases are handled as violations of people's civil rights.

Third, providing equal access—but too late—is also discrimination. This is the biggest difference between recent lawsuits and ones even fifteen years ago. For example, North Carolina State University came to an agreement with the OCR in 2000 regarding lawsuits brought by three students with visual disabilities who claimed discrimination, in part, because there were no accessible library services, student bulletin boards, class textbooks, computer access, and cafeteria services (International Center for Disability Resources, 2000). At the time, the settlement was made by asking the university to create the services that the students had complained were missing. It took them nearly three years to create policies, hire and train staff, and implement their plan (Reavis and Sitton, 2017), but the establishment of accessibility as part of the university's entire approach to designing their interactions for students has paid off in terms of fewer accommodation requests and better access to learning and campus services for all students, not just those with disabilities. However, notice that it took three years for North Carolina State to comply fully with the terms of the OCR agreement. These days, if a college or university cannot provide equal access in a timely fashion (meaning at the same time that other learners have access to the same information or interactions), that is also seen as discrimination, as each of the three narratives below will show.

These narratives offer a number of techniques that you can start using at your college or university to begin or strengthen your accessibility practices. Their common thread is the incorporation of the UDL framework as a means for assessing the location of gaps in accessibility programming and addressing outreach and design changes in a widening circle, from individual interactions and courses to departments and programs to the entire institution.

The Pennsylvania State University

In 2010, the National Federation of the Blind filed a complaint with the OCR "because a variety of computer- and technology-based services and Web sites at Penn State are inaccessible to blind students and faculty" (Danielsen, 2010). The ensuing lawsuit and consent decree outlined several areas of the university that were not accessible, including the banking system adopted by the university:

- The library web catalog was not fully accessible to blind students due to improper coding that prevents screen access software used by the blind from properly interpreting the site.
- Many departmental websites were not fully accessible to the blind, including, ironically, the website for the Office of Disability Services.
- The ANGEL learning management system, adopted and customized by the university, was almost completely inaccessible to blind users.
- Classroom [interactive] podiums were operated by an inaccessible touchscreen keypad, forcing blind faculty members to rely on assistance from sighted colleagues to utilize the podiums.
- Penn State contracted with PNC Bank to enable students to use their identification cards as debit cards. The PNC website was nearly inaccessible with screen-access software, and there was only one ATM on the entire Penn State

campus with audio output through a headphone jack so that blind students could use it privately and independently. (Danielsen, 2010).

The resulting settlement had far-reaching impact for the culture and operation of the university. Penn State

- conducted an accessibility audit;
- created policy statements and a timeline for implementing information and communication technology (ICT) accessibility measures;
- adjusted its procurement processes to take accessibility explicitly into account when purchasing products and services;
- changed its library website, university sites, and search processes to be accessible according to WCAG 2.0 Level AA standards;
- replaced ANGEL with the Canvas LMS;
- updated classroom-technology systems to be operable by faculty members with disabilities; and
- got PNC Bank to update its own websites and ATMs across campus. (Accessibility at Penn State, 2011)

Note that these actions do not presume that students or faculty members at the university must self-identify as needing to have barriers removed. The process of removing barriers proactively remains an ongoing process at Penn State today, and the systemwide changes that were implemented as a result of the agreement with the National Federation of the Blind—while requiring significant resources, funds, people, and time—have now positioned Penn State as a leader in accessible learning. The World Campus faculty development area of the university explicitly advises faculty members, web designers, and instructional support staff to utilize UDL principles to ensure compliance with the law (Kauffmann, 2014) as well as the consent decree (Bigatel, 2015).

Atlantic Cape Community College (ACCC)

Lest we think that smaller colleges and universities are immune to accessibility lawsuits because they do not have the deep pockets of larger institutions, the case of *Lanzilotti v. Atlantic Cape Community College* is instructive. Two students with visual disabilities who attended ACCC sued the college, and the National Federation of the Blind joined the suit. They reached an agreement with the community college after it erroneously required one of its blind students to have a sighted guide with him on campus at all times (whether he needed one or not) and the college failed to provide both students with accessible library, lab, and course materials. In the consent decree, the college agreed to a list of actions, including:

- Conducting a technology audit and . . . developing a plan to make all student-facing electronic and information technology used by ACCC accessible to students with disabilities;
- Making ACCC's websites accessible to blind students;
- Making ACCC's integrated library system and its website fully accessible to blind students;
- Developing a plan to provide accessible instructional materials, including textbooks, course materials, and tactile graphics, to blind students and to other students with disabilities at the same time that these materials are made available to students without disabilities;
- Requiring cooperation among faculty, staff, and ACCC's Disability Support Services office to handle accommodation requests made by students with disabilities;
- Reviewing and revising ACCC's policies and procedures for accommodating students with disabilities and for processing and resolving grievances brought by students with disabilities; and
- Requiring training of all personnel on the Americans with Disabilities Act and on ACCC's policies for accommodating students with disabilities, as well as training for such

students on their rights and the procedures available to them to enforce those rights. (Danielsen, 2015)

The phrase to note in the list above is that ACCC must "provide accessible instructional materials . . . to students with disabilities *at the same time that these materials are made available to students without disabilities*" (italics added).

Even if your college or university has a well-established process in place for receiving and acting on individual accommodation requests through your disability services area, if such responses are not timely in allowing students with accommodations to keep up with the course or get the same services as other students at the same time, this is now grounds for a discrimination lawsuit. Timeliness is the new driver for making accessibility decisions on campus.

The UDL framework offers a way of heading off such concerns before they arise. Many colleges and universities have resource concerns—too few people, too little time or funding—regarding making accommodations in a timely fashion. For example, obtaining an in-class note-taker for a student with a hearing disability at Northeastern Illinois University (NEIU) could take up to two weeks, enough time for a student to fall behind in a course. One part of UDL that the disability services office at NEIU adopted was to pilot having a designated note-taker in every course, regardless of whether any student had requested one as a disability accommodation (Lawson, 2016). The outcome of the pilot program included benefits for everyone in course sections who had designated note-takers: better overall performance on tests and quizzes, less reteaching of challenging concepts, and higher student ratings of their experiences at the end of the course.

The Ohio State University

Universal Design for Learning principles help in the design of all kinds of interactions on campus, not just those in the classroom. In 2009, a student with a hearing disability brought a suit at Ohio State University in order to request that audio announcements and play-by-play for sports games held in the university's stadium be cap-tioned so that the student could enjoy football games along with other fans. In the consent decree, the university agreed to

- caption on the north and south scoreboards all public-address announcements, emergency information, music, and other auditory information broadcasted into Ohio Stadium before, during, and after home football games, . . . without a written request for an accommodation or a completed and timely submitted Disability Needs Form; and
- activate the captioning of television broadcasts . . . on at least one half of the television monitors in the concourse of Ohio Stadium during home football games, without a writ-ten request for an accommodation or a completed and timely submitted Disability Needs Form. (*Sabino v. Ohio State University*, 2010)

The university also placed on its athletics website accessibility guides for fans visiting the stadium, along with a Disability Needs Form that could be filled out online in order to make requests beyond the terms of what was already taking place in the consent decree.

Note the language in the consent decree: "without a written request for an accommodation or a completed and timely submitted Disability Needs Form." In other words, the university is responsible for making its events accessible to as broad a range of fans as they reasonably can. It is not the responsibility of the fans to make individual requests each time they attend football games. This shift of responsibility from people with barriers to the institutions serving them is a key to why the UDL framework is so powerful: by providing information in mul-tiple ways (this is the "multiple means of representing information" tenet of UDL)—up front, and by design—we reduce the need for indi-viduals to have to ask for special treatment. In fact, the court sent a request around to other Big Ten football programs to request that they also make similar additions to their own stadiums, proactively, so that they would also be following inclusive-design practices in their ath-letic event programming.

Why "It's the Law" Is a Bad Place to Start

In each of the examples above, the agreement reached by the college or university included a self-examination for accessibility gaps, a specific set of actions to take that addresses the original complaints, and a longer-term set of goals that addresses the underlying inequalities in the interactions that take place under the aegis of the institution. These and other high-profile lawsuits have brought accessibility into the minds of faculty members, support staff, and campus administrators—largely from the perspective of fear: fear of being sued, fear of not doing the right thing, and fear of not having enough expertise, time, funds, or resources to be able to comply with the law or reduce institutional liability.

In one regard, having a federal law that mandates accessibility can actually produce a barrier to accessible practices being implemented on a wide scale. For example, most of the laws outlined above have been in force for decades, and all three of the lawsuits we highlighted had to do with colleges and universities not providing alternative access to information, materials, and interactions. It isn't as though the colleges and universities did not know about their legal obligations. In many cases, the feeling of knowing it's the right thing to do but being uneasy with redoing so many things leads to what psychologists call "analysis paralysis": we see that there is so much work to do, and because the scope of the task is so overwhelming, we do not even start. We even hide behind the excuse that our resources are no match for the legal requirements. So, what would a UDL adoption program look like if there were no legal requirement for accessibility?

Canada does not yet have a nationwide law that mandates accessibility, like the Americans with Disabilities Act does in the Unites States—but it is coming very soon. Quebec, where McGill University is located, currently has no provincial accessibility law either, so compliance with the law is not yet a primary driver for adopting UDL principles. Among North American public-facing institutions, many Canadian colleges and universities are leading the way on proactively adopting inclusive-design practices, but for a completely different reason.

Without the worry about legal compliance driving the project, the McGill UDL project team had the opportunity to do some listening first. They interviewed seventy-seven faculty members across five campus locations, asking them about their views on key project concepts such as their definition of fairness, their social models of practice, what barriers they perceived to learning, what stressors and facilitators of learning they saw for their students, their knowledge of the UDL framework, and their perception of student success overall. They also conducted interviews with students and pored through data about how many students were receiving individual accommodations at the university.

Armed with this information, the UDL project team created their UDL-adoption project based on the concerns-based adoption model (CBAM) framework (see American Institutes for Research, 2015) to determine what constituent faculty groups needed in order to feel supported through the change process of adopting inclusive design and UDL. The data collected were also the foundation of a grant from the Quebec Ministry of Education and Higher Education "for the development of a pedagogical online toolkit to facilitate the implementation of Universal Design for Learning (UDL) on campus" in collaboration with five other Quebec colleges and universities (Office for Students with Disabilities, 2016).

The team next examined policies about inclusion at their own and several similar institutions and came up with four drivers for the expansion of inclusive design and UDL at McGill University:

- **Resource management.** In their research, the McGill team saw that the number of students who self-identify as having learning barriers was increasing rapidly each year. Their conclusion is that "the traditional 'accommodation approach' begins to be inadequate."
- **Sustainable approach.** The traditional accommodations approach to disability is an ad hoc process of retrofitting, repeated each semester, for each course, for each individual student making a request. The process in itself is a nonrenewable use of resources and does not conform to

McGill's Vision 2020 objectives in terms of sustainable development.

- **Learner variability.** The complexity and diversity of diagnostic labels make retrofitting in the traditional way somewhat obsolete. Disabilities are increasingly varied and often invisible (mental health issues, learning disabilities, autism spectrum disorders, ADHD). The UDL team notes at least eight categories of barriers for which designers and faculty members would need to be prepared with individual accommodations.

- **Inclusive practices.** Most students reaching higher education have benefited from inclusive practices throughout their secondary education. The students have clear expectations for inclusion. The idea of self-identifying, disclosing a diagnosis, or requesting services outside of the class is foreign and unappealing to them. (Office for Students with Disabilities, 2016)

As noted in these four areas, data from interviews and listening sessions with faculty members supported the team's notion that their colleagues, when hearing "Universal Design for Learning" in the absence of a detailed understanding of the framework, tended mentally to connect it to their understanding of Universal Design in the built environment, and by extension, assumed that UDL had a limited impact only for learners with disabilities.

The McGill team also observed the negative emotional valence associated with the concept of UDL that we discussed in the introduction. Their adoption of the CBAM approach was designed specifically to reframe UDL in neutral or positive terms, as listed below:

- The university should use its resources in renewable ways (build once, use many times).
- With the adoption of UDL, faculty members and instructional designers do not have to be experts in responding to an increasingly complex universe of barriers.
- Students themselves expect their professors and university services to be inclusive.

The McGill University communication program is focused on faculty interactions and research into the efficacy of their own UDL measures. Staff members created a series of "Faculty Resources in 60 Seconds" to introduce the UDL framework through teaching strategies, workshops, and consultations. By reframing UDL away from the disability-services-only model, McGill University places inclusive design within a larger social model of push access that does not require people to have to pull, or make requests, in order to take advantage of inclusive practices.

Conclusion

Although McGill's UDL advocacy program did not need to (and indeed, couldn't) rely on legal requirements to support their efforts, it is still important for universities to look to the law as a foundation for UDL adoption. Just getting to the level of compliance with existing law can be tough for those of us who are working on shoestring budgets and with few human resources.

A cautionary tale is that of the University of California, Berkeley. In 2016, the university received an order from the U.S. Department of Justice to make more than twenty thousand video lectures and podcasts that were then "available to the public on YouTube, iTunes U and the university's webcast.berkeley.edu site" (Straumsheim, 2017a). Rather than incur the vast expense of captioning or transcribing such a large number of videos, the university decided in early 2017 to remove the majority of them from public access, requiring a Berkeley username and password to get access to the content. By removing the materials from public access, the university paid heed to the "economic realities of the tight budget climate."

The vice chancellor for undergraduate education said in a statement that "as part of the campus's ongoing effort to improve the accessibility of online content, we have determined that instead of focusing on legacy content that is 3–10 years old, much of which sees very limited use, we will work to create new public content that includes accessible features" (Koshland, 2017). The Berkeley solution does not take advantage of UDL. By continuing to frame the issue in narrow terms of disability services, the University of California, Berkeley, seems to be missing an opportunity to provide greater and freer access to content and materials. Instead, the decision to pull back content from wider access—ostensibly "to better protect instructor intellectual property from 'pirates' who have reused content for personal profit without consent" (Koshland, 2017)—results in more restricted access to materials.

Of course, by moving the bulk of its media resources off public venues, the university reduces the immediate need for making the materials accessible, adopting the wait-for-a-request stance that Andrew Lessman bemoaned at the beginning of this chapter. After the announcement, *Inside Higher Ed* published a follow-up article in which the author asked thirteen other large public and private universities whether they planned to emulate Berkeley and restrict access to or take down public-facing content. None of the five that responded said that they would, but a comment from Michael Ball of the University of Minnesota reveals the deeper issue: what should institutions do when government forces their hand toward broad accessibility? "For clarity's sake: The question *IHE* asked us (U of MN) was whether we were planning to follow Berkeley's action in taking content down. The question was not about how we would react to a letter similar to Berkeley's. A response to that second question gets very complicated very quickly and responding to that with conjecture wouldn't be responsible" (Straumsheim, 2017b). Indeed, more than forty scholars, administrators, and advocacy groups published an open condemnation of Berkeley's response to remove, rather than provide access to, the materials in question: "We acknowledge that remedial accessibility work—after-the-fact efforts to make content accessible—can be costly. Such work requires not only the addition of captions and audio descriptions but also checking to ensure that documents and materials can be read by screen readers or accessed on a variety of devices. That is why it is so important that leadership enforce accessibility policies from the beginning" (Vogler et al., 2017). We should definitely find opportunities to create bits and pieces of roles to advocate for UDL so our colleges and universities don't end up looking at mountains of work, as happened in the Berkeley case. In fact, the great disappointment of the scholars who published the open letter was that there were several points prior to the removal of the content where Berkeley could have taken action, when the problem was smaller in scope and more tractable.

There are several ways to address legal requirements in a positive way. For instance, create internships for graduate and upper-level undergraduate students, especially those studying education, organizational psychology, human resource management, social work, and related fields. Create a faculty-in-residence program by buying out a percentage of one faculty member's contract each semester or year. Consider partnering with third-party vendors. For things like captioning, some institutions send out any caption job for videos over five minutes long because the vendor will be faster and more accurate than in-house resources can be.

Many institutions have already devoted resources specifically to accessibility, but they tend to be siloed off from one another. Perhaps there is an accessibility person as part of the web-design or marketing team, and another specialist in the disability services office, and perhaps someone with an inclusive-design focus in the teaching-and-learning center. The best thing you can do on your campus is to get these folks in a room together regularly so that the conversation becomes about how the campus can make learner interactions go more smoothly and offer choices about those interactions wherever possible.

We argue that adopting the UDL framework is a way to draw a metaphorical line in the sand. But we also recognize that doing so is an individualized process, that each institution has its own mission statement, resources, and expertise in-house. By reframing the conversation away from "we must," we open opportunities to listen to the needs of our colleagues, to design learning interactions that help faculty members and staffers interact with the widest possible range of students, and, yes, to follow the law. In the next chapter, we will dive deeper into one potent way to do that reframing: students' mobile phones.

A THOUGHT EXERCISE

Connect with four groups at your institution:

- faculty leaders (members of the senate, tenured professors, directors of the learning center, department chairs),
- student services leaders (the registrar, director of financial aid services, writing center or tutoring center director, residence life, student athletics),
- administrative leaders (provost, deans, vice-president for academic affairs), and
- students (student government representatives, club leaders, your own students).

Do a ten-minute interview with at least one person from each group, in which you listen to their perceptions about legal compliance and best practices in terms of inclusive design for interactions with learners. Ask members of each group the following questions.

1. What laws govern accessibility at our institution?
2. What evidence do you see of inclusive practices already?
3. Are there opportunities to give wider access to the various interactions at our institution?

Reflect on the responses and synthesize a paragraph or two to define how your institution views accessibility in terms of what it must do and what it can do. This information will help to form your UDL implementation plan later in the book.

PART 2

Reframing UDL

CHAPTER 3

Meet the Mobile Learners

Meet Fatimah

Fatimah lives in Bay City, a small city about 115 miles north of Detroit, Michigan. Born in 1980, she is a combat veteran who served in Operation Dragon Strike in Afghanistan in 2010, a single parent of a twelve-year-old son and a ten-year-old daughter, a breadwinner with a job at Dow Corning, and a student taking courses toward an associate's degree in accounting at a community college near her home. Fatimah wants to keep up with her course work, but she has little time to study, mostly because she's always in motion. She lives only six miles from her job and two miles from her college, but she regularly logs more than 150 driving miles every week, thanks to grocery shopping, religious services, looking in on her elderly mother, and taking her two children to their extracurricular activities.

Fatimah would never talk about herself as a distance-education student; she drives to campus two nights during the week and Saturdays to attend classes. She benefits from the online, hybrid-format, and technology-enhanced courses that the college offers, though. She has to make sure that her children are in bed by 9:30 p.m. every school night. Thanks to the captions on her professors' video materials, Fatimah can turn off the sound and still follow along. Because one of her professors created audio podcast versions of the study guides for her course, Fatimah listens to the study guides in her car on her way to and from work, and then she studies with the PDF versions of the guides during her breaks and mealtimes at work.

Fatimah's challenge has never been distance. She lives within a thirty-minute walk of her community college, and she drives to various appointments, kids' sporting events, visits, and classes. She's a road warrior, for certain. She does not identify as having a disability, either. If we think in terms of barriers, defining them as "factors in a person's environment that, through their absence or presence, limit functioning and create disability" (World Health Organization, 2007, 230), then Fatimah's barrier is time, or the lack of it in her typically jam-packed daily schedule.

Because you are reading this book, you are likely a proponent of Universal Design for Learning, or you are at least curious about what it is and how it can help you in your design and teaching work. This chapter is all about why we haven't adopted UDL more broadly in higher education yet and how you can become something of a subtle evangelist for UDL in your faculty or staff meetings. How can you make the argument for adopting UDL principles at your institution? Well, for starters, stop talking about students with disabilities.

Emotional Valence

The theory of Universal Design for Learning (UDL) has only recently become buzz-worthy in higher education. Our colleagues in the K–12 world have been using it for years as a method for designing the interactions among learners and teachers to be as inclusive as possible. As you read in chapter 1, UDL is slowly gaining ground as a mental framework and design approach in colleges and universities; however, the perception among most higher education faculty members and administrators is that UDL is somehow tied to accessibility efforts on behalf of students with learning challenges, especially those who identify as having disabilities. This perception is unfortunate, since higher education faculty attitudes toward students with disabilities, as measured by study after study since the early 1980s, continue to be problematic, at best. The introduction outlined the way in which many faculty members experience negative emotions—explicitly or implicitly—when they think about accommodations for learners who identify as having disabilities.

And Fatimah? It's statistically likely that her professors created those video captions and audio versions of lecture materials, which she found so helpful, not because they were reaching out to all of their learners but to accommodate, in past course offerings, specific learners with disabilities. We want to argue that adopting and implementing UDL—which takes a lot of planning and effort—is best supported by changing the terms of the entire conversation about why faculty members and developers should adopt it in the first place. Let's stop talking only about the disability argument and adopt a completely different mind-set, one that doesn't automatically come with the negative emotional valence associated with disabilities; instead, let's reach out to students on their phones.

Mobile Learners

Fatimah is a member of the group of people between the ages of twenty and forty that was labeled the "digital generation" by scholars and thinkers such as Howard Gardner, Ian Jukes, and Ted McCain. The usual way that futurists talk about the digital generation is to see them as somehow separate from the rest of us, by dint of their use of technology. "Learning itself has undergone a transformation over the past thirty years. The Internet is changing the way that . . . college students gather and process information in all aspects of their lives. For Digital Natives, 'research' is more likely to mean a Google search than a trip to a library. They are more likely to check in with the Wikipedia community, or to turn to another online friend, than they are to ask a reference librarian for help" (Palfrey and Gasser, 2008, 239). It is problematic to think about a generation made up of digital natives, though, because technology use is not an age-based concern, and merely being younger does not confer expertise. Think for a minute about how you and the students at your institution use your mobile phones now. Regardless of your ages, all of you have likely become micro-coordinators alongside Howard Gardner and Katie Davis's "app generation." What they describe as a characteristic of teens sounds familiar to those who are much older, too: "Sixty-three percent of teens say they text every day with people in their lives, and the typical teen sends about sixty text messages per day. . . . And now, with the widespread use of app-filled smartphones, the range of operations that teens can perform on the go has extended far beyond phone calls and texting. . . . The app mentality supports the belief that just as information, goods, and services are always and immediately available, so too are people. Scholars in the mobile communication field have dubbed such in-the-moment planning micro-coordination" (Gardner and Davis, 2013, 94).

Of course, being a micro-coordinator is just a fancier way of saying that all of us have become very, very, *very* attached to our phones. And it's not just teenagers. Google collects massive amounts of data about how Internet users across the globe interact with their devices. Because it is far and away the most-used online search portal, Google knows not only what we search for but also how long we spend in given kinds of online tasks, what devices we are using to accomplish those tasks, and what our online habits say about our learning needs, especially as they relate to our immediate everyday tasks and goals.

In a 2015 report entitled *Micro-Moments: Your Guide to Winning the Shift to Mobile*, Google's team of researchers compiled trillions of data points into some eye-opening numbers about how closely our smartphones have become integrated into the rhythms of our everyday lives. Since 2010, the balance of Internet-connected device ownership, use, and dependence has shifted decisively away from place-bound computing and toward mobile Internet access.

> Millennials? They're really attached. 87% always have their smartphone at their side, day and night. That little device by our sides is transforming our lives, whether we actively notice it or not. It's enabling new ways of doing and learning things. It's helping us discover new ideas and new businesses. It's helping us manage our to-dos, tackle our problems, and inspire our plans.
>
> Mobile search behavior is a good reflection of our growing reliance: in many countries, including the U.S., more searches take place on mobile devices than on computers. Mobile is quickly becoming our go-to. When we want or need something, we tune in via convenient, self-initiated bursts of digital activity.
>
> Take the oft-quoted stat that we check our phones 150 times a day. Pair it with another that says we spend 177 minutes on our phones per day, and you get a pretty fascinating reality: mobile

sessions that average a mere 1 minute and 10 seconds long, dozens and dozens of times per day. It's like we're speed dating with our phones. (Adams, Burkholder, and Hamilton, 2015, 3)

The report from which all of this Google research comes is not intended to help educators to connect with far-flung and busy students. The report is meant to convince companies to spend advertising dollars to reach out to people who can't seem to put their phones down.

However, we academics can learn from what Google has figured out. Google calls most people's pattern of using their mobile phones "micro-moments." All of us—not just members of a particular generation—use our phones to help us make decisions in everyday situations like researching brands of toothpaste or comparing the quality of bed-sheet sets, all while we are standing in the store aisle. We place calls on our phones when we want to move from the world of information to the world of people. Once we find the set of sheets we want, we might then call the customer-service line for the store in which we are standing, to inquire about stock in other colors. We use our mobile devices to help us make decisions: Thai, Chinese, or barbecue? And which restaurant is closest? And which one also gets the best reviews on Yelp?

Google advises companies to create small, snackable pieces of content and interactions to which people can get access via different media, based on the choices (and devices) of the people who want to interact:

Here are three essential strategies that can help you win micro-moments:

- Be There. You've got to anticipate the micro-moments for users in your industry, and then commit to being there to help when those moments occur.
- Be Useful. You've got to be relevant to consumers' needs in the moment and connect people to the answers they're looking for.
- Be Quick. They're called micro-moments for a reason. Mobile users want to know, go, and buy swiftly. Your mobile experience has to be fast and frictionless. (Adams, Burkholder, and Hamilton, 2015, 6)

If you find that you are engaging in such micro-moments throughout most days, that you are snacking on information for a few seconds at a time, in the moment when needs or curiosity arise, then you are a part of the digital generation. Elizabeth Losh makes the point that the very labeling of a group of people encourages us to see them in a simplified, homogeneous fashion. "I've been a public opponent of casting students too easily as 'digital natives' for a number of reasons. Of course, anthropology and sociology already supply a host of arguments against assuming preconceived ideas about what it means to be a native when studying group behavior. I am particularly suspicious of this type of language about so-called digital natives because it could naturalize cultural practices, further a colonial othering of the young, and oversimplify complicated questions about membership in a group" (Losh, 2014). We want to broaden this concept to include many ways of interacting with one another and with technology, and to unmoor it from a generational definition.

In a significant sense, the terms *digital natives* and *digital generation* have been around longer than the connected-anytime-and-anyplace reality that they attempt to describe. For example, in 2008, John Palfrey and Urs Gasser described digital natives as being tech experts, but place-bound by their desktop and laptop computers: "In the Internet context, images and stories of this sort are accessible from any Internet-ready device—a laptop sitting around the house or a cell phone with a decent Web browser (though, to be clear, most Digital Natives rarely access the Web through these devices today)" (Palfrey and Gasser, 2008, 88). Only a decade later, that caveat at the end about how few people use their phones to go online seems almost quaint: today's eighteen-year-old college freshman can barely remember a time when web access wasn't part of mobile phone technology, and people in their thirties, forties, fifties, and beyond have largely adapted to a world in which mobile computing is simply part of the fabric of everyday life, even if they themselves might not be the savviest participants in that mobile culture.

Mobile learners are typically identified by the technology that they adopt or master rather than the historical epochs in which they live.

Only in recent memory has characterization of a generation taken on a distinctly technological flavor. In his studies of successive waves of college students, Arthur Levine (with colleagues) has discerned a revealing trend. Students in the latter decades of the twentieth century characterized themselves in terms of their common experiences vis-à-vis the Kennedy assassination, the Vietnam War, the Watergate burglary and investigation, the shuttle disaster, the attack on the Twin Towers in September 2011. But once the opening years of the twenty-first century had passed, political events took a back seat. Instead, young people spoke about the common experiences of their generation in terms of the Internet, the web, handheld devices, and smartphones. (Gardner and Davis, 2013, 50)

Our approach to defining the digital generation is to say that all people who use mobile technology on a daily basis for problem solving, information gathering, and social purposes—regardless of their age—are mobile learners. This definition allows for variation among the skill sets, background knowledge, and breadth of application that we all possess. This variation is key to our assertion that, as faculty members and learning designers, we should move away from a people-with-disabilities mind-set when it comes to UDL, and we should move toward a people-with-mobile-devices mind-set.

A Very Short (and Very Groovy) History of Assistive Technology

Now that over-the-air mobile bandwidth is robust enough in many places to support video streaming and other data-intensive uses of mobile devices, we are all growing increasingly comfortable with the idea of always being connected. For some of us, that comfort has grown into dependence. "Over two-thirds of smartphone users, 68%, say they check their phone within 15 minutes of waking up in the morning. 30% are willing to admit that they actually get *anxious* when they don't have their phone on them" (Adams, Burkholder, and

Hamilton, 2015, 3). Over a relatively short period of time, our mobile devices—especially our mobile phones—have had a profound impact on our communication patterns, our sense of connectedness, and how we go about our daily routines. Did you stop reading for a few seconds, somewhere in this chapter, because your phone chimed to alert you to a message or new content? You're not alone. But we micro-coordinators are not the first people to have used this kind of technology. In fact, the first ones beat us to it by at least forty years.

Who were these groovy people who were so far ahead of their times? People with physical and learning challenges were often the first people to use specific technology devices for communication and connectedness—this is one of the reasons that UDL has gotten so enmeshed with "people with disabilities" in our higher education mind-set. Such devices were, and still are, categorized as assistive technology, or AT. Try this thought experiment with us, and see how the shift from a disability approach to a technology-use mind-set has been slowly progressing since the 1970s.

Imagine, if you will, that it is 1977. *Star Wars* has just been released (just *Star Wars*, with no episode number in the title, because right now there's only one film). *Saturday Night Fever* is making John Travolta a household name for his good looks and disco moves, and great investment opportunities can be had in the gold chain and polyester leisure suit industries.

You are walking down the sidewalk, and you pass four people. The first person is standing on the sidewalk, looking at a movie poster in a store window, and he is holding up a device that magnifies the view onto a small glass screen. The second person is sitting with friends at a café table, pressing a button on a device that is sticking out of her ear. The third person you pass is seated at a desk in an office, and you can see that he is typing on a keyboard, but there is no paper coming out of the device, as you would expect with a typewriter. The fourth person is walking alone toward you on the sidewalk; he has headphones on, and he appears to be having one side of a conversation—with whom, you cannot tell.

In 1977, you'd likely think that the person looking at the movie poster had some sort of visual challenge. The second person is obviously adjusting a hearing aid to be better able to understand the conversation of her friends. The third person likely has a hearing impairment and is using a teletype machine, where the machine connects through a telephone handset to send coded signals to another person, who then reads what you have typed, line by line, on a small electronic screen. The fourth person is probably listening to music on his portable radio—and may be mentally unbalanced, poor fellow.

In 1977, all of these scenarios would be seen first (and perhaps only) through a disability lens. People with physical or mental challenges are using devices specially made to address their challenges, although what's up with that fourth guy?

Now, change only the date. It's today. There's still a *Star Wars* film playing, but now we're up to Episode 9, or 10, or 4½, or whatever franchise reboot they're working on. The hot movie star and fashion trends have moved on: now it's Ryan Reynolds and lots of plaid everywhere.

You walk down the sidewalk again, and you see the same four people. The assumptions available to you are very different. The man holding his device up to the movie poster? He's on his phone, taking a picture or scanning a code. The lady adjusting something in her ear? That's a Bluetooth phone headset, no? The man in the office is obviously tapping away on a tablet device. And the person who is talking to the empty air? Heck, everybody is talking to the empty air—we're all on our mobile phones, with ear buds and inline microphones, blithely conversing with our spouses and kids and colleagues.

Notice that today the devices that the four people are using still fall into the category of assistive technology. They just aren't intended to be used only by people with disabilities anymore. It's not exceptional or weird, these days, to see people using portable technology devices. Of course, the use of technology to assist people in lowering barriers is still with us. In fact, we might be wrong about the lady adjusting the device in her ear—it might still be a hearing aid today. We might be wrong about the gent taking that photo of the movie poster—it might be a magnifying device, after all.

And that's why we're introducing you to the world of the mobile device "generation," and why we're including you in it too. We're now in a culture where the augmentation of human abilities isn't just the stuff of science fiction. Most of us have assistive technology devices in our pockets, and we're not carrying them around because we need them to address physical or mental barriers. So, good-bye negative emotional valence. Now, let's talk about how you can make the case to your colleagues and administrators for adopting UDL on a broad basis in your department, college, or university.

Two Kinds of Digital Divide

When was the last time you heard a senior campus leader talk about the need to increase student retention? It probably wasn't too long ago. Senior leaders often talk in terms of reaching out to the most vulnerable learner populations: "we must do something that would help our most at-risk students to stay with us." One of the symptoms of socioeconomic inequality has recently become a potential means of supporting at-risk students, which is music to administrative ears. Student services areas in higher education live and breathe strategies for retaining students. They are told to provide services, to help students with their academic and nonacademic college experience: retained students are key drivers of institutional success.

You have heard of the digital divide, in which people who can afford the latest technology get better access to information and connectivity than those who are unable to keep up. A place-bound computing model held sway up until about 2010, and the digital divide was an established phenomenon: those who could buy computers and Internet services for their homes were the haves. Then something curious happened: access got remarkably less expensive. In a 2015 study, the Pew Research Center discovered that a growing number of people who would otherwise have been included in the have-nots are opting to buy smartphones as their only Internet connection:

> 64% of American adults now own a smartphone of some kind, up from 35% in the spring of 2011. . . . 10% of Americans own a smartphone but do not have broadband at home, and 15% own a smartphone but say that they have a limited number of options for going online other than their cell phone. Those with relatively low income and educational attainment levels, younger

adults, and non-whites are especially likely to be smartphone-dependent. . . . Smartphones are widely used for navigating numerous important life activities, from researching a health condition to accessing educational resources. Lower-income and smartphone-dependent users are especially likely to turn to their phones for navigating job and employment resources. . . . young adults have deeply embedded mobile devices into the daily contours of their lives. (Smith, 2015)

What interests campus leaders in these statistics is that more and more people whom we used to serve poorly (or not at all) in higher education now have the means of connecting with learning opportunities in, as Google has phrased it, the micro-moments of their lives. In the same Pew Research Center study, we learn that 30 percent of American smartphone owners have used their smartphones "to take a class or get educational content" (Smith, 2015). One intriguing opportunity that smartphone ownership affords us is that we can now interact with practically all of our learners outside of formal class time, especially if we design those interactions to help them make sense of the information overload that many of them are experiencing. "Digital Natives are doing the same things their parents did with information, just in different ways. While they may not be learning the same things through the same processes, it's not the case that Digital Natives are interacting less with information. They are simply coping with more information, and that information comes to their attention in new ways—offering new possibilities for engagement" (Palfrey and Gasser, 2008, 244).

Ignore the problematic digital natives label and think about the impact: if our learners are now drinking from the metaphorical fire hose of information, UDL allows us to help them be intentional about how they take in, evaluate, and share information. There is further hope that when you talk about UDL to your colleagues and campus leaders they will listen when you couch its benefits in terms of reaching learners on their mobile devices: "Mobile technology is ubiquitous in the lives of today's college students. Although 83 percent of adults between the ages of 18 and 29 own a smartphone, mobile device ownership among college students is even higher; according to a 2014

EDUCAUSE report, 86 percent of undergraduates owned a smartphone" (Chen et al., 2015). The upward trend toward nearly universal smartphone ownership is borne out by the data trends in the annual EDUCAUSE survey. The 86 percent figure reported above by the EDUCAUSE Center for Analysis and Research (ECAR) in 2014 was bested in both 2015 and 2016: "student ownership of digital devices continues to grow despite approaching market saturation for laptops and smartphones. From 2015 to 2016, smartphone ownership increased from 92% to 96%" (Brooks, 2016, 5).

Students aren't yet using their smartphones for formal course-related learning in large numbers. They're more likely to be engaging in those micro-moments Google talks about. "Mobile learning in U.S. higher education is on the rise. College students use their mobile devices mostly for self-directed informal learning rather than in the formal academic context, however, which makes it challenging to get an accurate picture of academic use" (Chen and Denoyelles, 2013).

Perhaps this puts the wrong end of the telescope to our eye, though. We have now uncovered the second type of digital divide, the one between (1) how and when students are typically able to learn and (2) how faculty members and designers create learning interactions.

This is not to say that faculty members need to be tech savvy in order to adopt good UDL strategies. We will address some low-tech and no-tech UDL strategies in chapters 6, 7, and 8. However, at many colleges and universities, the percentage of faculty members who provide interactions for their learners beyond the time and space of the physical classroom remains relatively small. For these few academics, this going beyond provides benefits to students and faculty members alike (Davies, Schelly, and Spooner, 2012, 198) by allowing learners to shift, select, and schedule their study time better to match their available free time.

There is a big opportunity to unite students' willingness to learn using mobile devices and faculty members' creation of learning interactions that make use of such devices. In fact, many faculty members who use the learning management system (LMS) as part of their courses today use the LMS like a giant electronic filing cabinet—just storing materials, handouts, lecture notes, and the dreaded narrated

PowerPoint slides. In *Dancing with Digital Natives*, Sarah Bongey argues that much of the publisher-provided multimedia content that comes with our textbook orders is poorly designed window dressing: "[We stress] the need for any delivery method to assist students in developing a visual framework, [and we] disparage publishers and instructors who create and distribute illustrative material of poor quality—solely to include some visual interest. . . . We're better off with accurate verbal descriptions than inaccurate full-color moving images. So, in that way, the technology that allows easy animation can be a hindrance, and, to tell the truth, that is mostly what [we] see today. The potential is fantastic, but the reality is extremely disappointing" (Bongey, 2011, 281).

The point here is that just putting all of our old slides and speaking prompts into an online repository doesn't mean that we're engaging with our learners. UDL, especially when we see it through a mobile device outreach lens, helps us to counteract the filing cabinet approach to online course materials and interactions. A quick UDL approach might be for faculty to utilize the discussion board on the LMS to promote discussion both within and outside of formal class interactions. We will examine this more deeply in chapter 5 when we introduce the plus-one way to think about UDL. Faculty members and designers could go one step further and provide specific prompts based on class discussion or the readings in order to help develop students' thoughts into well-versed opinions. This not only increases student knowledge of the subject, but also increases their confidence to speak to the subject in a manner (whether in class or online) that is comfortable to them.

While Google has determined that most people with smartphones are finding snackable content for answering specific questions and learning about processes, comparatively few faculty members and designers utilize or develop online content that supplements their courses in ways that are easily experienced on phone screens. Later, we will examine the concept of responsive design, in which content automatically rearranges itself to work well on varying screen sizes. For now, though, think about all of the students whom we aren't yet reaching when they have a few minutes here and there throughout their day for learning. For "digital natives" in this passage, substitute "mobile learners," and things will start to click: "The first generation of digital native learners [is] growing up, graduating, and making inroads in the workplace. New cohorts of natives are entering our classrooms every year. While these students may seem very comfortable with the technology used in the classroom, they will need solid skills to help them wisely navigate the use of digital technologies and truly be in a place where they can constructively and reliably leverage the continual and lifelong learning opportunities that the digital age offers" (Bongey, 2011, 286).

In old kung fu movies, the phrase "when the pupil is ready, the teacher appears" is often invoked to explain the uncanny timing of the hero's supposedly accidental meeting with the wise elder who teaches the hero new skills. In the realm of UDL, the pupil has been ready for a while, now, and the teacher had better hurry up and appear.

College students—whether eighteen-year-olds or returning adult learners—are already using their mobile devices in learning situations both formal and informal, such as doing homework, working on course projects, and settling curious questions with their smartphones. In fact, owning a smartphone is an enabling factor that leads to greater learning inquiry behaviors. "Students who own devices use them for learning. However, comparisons between the 2012 and 2014 data show that use for learning depended on the type of device the student owned. Percentages increased considerably among smartphone owners (from 58 to 77 percent)" (Chen et al., 2015). If students are ready for anytime-anywhere learning interactions, UDL is a good framework for creating such elements in our courses and programs of study, and we already have the tools to be able to design our interactions so that students on mobile devices can interact with materials, one another, and us. "In fact, undergraduate college students who were surveyed on their perceptions related to the use of an LMS to support instruction and promote UDL reported high levels of engagement and satisfaction, with 98 percent saying that they would make a special effort to enroll in future courses that used the LMS this way" (Bongey, 2011, 277). Every year, our colleagues at EDUCAUSE survey tens of thousands of undergraduate students across the United States and in fifteen other countries. Their survey asks about students' familiarity with and ideas about the use of technology in the learning process. A recent conclusion from their survey shows that students are not only ready for their professors to make content and interactions more accessible to them on their mobile devices, more and more students would prefer such access.

The popularity of mobile technologies among college students is increasing dramatically. Results from the ECAR study on students suggest that many undergraduate students bring their own digital devices to college, favoring small and portable ones such as smartphones and tablets. Although students still rate laptops (85 percent) as the most important devices to their academic success, the importance of mobile devices such as tablets (45 percent), smartphones (37 percent), and e-book readers (31 percent) is noticeably on the rise. Increasingly, students say they want the ability to access academic resources on their mobile devices. In fact, 67 percent of students' smartphones and tablets are reportedly being used for academic purposes, a rate that has nearly doubled in just one year. (Chen and Denoyelles, 2013)

Further, we are at a tipping point, technologically, where the number of mobile device operating systems now outnumbers desktop operating systems for the first time (see fig. 3.1). That is, for the first time in history, more people own mobile devices than own desktop devices.

So, if the students are ready for us to design our interactions so they can take place on their mobile devices, why haven't many of us done so, or at least begun the experiment? In many cases, teaching and technology are seen as being in conflict. Technology is often perceived as an intrusion from outside the teaching dynamic. "Despite being busy stage-managing increasingly complex PowerPoint presentations or elaborate clicker quizzes recommended by instructional technologists, professors notice student apathy and preoccupation, and their feelings do get hurt. Bring up the subject of student engagement and digital distraction at any faculty gathering and brace yourself for tales of woe involving laptops, cell phones, and other instruments of pedagogical subversion that seem to further distance instructors from

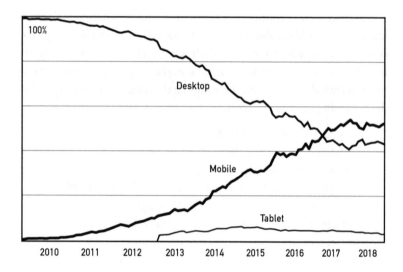

100%

Desktop

Mobile

Tablet

2010   2011   2012   2013   2014   2015   2016   2017   2018

Figure 3.1: Desktop vs. mobile vs. tablet market share worldwide (StatCounter Global Stats, 2018, used under CC BY-SA 3.0 license)

their students" (Losh, 2014). While it is tempting to see mobile devices as instruments of pedagogical subversion, such a view assumes that students wish to use their devices only for noninstructional purposes, and that is simply not so.

Even advocates for the use of UDL sometimes mistake greater access with a lessening of meaning or contact. Jason Palmer, writing in the *Cleveland Law Review* in 2015, assumes that having a choice of interaction methods means that students are somehow receiving a subpar educational experience. "The relationship between engagement and student success is critical to the growth and development of self-efficacy in Millennial students. One aspect of engagement is personal interaction with faculty and fellow students. While advances in technology, such as IMs, SMS, and social media, have provided new means for students to communicate, these electronic communications have removed interpersonal dynamics from face-to-face interactions, with a resulting dehumanization of the communication experience.

Students have grown accustomed to this lack of interpersonal communication and have allowed it to permeate their educational experience" (Palmer, 2015, 694).

Here is where our argument about UDL and mobile devices really provides an advantage over the viewpoint that one should adopt UDL only for learners with disabilities. What Palmer is bemoaning is the unfettered, unstructured, and unguided nature of most instant communication. If all of our learning interactions were akin to Snapchat sessions that expire soon after their creation, we'd be right in saying that the result is dehumanizing. UDL allows us to design interactions that counter the kind of depersonalization that can accompany technological mediation. It provides a mind-set, structure, and choice architecture for learning that is independent from real-time, place-bound interactions. It encourages more, not less, interaction and communication, and the reason is a little counterintuitive.

This Is Not the Future You Are Looking For

We have to go all the way back to the 1940s, where a far-seeing thinker predicted what the information-age college or university might look like. In a now-famous essay called "As We May Think," Vannevar Bush predicted in 1945 that people in the future would construct their own "traces" in collections of all of their books, magazines, photographs, notes, letters, and documents. Bush called the machine for storing and indexing these items (on microfilm) a "memex," and today we recognize his logic as prefiguring the hypertext structure of the Internet.

Such a self-contained encyclopedia-style model meant that Bush got one thing very wrong: he assumed that each person would have his or her own memex that wasn't connected to anyone else's. Individuals would be responsible for building their own memexes, and the burdens of creation, study, recall, and demonstration were pursuits for individual people, working alone with their customized collections of information.

Bush's essay predicted that we would live in a face-to-face world where information was stored in ever-smaller physical locations:

libraries, encyclopedias, microfilm. When, with the advent of the Internet, recorded information became untethered from a physical form, we leapt beyond just storing information and started actively sharing and creating it ourselves. We are now used to being connected, both in terms of social relationships and being digitally plugged in. In books with titles like *Hamlet's Blackberry, You Are Not a Gadget,* and *The Winter of Our Disconnect,* authors today grapple with what it means to be a human being in the actual world and a presence in the online world simultaneously.

This is how you will become a subtle evangelist for adopting UDL at your institution: not by making the argument that UDL helps learners with disabilities, not by talking about the return you get for the work you put into your course interactions—although both of these are powerful and true outcomes of adopting UDL. No, you will win over your colleagues when you talk about how the changes you make in your own teaching or design have helped to save you work, bother, or time. You can make the argument for a number of different ways of approaching mobile device learning, so long as you are able to show others the choices that you provide to your students about how they bring their connected selves into the learning space with you. Bailin Fang's ideas in *EDUCAUSE Review* about wireless devices in the classroom support our idea of reframing UDL as a mobile access strategy; notice the parallels between the types of learning that Fang advocates and the multiple-means approach of UDL:

> Once we start to think beyond the traditional concept of learning as classroom lectures, many new opportunities for learning unfold:
>
> - Behaviorist learning, in which mobile devices are used to create stimulus-response connections such as content delivery through mobile devices.
> - Constructivist learning, in which mobile devices support student construction of knowledge.
> - Situated learning, in which mobile devices are used in authentic context and culture.

- Collaborative learning, in which students learn with their mobile devices through social interactions.
- Informal and lifelong learning, which happens outside of a formal education context.
- Teaching and learning support, in which mobile devices and their associated resources are used not for actual learning but for support of human performances.

If institutions broaden the scope and definition of "educational value," unique uses for mobile phones, laptops, or other wireless access devices can positively affect student learning and student life in general. (Fang, 2009)

UDL allows you to go beyond merely giving your students information, too. It's all about designing interaction in the learning experience and providing learners with choices about how they interact. However, giving information is a great way at least to start thinking about UDL. "Reading is not students' only consumption behavior; they also use their devices to read blog feeds or check microblog updates, listen to podcasts, and watch lecture videos. According to Scott Hamm, easy access to content reduces the cognitive load for learners in that knowledge does not always stay in the head, but it can be located in the world. . . . Having materials easily available in a mobile device frees up mental bandwidth and lets students focus more on learning important concepts, while also letting the knowledge base remain, literally, in their hands or pockets" (Fang, 2014). Note, though, that this example is only a strategy to get started. When people do not have mastery of information and just look it up in order to examine topics in a cursory or introductory fashion, their thinking tends to be shallower. For example, students who don't have their core math precepts memorized are less successful at higher-order math problems than students with a baseline of memorized facts. We will examine strategies for deeper and higher-order engagement in the coming chapters.

Students with mobile devices also present an opportunity to increase learner engagement, if done in an intentional way. In a 2016 webinar, "Leveraging Mobile Devices to Further Teaching and

Learning," Julius Su commented on how his institution was making ubiquitous interaction the watchword for learner engagement.

> We do have some data on student success. We developed a micro-assessment technique to really compare and isolate—not tablets because it's not about the technology—but really how they're used, so we found that the impact was really key to active learning. A famous phrase that began to circulate around our campus was "the students can no longer escape learning," because in the classroom, they simply had to learn, but they had to actually draw out, for example, mitosis, and submit the picture of it right there in class, so there was greater positive pressure to engage. What we saw was that the A students were going to get As no matter what, but it really helped the D students come up for Cs, and the C students come up for Bs, and so on. It really helped those who needed it the most. (Su et al., 2016)

The technology itself is almost beside the point, here. The professors in the example created alternative methods for giving students the content for their biology courses, adding various ways for the students to show that they indeed understood the concepts. The choices that students had (watch a simulation or read the process steps, write an essay or film an experiment) helped them to be intentional about their interactions with the material, with each other, and with the professor.

We will examine the nuts and bolts of UDL in the next chapter. Now you have the rhetorical and neuroscientific firepower to be able to make a broad-based argument for adopting UDL principles at your institution. UDL is a way to reach out to students via their mobile devices and offer them choices about how they get information, demonstrate their skills, and stay engaged.

Meet Stan

Remember Fatimah, the adult learner whose story opened this chapter? We want to close with another student's story that could serve as the next step for Fatimah. We recently talked to Stan, who is twenty years old, from a working-class Latino family on the southwest side of

Chicago. Stan's parents never went to college. They came to the United States years ago, before Stan was born, and both of them still work in the Nabisco bakery near their home. Stan works part-time at UPS, and, in 2016, he was studying at Northeastern Illinois University to become an accountant.

Because money is sometimes tight in his family, Stan had to decide whether to buy a computer or a smartphone. He went for the phone in order to stay connected to family and friends. He doesn't check his college-provided e-mail account every day, but it seems as though he checks his text messages on his phone every few minutes that he is awake. Stan sometimes experiences "phantom vibration syndrome" (Drouin, Kaiser, and Miller, 2013), where he feels that his phone is vibrating against his leg to indicate a new message—but it's really not.

Stan's accounting professor has adapted her teaching materials and interactions to take advantage of the fact that Stan and his classmates all have smartphones. She posts her lecture notes as text files, alongside short screencast videos that show her working through various problems and talking about the steps. She also allows students to demonstrate their skills in traditional ways, like creating a spreadsheet, or in multimedia ways, like screencasting their own accounting practices. The professor shares examples from students in previous classes, and she links to lots of materials and examples from other accounting professors, as study aids for her own students.

Stan told us, "I don't understand why all of my professors don't do what she does. She's pretty flexible about how we get from 'I don't know' to 'let me show you.' And she provides examples and examples and examples until at least one of them sticks." Stan watches his professor's videos over and over—pausing, replaying, and snacking on different pieces of content whenever he finds a few minutes to study throughout his day. What Stan is experiencing is not new. Fang's "fluid learning" construct shares many tenets with UDL, for example:

> Instead of mobile learning, I call this second-generation mobile learning fluid learning, which focuses on the flow of learning between mobile and non-mobile devices, such as desktop computers. Fluid learning is enabled by a consideration of five attributes

when designing content or instructional activities: neutrality, granularity, portability, interactivity, and ubiquity.

- **Neutrality.** Content must be produced to be accessible via various devices and platforms.
- **Granularity.** Educators must re-present content in smaller units when possible so that students can access them anywhere, anytime. A major benefit of mobile devices is that people can use them to fill in little gaps of time when they are waiting in line at the box office or waiting on a meal in a restaurant.
- **Portability.** Content must be transferable across platforms. One reason Evernote has gained popularity among educators is that users can easily access it on most smartphones and computers.
- **Interactivity.** Learning flows when it is active and interactive; when learning stagnates, it is finished. Using various devices not only makes content consumption and creation easier, it also creates possibilities of interaction—with content, among students, and between teachers and students.
- **Ubiquity.** Fluid learning does not limit learners to the time they spend using devices. Fluid learning flows out of classrooms into multiple social contexts that provide authentic learning opportunities. (Fang, 2014)

The five characteristics of what Fang calls fluid learning echo the UDL framework of multiplicity, choice, and engagement.

In fact, by thinking about UDL through a mobile-learning lens, we can avoid one last potential pitfall: seeing the so-called digital generation as a homogeneous and well-defined group:

[There are] four potentially destructive cultural clichés about how "they" are different from "us":

- "They all have access to networked digital technologies. And they all have the skills to use these technologies";
- "And they're connected to one another by a common culture";

- "They are joined by a set of common practices"; and
- "Digital natives can learn to use software in a snap." (Losh, 2014)

Although the rise of mobile computing on cell phones has enhanced the technological abilities of many youth from low-income homes who grew up without access to desktop computing, the ability to tinker meaningfully becomes increasingly difficult with such black-boxed devices that rely on business models that perpetuate a push toward miniaturized components, planned obsolescence, proprietary code, and noninterchangeable parts. "I might say . . . that there are huge curricular costs to assuming knowledge transfer without obstacles, and that the term digital natives has been widely adopted by news outlets relatively uncritically, even as researchers point to how poorly digital natives may score on tests of basic digital skills, many of which depend on an ability to read fine print rather than respond to showy technical wizardry" (Losh, 2014). This is a good point on which to close our chapter: most people adopt various kinds of technology, smartphones among them, for practical reasons. The technology allows them to meet specific needs.

Conclusion

A recent study shows that 85 percent of Facebook videos are now watched without the sound turned on (Patel, 2016). People and companies who post video content to Facebook are now open-captioning their videos, meaning the captions display without the viewer having to select them or turn them on. Why does such a trend exist? People using Facebook are often in places where audio would be intrusive. The most common way to look at Facebook is through one's mobile phone, and video creators realize that "no sound" should not be a barrier to "this looks interesting," so they caption their videos. Note that the captioning is done not to accommodate potential Facebook users with disabilities, but for a more practical reason: access. In our reframing argument about UDL, we advocate taking the end of the word *accessibility* off and thinking only about access when we design the interactions that learners have with content, with each other, with their instructors, with support areas of our colleges and universities, and with the wider world.

Remember Google's concept of micro-moments? Those are predicated on meeting specific needs: people's needs for information, support, options. In this chapter, we looked at the ways in which just about everyone who is a learner is also a user of technology in some form. We examined how most people switch among many modes of taking in and expressing ideas. Learning styles don't exist, at least not as a destiny, fixed in place and immutable; we prefer to talk about learning preferences, which are dependent on learners' inclinations but also on their environments and constraints in the moments when learning takes place. For example, in Jason Palmer's review of how law students used UDL-varied materials to study for courses, he discovered that "significantly, as many as 50–70% of the population are 'multi-modal learners,' those who prefer to use two, three, or even four different learning styles" (Palmer, 2015, 701).

While there may not be a single age-bound or technology-bound digital generation, most of us use our mobile devices for learning needs—and many of us turn to our mobile devices first when we want to find out about something that we want to explore. One of the biggest challenges in adopting UDL in a program or at an institution is that it is often perceived as being only for people with disabilities.

Now you know that UDL helps us to reach out to learners across not only the ability spectrum, but the technology spectrum as well. You now have a well-structured and detailed argument to make when a colleague suggests that UDL is too much work for too few students. "Applying Universal Design for Learning principles to information resources, faculty-student interactions, and assessments will maximize student learning and increase self-efficacy in Millennial students" (Palmer, 2015, 679), as well as the rest of us who have mobile devices too.

A THOUGHT EXERCISE

Take a moment to list three learning tasks that we can do today with the phones in our pockets. Interpret the concept of learning tasks broadly—think about any time that we want to learn or review information, processes, or knowledge.

Next to each of the three items on your list, estimate the amount of time it takes to accomplish it.

Finally, think back to the pre–mobile phone days, and estimate how long it would take to accomplish the same or similar things.

Learning Tasks	Time with Mobile Device	Time without Mobile Device
Check my course schedule	*30 seconds (check course website)*	*2 minutes (find the paper syllabus)*
1.		
2.		
3.		

Given the chart, can you identify areas of learning that require body and brain without technological intervention? If so, what are they?

For the areas of learning that are better done without technology, what kinds of interactions might you have that still diversify the learning experience but without technology (e.g., speaking to experts, peer-guided facilitations, site visits)?

How might having choices and control in those interactions make them go more smoothly?

CHAPTER 4

———

Engage Digital Learners

———

Meet Philip

Until he moved to the University of Nevada, Las Vegas, in 2016, Philip Voorhees was the assistive technology and accessibility specialist for the Tennessee Board of Regents. For years, he has been an advocate for the educational rights of people with learning challenges, and he recently told us about an aha moment about the scope of the work he did for public colleges and universities across the state of Tennessee. Voorhees was talking with Ron Stewart, a managing consultant at AltFormat Solutions, about the amount of effort that many faculty members and support staffers put into providing accommodations for people with disabilities.

Voorhees wondered why so many faculty colleagues provided the same types of accommodations for students in their courses, over and over again. For instance, Voorhees seemed always to be working with faculty members who needed to have their video content captioned when students with hearing disabilities came into their courses. For some faculty members who went through the process of receiving accommodation requests and then requesting help from Voorhees and his team, the need to be proactive about alternative formats for video never really seemed to sink in. They tended to wait until accommodation requests happened in each of the courses they taught before they took action.

Voorhees was puzzled why more faculty members didn't take action across all of their courses, especially after they saw the benefit of responding to specific accommodation requests. He was dismayed that, despite good efforts over the past decade to train faculty members about the benefits of adopting Universal Design for Learning practices, few colleagues put them into effect. In fact, fewer than 10 percent of faculty members in North American colleges and universities report actually implementing them in more than one course (Lombardi, Murray, and Gerdes, 2011, 255).

Stewart responded by talking about how, in his opinion, most accommodation requests are driven by incomplete or poor design in the first place, and he shared a story about usability testing for websites. In the early days, websites were put together mostly by people who had a need to share information: this is what we sell; these are the results of our research; here are seventy-five witty sayings from Oscar Wilde. The content itself was the design, and there were few thoughts given to how people actually used the materials. Then, interaction designers started to do research into how people actually looked at web pages: where their eyes went first, how they employed an F-shaped pattern when reading (or, more often, skimming) through the content on screens of information (Galitz, 2007, 136), and how they adapted quickly to any structure intended to curate the information on the screen (Nielsen, 1995). Websites like WebPagesThatSuck.com (Flanders, 2015) even popped up in the mid-1990s to make fun of other sites that had poor usability, in the hopes of raising awareness about—and stamping out—poor techniques that were in common use (and yes, it's still there, every year bravely pointing out other sites that are needlessly difficult to use).

Voorhees thought about how there isn't (yet) a course-designs-that-suck resource to show faculty members and course designers how not to put together their interactions. A further thought struck him. "Wait a minute. How many of the requests for specific accommodations come in that are really mop-up jobs after poor or incomplete design in the first place?" It turned out that it was a lot of them—nearly half of the requests received over a six-month period (Voorhees, 2015).

Engagement

Course interactions that are designed to be as barrier-free as possible allow learners to select how they want to engage with the material based on their learning needs. A good example of this happened to Karen, a graduate student working toward her MBA at a large public university in the midwestern United States. Karen is a single mother with two young children, a five-year-old daughter and a two-year-old son. She has to put the kids to bed at 9:00 p.m., and she uses the hour and a half after that for studying and homework for her courses. Recently, many of Karen's professors started to create videos to help students to review course content. Her classmates were enthused about being able to watch the video roundups in order to prepare for exams.

Karen was stuck, though. She didn't want to watch the lectures at night because the sound might prevent her children from getting to sleep. She didn't want to plug in headphones, either, because she wanted to be able to hear her children while she was studying: shutting them out of her attention wasn't an option. Fortunately, shortly after Karen's professors posted their videos, the university's media services area augmented them with captions. The captions allowed Karen to study during the evening without waking her children.

Reasons to adopt UDL go way beyond learners with disabilities; in fact, the biggest benefits of UDL have to do with removing barriers for everyone: deployed military learners, traveling sports teams, international students, and yes, students with disabilities. To move beyond today's 10 percent adoption rates, we have to make the case for UDL being worth the work we put into it and beneficial to the widest range of learners. Figure 4.1 shows three ways that resources can be allocated to the interactions in our college courses.

As in Karen's story, higher education in general is poised to move beyond providing everyone with the same resources and interactions (equality), and we are even ready to start moving beyond accommodating differences and challenges as we have been doing on an individual basis for many years. At the University of Central Florida, online courses are offered less to reach out to learners beyond campus, and more to expand offerings based on people's schedules (equity).

> Our online students are more digital than they are distance. What that really means is that we have students who are taking all online courses, or all face-to-face courses, and most of them are taking some mix of the two at any time in the semester. . . . From the students' perspective, what they tell us is they want

EQUALITY VERSUS EQUITY

In the first image, it is assumed that everyone will benefit from the same supports. They are being treated equally.

In the second image, individuals are given different supports to make it possible for them to have equal access to the game. They are being treated equitably.

In the third image, all three can see the game without any supports or accommodations because the cause of the inequity was addressed. The systemic barrier has been removed.

Figure 4.1: Equality versus equity (Froehle, 2016). Used with permission.

that flexibility. They want the flexibility, especially time, to be able to take [a course] when they can fit it into their lives. They may drive out to the campus if they work downtown three days a week and take face-to-face classes and then fill up their schedule with online courses so they can work downtown on Tuesdays and Thursdays, let's say. About half of our students work 20 or more hours a week. (Young, 2017)

We are ready to adopt the mind-set of removing barriers by providing choices—a both/and way of thinking. This is how we can best advocate for wider adoption of UDL principles and get beyond the 10 percent of faculty members who now use UDL. Think back to our earlier chapters where we met some mobile learners—it's for them that the promise of UDL is most broadly fulfilled. UDL also happens, fruitfully, to reduce the need for specific disability accommodations.

Here We Are at the Starting Line

This book is structured as a practitioner's guide, with two related but distinct purposes. First, we want to share ways to get more people on campus involved in designing interactions that include a wide range of possible participants—we want to make our readers into subtle evangelists for UDL practices. Up to this point, this book has largely focused on this aim. Now, it's time to turn to the practical hands-on application of UDL, both in terms of designing new interactions in an inclusive fashion, as well as in terms of examining existing interactions and retrofitting them to be more inclusive.

This latter goal is the tougher one: many faculty development staffers and faculty members fail to move from a mind-set that agrees it's a best practice to be inclusive to one of actually implementing changes. Think about all of the media elements, text files, and design elements in each of the credit courses taught at your own institution. Now think about the work that would need to happen in order to make all of those items accessible. Seen from this perspective, analysis paralysis soon sets in: how could we even decide where to start, let alone how to go back and redo or add to every single thing in our courses? Who will train our media services people, teaching center staff, and faculty members? What processes will we need to put in place in order to make sure that we're 100 percent compliant? And how will we get faculty members to view mobile technology as a UDL possibility rather than just a hindrance in the classroom?

Fortunately, this sort of mind-set contains a few assumptions that don't need to apply to our decision about where and how to begin. One assumption is that, in order to be effective, UDL has to be an all-or-nothing proposition. This kind of thinking is bolstered by the legal requirements in the United States and some Canadian provinces that all media and web content must be accessible. The reality is that institutions often do not have the financial and human resources to go back through content that has already been created in order to make it accessible; when colleges and universities get sued for inaccessible materials (Lewin, 2015), courts often accept plans that draw a line in the sand for all new materials going forward and that focus plus-one efforts (more on this in the next chapter) on existing materials that provide broad access benefits to all learners.

Another assumption is that changes have to happen across the entire institution, all at once: everybody needs training, all course environments need to be updated, and so on. Rich Culatta has worked in the U.S. Department of Education Office of Educational Technology and is now the chief innovation officer for the state of Rhode Island. He views UDL through the lens of user experience, or UX, testing: "Often, we get to scale faster by making small changes quickly and stacking them together. . . . In higher education, we can learn a lesson from industry by adopting the concept of the MVP, or minimally viable product" (Culatta, 2016). In other words, we should drop the assumption that we have to wait until all of the elements in our course interactions are accessible and start by identifying a limited number of places where good design will save effort and prevent confusion for our students (and for our faculty members and support staff too).

There is one last assumption that is easy to make about UDL, especially for those of us in higher education, and that is the idea that it is a digital phenomenon. When we have spoken to colleagues at colleges and universities throughout North America, we tend to hear similar themes in people's comments, such as the following:

- "I don't have any students with disabilities in my class this semester, and even when I do, I just send them to the Disability Support Office, because they know how to use the special technology that students with disabilities need."

- "I teach some online courses, but no one has said that they have a problem with my materials or interactions, so they must be okay as they are."

- "I teach only face-to-face courses, and no one has said that they have a problem with my materials or interactions, so they must be okay as they are."

- "I am already doing UDL because I have posted my readings and lecture notes into the LMS in PDF format as well as Microsoft Word format, so people can use screen readers if they need to."

- "I'm not very tech savvy, and I don't have any videos that need captioning."

Based on our conversations with faculty colleagues over the last twenty years, as well as more than thirty years of research about faculty attitudes toward students with disabilities (see Benham, 1997; Bento, 1996; Bigaj, Shaw, and McGuire, 1999; Cook, Rumrill, and Tankersley, 2009; Fonosch and Schwab, 1981; Houck et al., 1992; Lombardi and Murray, 2011; Murray et al., 2009; Murray, Lombardi, and Wren, 2011; Nelson, Dodd, and Smith, 1990; and Zhang et al., 2010), we argue that this last assumption—that UDL is a technique that benefits only a small segment of learners who require technological accommodations—is held by many of us in higher education today. Such an assumption goes a long way toward explaining why only about one in ten faculty members is actively using UDL as a way of structuring the interactions in our college courses. For many faculty members, designers, and campus leaders, the thought of adding technology to existing courses can be overwhelming.

We've spent some time showing how UDL is not just for students with disabilities. Now, let's take a moment to talk about why it isn't just a digital phenomenon, either.

UDL in Physical Spaces

Must everyone have a smart phone or mobile tablet in order to benefit from UDL? Nope. It is true that the power of a UDL approach is amplified when we design learning interactions that extend beyond the time we spend in the classroom or in face-to-face services, and that usually means using technology. UDL started out in the K–12 world, however, as a means of designing place-based learning interactions. UDL's in-person interactions are relevant both to on-ground courses and to student-services areas in colleges and universities.

As a starting point for colleagues who may be tech-averse, here are a number of concrete examples of low- and no-tech UDL in action on campus.

- **Posted lesson goals.** Having goals helps students know what they're working to achieve. That's why goals are always made apparent in a UDL classroom. One example of this is posting goals for specific lessons in the classroom. Students might also write down or insert lesson goals in their notebooks. The professor refers to lesson goals throughout the lesson itself as a method of grounding the students' learning.
- **Assignment options.** In a traditional classroom, there may be only one way for a student to complete an assignment. This might be an essay or a worksheet. With UDL, there are multiple options. For instance, students may be able to create a podcast or a video to show what they know. They may even be allowed to draw a comic strip. There are tons of possibilities for completing assignments, as long as students meet the lesson goals.
- **Flexible work spaces.** UDL promotes flexibility in the learning environment. That's why in a UDL classroom there are flexible work spaces for students. This includes spaces for quiet individual work, small- and large-group work, and group instruction. If students need to tune out noise, they can choose to wear earbuds or headphones during independent work.
- **Regular feedback.** With UDL, students get feedback—often every day—on how they're doing. At the end of a lesson, teachers may talk with individual students about lesson goals. Students are encouraged to reflect on the choices they made in class and whether they met the goals. If they didn't meet the goals, they're encouraged to think about what might have helped them do so. (CAST, 2014a)

Another way to approach UDL for in-person interactions across campus is to plan for interactions to happen twice, using different methods or media. For example, a class meeting that covers government structures might include prereading of the transcript of a video clip from a TV interview with an expert in the field, then a viewing of the clip in class, followed by a discussion about the relevant concepts.

The readings and video contain the same content, and learners can choose where (and how) they direct their attention.

Likewise, in student-facing service areas of colleges and universities, the do-it-twice approach yields low-tech and no-tech benefits. For your institution's application process, provide a paper application form that can be mailed in, as well as a fillable online form. At the registrar's office, have handouts that explain the registration process with a numbered text-based narrative on one side and a pictorial flow chart on the other (with the same text on each side). In the tutoring center, provide paper, pens, scissors, and glue for long-form drafting and literal cutting and pasting, as well as higher-tech options like laptops and tablets.

The Faculty Four

Expanding the scope of what UDL helps us to do in higher education as well as narrowing the scope of how to get started (as we will see in the next section of this chapter) helps us to make the argument for why a UDL approach is worth the effort. This is often the hardest sell for adopting UDL principles. Our colleagues among the staff, in the faculty, and on the leadership team can hear all of the arguments we've made so far and respond with "yeah, that's a great goal, but who's going to pay for the time and energy that we will have to invest?" This is why we can get beyond 10 percent of faculty members by setting an achievable bar for beginning UDL.

Narrowing the scope of what we need to do first is one more way to make UDL more approachable. Jordan Cameron and Jim Cope at Kennesaw State University recently came up with the Faculty Four: a set of access-expanding techniques that all faculty members and support staff at their university would adopt in order to reduce or remove barriers for learners and faculty members using technology as part of their teaching and learning interactions. The Faculty Four program trains the university faculty and staff in the following simple but broadly effective techniques.

- **Alternative text.** All visual resource provided to learners, including still images, animations, and videos, are tagged with descriptive metadata. In plain language, designers always provide ALT-text descriptions for visual elements.

- **Accessible documents.** Text-based files are created to be friendly to alternative access methods. Designers employ a consistent semantic structure within files and use the accessibility-checking features of the software used to create files, such as the process outlined in the Kennesaw State Microsoft Word accessibility tutorial (Kennesaw State University, 2016). This has the broader advantage of making files discoverable, indexable, and searchable.

- **Captions, transcripts, and audio description.** The university trains support staff, developers, and faculty members in the basics of creating video captions, transcripts for audio and video content, and how to note descriptive audio (describing in text significant audio cues that happen within audio and video clips). Readers interested in more can see the U.S. Department of Education's Described and Captioned Media Program (DCMP) website at captioningkey.org.

- **Choosing accessible third-party resources.** The university trains staff members in the procurement and accounts areas, as well as those who make purchasing decisions for departments and service areas, in how to review vendor tools for accessibility, including how to read a Voluntary Product Accessibility Template (VPAT) self-disclosure document and how to perform basic accessibility testing. Just making accessibility a criterion for purchasing decisions is a key step toward reducing or removing barriers proactively. (Cameron and Cope, 2016)

The success of the Faculty Four program is twofold: it purposely teaches a small set of skills that everyone involved in the development and implementation of teaching interactions can master, and it provides university resources in the form of trained support staff members who can help put the good ideas into practical use (Cameron and Cope, 2016), a good use of the coach-the-coaches approach for which we will advocate in chapter 6. A further benefit of the Faculty Four approach is that many faculty members are already doing at least some of these practices, which allows them to tie their interactions explicitly to goals and objectives in order to bring them under the UDL umbrella of practices.

You will learn some specific UDL practices in chapters 8, 9, and 10 that apply to individual courses and to programs of study. Right now, let's focus on practical steps for implementing UDL in the spirit of the Faculty Four. How can we reach out to our connected learners and expand access for everyone in an approachable manner? Think "20, 20, and 20," as in strategies to implement in the next twenty minutes, twenty days, and—thinking longer-term—twenty months.

UDL in the Next Twenty Minutes

The first phase in implementing UDL is just to do something. There are a number of techniques that faculty members and those who support them can implement in relatively quick fashion—say, twenty minutes' worth of work. These sorts of UDL practices are not meant to be comprehensive accessibility solutions, and they do not substantially reduce the need for specific accommodations when students with learning challenges come into the courses and situations where they are being applied. They are starting points that create pathways for all students who are deeply engrossed in their mobile devices to have choices in how they take in and share ideas and skills while staying motivated and engaged.

Further, these twenty-minute UDL strategies are great examples that do not involve a large investment of time and work. For skeptical colleagues, and even for those of us who count ourselves among the UDL early adopters, these twenty-minute processes help to show the value of doing inclusive-design work once and reaping the benefit repeatedly in the form of fewer student questions, fewer requests for accommodations, and greater student learning gains.

Twenty-Minute UDL: Step Zero

In order to know where to apply any of the twenty-minute strategies we will talk about in this chapter, it helps to identify the places within a given course where UDL strategies offer the greatest benefit for faculty members and learners. Most faculty members, if they have taught a course a few times, know where these pinch points are. In fact, they often engender water-cooler stories that start with "can you believe that my students. . . ." Try this thought experiment. Call to mind a course, one that you have taught a few times or one for which you were part of the development team. Now, think of specific examples of the following criteria. Where do learners always

- bring up the same questions every time the course is offered,
- get things wrong on quizzes and tests, and
- ask for alternate explanations?

For example, the professor of a freshman-level biology course might call to mind the fact that students always get bogged down and ask a lot of questions in the second unit of the course when the topic shifts to discussions of Mendelian inheritance, especially when learners are asked to draw Punnett squares based on data about the traits of parent organisms (Punnett squares are the charts that list the possible outcomes of crossing dominant and recessive traits in breeding—an early way to record genetic selections). When students take the midterm examination, most of them do poorly on questions that have to do with Punnett squares.

The professor remembers that she gets multiple e-mail messages, phone calls, and in-class questions around this pinch point, and often has to do significant reteaching and review after the midterm exam. This pinch point is an excellent place to begin a retrofit with UDL principles, if for no other reason than to save the professor effort in the future. Research shows that it tends to increase student persistence, retention, and satisfaction as well (Wine et al., 2011). Once you have some step-zero knowledge about where to apply UDL, it's time to design and implement a few UDL strategies.

Twenty-Minute UDL: Step 1

Look through the course interactions and identify elements that are single-stream, meaning that there is only one way to get access to the information. Your examination of the course should go beyond just looking at the materials being shared with learners. Look, too, at the discussions and conversations that learners engage in throughout the course: do they take place only in the classroom, out loud? Only in the learning management system (LMS) via keyed-in text? How can students tell whether they are keeping up with the course's demands—via text, spoken feedback, subtle eyebrow-raising on the part of the professor?

Some common single-stream course elements are lecture notes that are text-only, slide presentations that exist as visuals on a screen, and instructor-created unit introduction video clips with information that exists only in the videos themselves (such as a preview of the topics to be covered in the coming unit). Find out where your list of single-stream content and interactions intersects with your list of pinch points in the course: these are the places to start doing some twenty-minute UDL.

Let's look at three examples from undergraduate courses in math and biology and a graduate-level English course. In the math course, the professor already provides text-based notes on how to approach sample problems, with the steps outlined with equations and text. This, by the way, is a great foundation on which to build: most faculty members and designers are already using text heavily in our courses. Text is usually our default mode.

In the biology course, the instructor has taken her existing PowerPoint slide decks that she has used for years in the face-to-face environment and posted them in the LMS course environment for learners to use as class notes. Not only are the slides inaccessible unless learners have PowerPoint on the devices they are using for access (making smartphone access chancy at best), but the slides themselves are mostly just bulleted lists of text elements that serve as reminders for an already expert audience: the instructor. This resource is both single-stream and also cryptically incomplete without the professor's explication of each bullet point.

The professor in the graduate English course was an early adherent to the just-add-technology movement. She recorded brief video segments to introduce each unit, each assignment, each classwide discussion, and even each of the eight parts of the course syllabus. Students see and hear the professor talking to them about the concepts, processes, and requirements of the course.

Two- to five-minute videos are a great way to reach learners where they are and increase instructor presence outside of face-to-face interactions. These videos are all single-stream because there isn't a consistent way to get the content in them other than to watch the videos—and some videos contain instructions for assignments that aren't included anywhere else. Think about the learners who prefer to read the content, who can't get the video due to a poor connection, or who can't have the sound on. Even, or perhaps especially, developers and faculty members who are techies can benefit from the opportunity to move down the complexity scale in order to practice UDL. It's not always a process of moving up to more technology or more complexity.

Twenty-Minute UDL: Step 2

Once you have found single-stream course interactions that are part of the pinch points in the course, it's time to brainstorm expansions into one new medium, method, or expression for each. This is the type of thinking that makes UDL a manageable and iterative process. List those places where learners express barriers, then find just one way to provide a choice about how to address the barriers, or, better yet, remove the barriers. But let's take it one step at a time and revisit our courses in math, biology, and English to apply some twenty-minute UDL.

For the math course that already has a number of static text-based resources in the form of proofs and action steps, the professor builds on that good foundation with a strategy of recording screencasts of the instructor actually doing the same proofs or problems, in real time, with explanations of each step. The instructor selects which videos to create first by remembering the three pinch points in the course, and then creates video resources for those parts first.

For math—where there are a lot of special symbols, diagramming, and spatial thinking—the professor uses a pen and paper to work through problems longhand, with the camera positioned above the paper so viewers can see and hear the thinking that is going into each explanation. The visuals and audio reinforce the purpose of the examples and create alternate channels for learning that go beyond the text-only resources that were already in the course. Now learners can choose how they study the problems, looking at the text version, the screencasts, or both. The instructor has also created a presence that goes beyond the classroom and formally structured learning time.

Screencasts don't have to use fancy technology, although it's out there (our math professor could have purchased a recording pen and special paper, for instance, to do a pen-cast of the lesson). Free tools exist for recording the screen plus microphone input, and like our math professor, you can also point a video camera down at a piece of paper and do a paper-cast of yourself doing the work longhand too. Each of the videos produced this way takes about twenty minutes, from setup to recording to uploading and sharing. And for the mobile learner, these videos are wonderful resources. Think of students who might be commuting to school using public transportation; they can watch these videos as they travel.

Just having an outline or transcript of the content in a video gives access beyond the video itself. Not only are text files smaller and easier to download under low bandwidth conditions, they (and captions) are searchable. The math professor's students started searching for specific phrases or concepts, which meant that, when studying, they went directly to the resources that mentioned them. UDL allows learners to home in on the resources they need to do targeted studying. The professor found that she took about twenty minutes to listen to and caption each of her five-minute videos—and she saved a lot of time by contracting out to third-party captioners when the videos were longer.

The twenty-minute UDL techniques also extend to engagement techniques, especially in terms of options for self-regulation (e.g., providing estimates of how much time students will need to read or watch course materials), options for sustaining effort and persistence (such as recording audio and text-based announcements for learners to keep them motivated and informed), and options for recruiting interest (like pointing students to news stories or examples from popular culture of course concepts being applied by people like themselves).

Learners can also demonstrate their skills in varied ways using twenty-minute UDL approaches. For example, in about twenty minutes, you can expand an assignment so that learners can complete it successfully via a text-based response (say, the traditional three-page paper) or an audio recording (a link to a five-minute SoundCloud file, perhaps). As long as all learners have to meet the same objectives regardless of format, the assignments can be graded using the same criteria and measurements—and the changes to the assignment likely won't take even twenty minutes each.

To wrap up how you can think about twenty-minute UDL, remember to think about UDL as design intended to provide choices for all of your learners (not just people with disabilities). Find pinch points in your interactions: UDL helps most at the part of the interaction where learners always have questions, get things wrong on tests and quizzes, or need more viewpoints to better understand concepts. Once you know where the pinch points are, brainstorm and create new media, methods, or expressions that you can implement in about twenty minutes.

UDL in the Next Twenty Days

Once you have started to implement the kinds of twenty-minute UDL changes in your courses, you will start to see the impact on how well your learners recall concepts, stick with the course, and demonstrate knowledge and skills. The next level of planning for adoption of UDL is to sketch out two paths through the course that allow learners the choice to engage in a more text-based or media-based interaction with the course. This twenty-day planning focuses on allowing learners to exercise preferences and choices at regular intervals, as well as keeping learners engaged through the design of specific interest points throughout the progression of the course.

Twenty-Day UDL: Step 1

Start your twenty-day planning by thinking of the interactions in your course where students work with materials, with one another, with you, and with the wider world. Plan out a way that students could have many of those interactions using only media, and then create a separate similar plan focused only on text.

To create the media path, see if you can go through an existing course (or, even more effective, ask your learners to do so) by finding and using nothing but media files or interactions with media elements such as videos, audio clips, slide shows, links to interactive learning objects, and the like. Once you have created the list of existing media elements and interactions in the course, ask where learners would find gaps or be confused about what to do next. Also, which media files (or interactions with media) can become anchor points for learners as they move through the interactions in the course? Think of items such as video directions for assignments, audio study guides, and image-based signposts to show students where they are in the progression of course topics and work. Figure 4.2 shows a media-path assessment for a module in a course on copyright that Tom Tobin teaches at the University of Illinois.

This media-path assessment method works equally well with technology-enhanced and online courses and with planned interactions and low-tech strategies in the face-to-face classroom. For example, in a history course, highlights of a media path might include a video welcome to the course, audio signposts at the beginning and end of each unit, video lectures from the instructor, still-image study guides with timelines and pictures of noted historical figures, and spoken feedback from the instructor on learner presentations. It might be tempting to map out the text-based path through your course first. We suggest doing the media path first because most college and university courses are not designed from a media-interaction basis, so making your media-element path map first will show more plainly where there are holes or gaps that students might encounter as they move from one interaction to another in the course.

Module 5: Licenses and Permissions

Element	Interaction	Formats Now	UDL Alternative
Overview	Materials	All text	Three-minute video 
Resources	Materials	PDF with links to websites, videos, and practice guides	✓ (already exists)
Readings	Materials	All text	Read-aloud option? 
Discussion	Students, instructor	Key text into LMS or link to audio or video	✓
Reflection assignment	Concepts	Microsoft Word or video response	✓
Course project, part 2	Wider world	Create a web page with various media or design one using text descriptions	✓
Wrap-up	Concepts	All text	Read-aloud option?

Figure 4.2: Media-path assessment for copyright issues in online education course

Once you have mapped a media path through your course, create a similar map for text-based elements and interactions in the course. This is likely to be the easier path to chart using existing course content. Go through an existing course (or ask your learners to do so) by finding nothing but text files or interactions with text. Again, ask where learners would find gaps or be confused about what's next. What text files (or interactions with text) can become anchor points for learners to move through the interactions in the course? Think of items such as agendas that show students what's coming, checklists that help them to stay on track with assignments, and the humble-but-effective instruction sheet for assignments. Figure 4.3 shows what such a text-only analysis looks like for a module in the same copyright course.

A text-only path can work equally well in technology-enhanced and online courses as with low-tech strategies in the face-to-face classroom. For example, in a macroeconomics course, highlights of a text path might include the syllabus, a text welcome to the course, the directions on assignment sheets, e-mail messages from the instructor to keep learners on track, and written feedback on learner assignments.

Twenty-Day UDL: Step 2

After mapping out the media and text paths through your course, the goal is to create two full paths so that learners can choose one or the other (or switch back and forth as they prefer) all the way through the course. The two-path implementation of UDL principles focuses on two kinds of interactions in each path. Especially where there are gaps or areas where learners might be confused about what comes next, create one of two interactions: action choices or interest points. For every interaction where you wish to redesign an existing element or create a new one to fill out a full media or text path, creating action choices or interest points allows you to avoid creating what Richard Culatta calls "nexter courses," where the course consists of information presentation only, and the only interaction is where students click the Next button to move to the next piece of content (Culatta, 2016).

Module 5: Licenses and Permissions

Element	Interaction	Text Path
Overview	Materials	HTML web page, downloadable Microsoft Word file
Resources	Materials	HTML web page, downloadable PDF
Readings	Materials	Links to resources in university library system. All have full-text alternative versions, including video and audio resources
Discussion	Students, instructor	Learners can key text into the LMS tool
Reflection assignment	Concepts	Microsoft Word response is one option
Course project, part 2	Wider world	One option is to design elements of a web page by using text descriptions
Wrap-up	Concepts	HTML web page, downloadable Microsoft Word file

Figure 4.3: Media-path assessment for copyright issues in online education course

To create an action-choice interaction, focus on key areas where learners can choose how they respond to course interactions. Offer multimodal ways for learners to communicate with one another and the instructor. Instead of just asking learners to post text-based messages on a discussion forum, for example, offer learners the choice of responding via text or by posting an audio or video response. Provide choices in how learners respond to assignments. If an assignment calls for a three-page essay, allow learners to create a five-minute video response. So long as the same objectives are being used to assess learner performance, the format learners use to demonstrate their skills need not be limited to just one.

An advanced option: offer learners one or more self-defined assignments: provide them with the grading criteria, and learners are responsible for creating the instructions and then doing the assignment according to their own instructions. Creating action choices turns single interactions such as discussions, assignments, and demonstrations into multimodal opportunities for learners to choose how they want to move through the course best. Just having choices about how they travel through the course leads to greater learner persistence (Godfrey and Matos-Elefante, 2010, 12–14).

Twenty-Day UDL: Step 3

The final phase of twenty-day UDL is to test the interactions you have designed and take note about the gaps or points in the interactions where learners express confusion. Those pinch points become your road map for creating anchors in the interactions. Anchors are task-specific elements in the media path or text path that offer choices, encouragement, or alternatives. For example, if learners using the media path always ask what parts of a unit 5 video apply to the test or assignment, create an anchor to go along with the video, such as a brief instructor-led video introduction (yes, a video introduction to a video is perfectly all right). Likewise, if learners say that, in the text path, they have trouble learning the materials that begin unit 8, look at the overview for unit 7 and create an anchor, such as a study guide or a document that talks about how to connect unit 7 knowledge to forthcoming course ideas.

In addition to our course interactions, the practice of creating anchors can be particularly effective in student service interactions. At the registrar's office, ask students how they interact with staff members (or better yet, observe them), and recruit students to interact with the registration web interface while designers watch. At the points where students experience gaps or always ask questions, create point-of-need alternatives, such as a looped video that walks students through the types of forms they need to have filled out before they speak with people at the registration counter. If that video is captioned, it can play on screens near the people waiting in line—and it can also be placed on the registrar's website, too, in order to provide ahead-of time and just-in-time interaction. This is different from Universal Design, which applies only to the built environment, such as having a few service counters that are friendly to seated patrons.

The idea in any higher education context, whether in course design or student-services interactions, is to offer choices to learners so that everyone's experience is smoother and all of the interactions in which they engage can be accomplished in more than one way. The only way to design interactions to be as open and user-friendly as possible is to know for certain where those pinch points are, and for that you need to have data.

UDL in the Next Twenty Months

After implementing twenty-day paths through the interactions in your course or student-facing service, the final step is to move beyond anecdotal observations of effectiveness. Most of the strategies in the twenty-day UDL approach allow us to get to the level of compliance with laws or best practices: we've offered a way for learners to interact, demonstrate skills, and stay motivated throughout our courses and service points. The mind-set to adopt for twenty months is one of collecting data in order to target UDL applications where they offer the most benefit, including the higher education institution as a whole.

This is not to say that the goal of applying UDL principles is merely to apply UDL in narrow or limited ways. Finding the pinch points of a course or service interaction in twenty-minute UDL allows us then to branch out to multipath UDL in twenty days. Once the broad access possibilities are covered, we can turn our attention to expanding access in the places where we can measure the greatest impact.

An overview of twenty-month UDL might follow this pattern. At the beginning of your twenty months, collect completion and usage statistics about resources in existing online courses. Ask students to share their use cases about how, when, and where they interact with the content, their classmates, and with the instructor in your existing online course. For example,

1) What devices do they use to view and interact with tools and content?
2) How much time do they spend learning how to use course elements?
3) What elements of the course gave students problems?
4) Did any cause students not to use specific items?
5) Were students unable to get to or use any parts of the course?

Map and build one alternative path through an existing online course, beyond the text-only and audio/video-only paths that already exist. Share the possible paths through the course with your current students, and ask for their feedback about which parts need multiplying soonest. Collect completion and usage statistics about the resources in your UDL-augmented online course for a pre- and post-change analysis.

Twenty-Month UDL: Step 1

The first step in the long-term application of UDL principles is to determine which UDL practices have the greatest impact on learner success by collecting data about what actually works. Your institutional-research staff can help you identify where to look for data to support your analysis, such as the LMS, student information system, or the registrar's database. Collect both quantitative data, such as time spent on various elements in the LMS, and qualitative data. Interview learners to obtain use-case information: how, when, and in what contexts do they interact? Having use-case data allows us to study interaction patterns from previous offerings of a given course and resource-use trends in student service areas. In your initial data collection, look especially for places where you have not yet applied UDL principles in order to provide learners with choices: do learners use or interact with such materials and elements less frequently? For face-to-face courses, you can quantify interactions by examining learner usage of fixed-format elements, such as how often learners visit the syllabus content in the LMS.

The next stage in collecting data is to ask some meta-interactive questions. How much time do students spend learning how to interact?

In other words, how much cognitive load is required just to learn new systems or processes before learners can even begin to interact around the course concepts? What are the ground rules for communication, and are they articulated clearly? Ask learners how much time they spent learning those ground rules. What tools do learners need to use, either in the LMS, when engaging with third-party online tools, or in the face-to-face environment? Are these standardized across similar experiences (i.e., every course uses the same core structure and tool set), or must learners adapt to new structures every time they encounter a new course?

Pay special attention to pre-interaction challenges or obstacles that cause learners not to engage in some interactions because "people have a strong, intuitive drive to reduce cognitive dissonance, the coexistence in the mind of conflicting ideas. In general, people do not tolerate inconsistency well" (Gorman and Gorman, 2017). For example, if your online courses all allow learners to use their mobile devices to engage in course discussions, but the form for applying to the program is a read-only PDF file that must be printed out and scanned, the application form presents a barrier for mobile device–dependent learners.

Create opportunities to collect open-ended data from learners at regular intervals during courses, and perform exit interviews for as many people who drop and withdraw as possible and use the results to simplify and expand. Lower the barriers that you find near little-used interactions and expand the ways people can engage with interactions that get used most.

Twenty-Month UDL: Step 2

When you have the data about which interactions in your course or service area are being underutilized, or where there are barriers to broad usage and adoption, you can now map and build a maximum-use alternate path. Let's look at how a math course and biology course used data-based analysis to expand the most useful parts of the interactions in each course.

In the math course, the instructor already had a number of examples for students to work through. Both on the course's LMS pages and in the form of paper handouts for face-to-face course meetings, text-based problems and static drawings were plentiful throughout the course. Because there was already a text-based path through the course, the instructor asked questions of the students throughout the course that measured how often they interacted with the worksheets and sample problems. Students responded to three anonymous surveys at the ends of the first, second, and third quarters of the course that asked, for instance, "for this unit, there are ten sets of sample problems: four are handouts and six are found in the course's LMS environment. How many of the sample problem sets did you complete? In what formats?" Based on students' self-reported data and the analytical data from the LMS that showed how many students visited each sample problem page, the instructor realized that students were seldom practicing with the sample problem sets, even when doing so correlated strongly with higher scores on graded tests.

The math instructor worked with an instructional designer to test a series of voice-narrated pen-casts—videos that showed the instructor working through sample problems. The instructor did pen-casts for problem sets where learners most consistently earned poor scores on tests in previous semesters, and created the pen-casts to provide information to offer cognitive pathways that text-based sets of steps did not.

The instructor and designer monitored the use of the pen-casts and the text-based sample problem sets over the next two semesters. Overall, student use of text problem sets remained steady, and the use of the pen-casts quickly exceeded the rates for the text-based sets. They also noticed two positive trends: students were choosing which format to use for studying, with some students abandoning text in favor of the video walk-throughs, and others choosing to work with the text-based examples. A significant number of students fell into a both/and category, interacting in either modality—and sometimes both—in each unit of study. The aggregate increase in student use of the study materials also correlated strongly with an increase in test scores in previously weaker areas of performance.

Based on these findings, the instructor and designer concluded that just having the choice of format was a powerful incentive for learners to select one or the other in a situational way. Their formative survey results included learner comments such as "I could listen to the problems when I was driving to work, and then work on them with the worksheets when I got home," and "I watched the videos over and over until I figured out where I was going wrong in my practice sessions." To cap off the long-term UDL project, the instructor created a series of one-minute screencast walk-throughs for the core elements in the syllabus, too, and created short videos to introduce interactive elements of the course so that students had choices about reading text or watching video in all of the places where the instructor introduced new information or directions.

The "before" state of affairs in the biology course was a series of slide-show presentations with the bullet point outline of what the faculty members said in the face-to-face environment. Many instructors employ such memory-aid presentations as they lecture and interact with learners: the presentation materials are there more to jog the memory of the instructor rather than to serve as resources for learners directly. The biology instructor had shared the series of presentation files with students, ostensibly as a basis for note taking or studying.

The statistics collected over two semesters painted a different picture: students downloaded or visited the pages in the LMS that contained the slide presentation in early weeks of the course, but fewer and fewer students opened the files as the weeks progressed. Anonymous surveying further revealed that students perceived the slide presentations to be incomplete, difficult to understand, and divorced from the content of the instructor's lectures themselves, which students found to be useful because of their interactive nature.

The response from the design team was to record a series of audio podcasts with lecture content that supported the interactive elements in the course, including the syllabus, assignment directions, discussion introductions, lecture materials, and lab work. The instructor essentially used each slide in the existing presentation files as the basis for each one- or two-minute podcast. The instructor decided to host the audio and the resulting text-only files on a separate web page so students did not have to log in to the LMS or download files to use the alternative-format resources. Learners could listen their way through the entire course—but still demonstrate key skills by performing lab experiments and creating reports (either audio or written).

The resulting data showed that the time the instructor invested in the audio and text alternatives was well spent. The instructor noted fewer instances of needing to reteach concepts, and the resources website was consistently used by nearly the entire class throughout the semester. Students responded to anonymous surveys with comments such as "I read the text lecture recaps and then I chop them up to make my own self-quiz questions," and "I read the lab directions ahead of time, and then I listen to the audio directions for the lab work while I am in the lab."

This kind of long-term UDL thinking about access also bears good fruit when we collect data about student-service interactions. When the tutoring center wants to expand their reach and adopt remote tutoring, data about the students who do not use their services now are essential. A college or university procurement office can help operational areas like writing centers and tutoring services to purchase technology to support remote interactions. For twenty-month UDL, you can feed data into the procurement process about the characteristics of your potential learner clients.

1) How many of them feel that they would use the services of the support area but cannot make time to do so?
2) How many of them have regular access to mobile communication devices?
3) How often do they check their various accounts?
4) How familiar are they with common real-time communication technologies, such as video chat and interactive screen sharing?

The information you learn from asking these kinds of questions about your current and possible audiences of learners will create a series of requirements for the tools you adopt. Once you know how you wish to design the interactions with your students, the partnership with the procurement office to find the right platform will have accessibility as a set of requirements from the beginning, and that's an especially deep way to apply UDL principles.

Some UDL Caveats

As you think about the interactions that learners have with materials, one another, instructors, and the wider world, it can be tempting to adopt an approach that focuses on making more formats in order to require all learners to experience various media types. This is not UDL, but merely multimedia. The rule of thumb is to create choices, not merely multiples. A wrong way to adopt UDL would be to create, say, a text unit introduction, a video lecture snippet, and an audio set of directions for the unit's assignment—and then make learners experience them all, in sequence, in only those formats. UDL is not about making learners cycle through variety but, rather, about providing choices so learners can decide how they want to experience interactions. Each of the items listed above should have at least one choice: for example, the text-based unit introduction might be presented via audio as well.

Also, don't forget engagement and action choices. Designers can get hung up on creating alternative formats for content and neglect making alternatives for keeping learners motivated and on track. Design choices about how and when learners can choose how they demonstrate their skills. That way, when you find out how, when, and why learners interact with you and with materials in your courses, you can later analyze the impact that your UDL changes have on student persistence, retention, and satisfaction.

Conclusion

All of the strategies listed above help to reduce the need for specific accommodations in the future and bring similar benefits to a wider audience of learners, learners like Zakiya Acey, an Oberlin College student who was interviewed in 2016 by the *New Yorker* about the challenges of being an undergraduate at a diverse liberal arts college:

> "We need to be able to get what we need in a way that we can actually consume it." He pauses. "Because I'm dealing with having been arrested on campus, or having to deal with the things that my family are going through because of larger systems—having to deal with all of that, I can't produce the work that they want

me to do. But I understand the material, and I can give it to you in different ways. There's professors who have openly been, like, 'Yeah, instead of, you know, writing out this midterm, come in to my office hours, and you can just speak it,' right? But that's not institutionalized. I have to find that professor." (Heller, 2016, 55)

Acey's experience of having to "find that professor" lends weight to the need for all of us in higher education to become subtle evangelists for designing our interactions with learners to be as inclusive as possible. In the next chapter, we'll examine how to get beyond our current 10 percent adoption rate by doing something simple: expanding the pool of people on campus who know about UDL.

Remember Philip Voorhees, from the beginning of this chapter? We learned about his story when he shared it with colleagues at the 2016 Tennessee Board of Regents eCampus statewide course-designer conference. Many of the conference participants echoed the idea that by designing engaging and accessible interactions we reduce the very need for accommodation requests. As Jon Metz, a website accessibility consultant in Washington, DC, recently wrote,

> People in my field love to tell designers and developers that accessibility is a User Experience (UX) problem, but getting your project to work with A[ssistive] T[echnology] is better thought of as a User Interface (UI) problem. . . . While they are very important for testing, screen readers are not testing tools. To be honest, people with disabilities are not running around with AT checking to make sure websites and software work correctly. They're using it as a means to overcome a technological barrier that would normally keep them from doing something you and I take for granted. (Metz, 2016)

While we will never wholly eliminate the need for specific accommodations, we can do our students and ourselves a huge favor by removing barriers and creating engagement as a first principle in any course or interaction design or redesign process. This saves the efforts of our design teams later on so they can respond to the most specific accommodation requests, rather than accommodation requests that actually point out usability and design flaws.

A THOUGHT EXERCISE

Think of your own courses or those of the faculty members you support. Over the past few years, how often have you had to scramble to provide accommodations to individual students when the requests came in unannounced? Use the worksheet below to think through if and how an accommodation request could benefit other students.

Course/Interaction: _____

Accommodation Needed	Time to Implement Accommodation	Accommodation or Inaccessible Design?	How Many Students Were Helped by the Accommodation?
Note taker	*2 days*	*Inaccessible design*	*1*

CHAPTER 5

Adopt the Plus-One Approach

How Not to Do UDL

In 2016, Tom Tobin visited a university to facilitate a faculty development workshop. As he was arranging his materials, distributing handouts, and organizing his workspace, a faculty member came into the room, introduced herself, and said, "I made *all* of my lectures accessible last semester for my 300-level history course. I recorded all three lectures a week for the entire semester, and I made sure that students with hearing challenges could still experience them."

Tom smiled politely and asked, "Oh, you did? So how did that work out for you?" He suspected what was coming next but let the faculty member share her story. She said, "I'm exhausted. My teaching assistant is exhausted. After each recording, we spent about six hours per lecture finishing the editing, creating captions, creating text transcripts, and uploading the files. It took so much time. And I'm not sure it was worth it, even though the law says I have to do this."

Of course they were exhausted. A three-credit course meets for approximately an hour three times a week over the course of a typical semester. That's a minimum of forty-five hours of video-recorded lectures. Add another six hours to each of those one-hour video segments and the whole idea of creating an accessible version of the course seems impossible, especially on top of all of the other responsibilities that faculty members and students have.

Tom was curious: "Wow, that's a lot of time spent in the recording studio. What kind of feedback did you get from your students?" The faculty member said, "That's the thing. I'm not so sure my students even watched the videos. Very few came to class prepared. Eventually,

I figured that the videos were there if students wanted to rewatch a lecture or if they missed class. I guess I don't see the point of creating all of these alternative video and text versions of the interactions in my course. It took too much time, and it didn't seem to matter to the students anyway. At least I can say I tried it, but it's probably not something I would do again."

Too Much Work!

The professor in Tom's story above was following one of the tenets of Universal Design for Learning: giving learners multiple ways to get information. As you read in chapter 1, the core elements of UDL, as defined by the neuroscientists at the Center for Applied Special Technology (CAST), stimulate three brain networks that help us to learn and retain what we learn:

- **Affective networks.** Engagement: for purposeful, motivated learners, stimulate interest and motivation for learning.
- **Recognition networks.** Representation: for resourceful, knowledgeable learners, present information and content in different ways.
- **Strategic networks.** Action and expression: for strategic, goal-directed learners, differentiate the ways that students can express what they know. (CAST, 2018)

When implemented as part of an overall plan for designing the interactions that learners have with course materials, with one another, with the instructor, and with the wider world, this three-pronged approach does indeed offer learners engaging, choice-filled learning.

Too often, though, faculty members and instructional designers approach UDL from an accessibility mind-set. The professor with whom Tom spoke was not looking to identify the best places to adopt accessible design in her course (as you will read about in chapter 6); rather, she focused on the one part of UDL that most people have heard about: creating text-based alternative versions of multimedia resources. Instead of choosing which parts of her course materials would best serve learners if they had alternative versions, the professor rigidly created both captions and text-transcript files for every lecture video she had created, citing "it's the law" as the reason she had undertaken the work. And the process of doing so left her exhausted.

In many of our conversations with faculty members, administrators, and support staff across North America, this sort of approach is all too common. People focus on a narrow part of the inclusive-design process, usually having to do with videos and captions, and they spend considerable time and effort fulfilling what they think is a legal mandate to cover every possible access method for the content in the materials (think back to chapter 2 and the it's-the-law mind-set). There are two problems with such an approach. First, it creates extra and often unnecessary labor for everyone involved. Second, it relies on a mistaken notion of why the work is needed in the first place. This is why we want to put forward UDL as simply a means of plus-one thinking about the interactions we have with our learners.

Why Don't All of Us Get UDL?

If you take away nothing else from reading this book, remember this: UDL is a way of thinking about creating the interactions that we have with our learners so that they do not have to ask for special treatment, regardless of the types of barriers they may face—time, connectivity, or disability. If you forget which brain networks go with which strategies, or you need to refer back to the reference sheet of menu options for UDL, go ahead and refresh your memory using the resources in this book and the ones to which we point you. One of the key things that the authors recognized as we did research for this book is that no two institutions of higher education are the same. The process by which your faculty, designers, leadership team, and campus as a whole consider UDL will differ. So please refer back and interpret those strategies with your own situation in mind. One of the reasons we want to simplify UDL is that most of us in higher education are already pretty busy, mentally speaking.

Susan Yager identifies three constraints on faculty members' awareness; they also apply equally to everyone involved in the design and delivery of instructional interactions for colleges and universities.

We argue that these three constraints go a long way toward explaining why so few faculty members, department chairs, and deans have adopted UDL practices across the board, despite their proven effectiveness.

The first of Yager's constraints is time. "Textbooks and supplies are sometimes obtained just before term begins; films and videos may be ordered without being previewed; or older media and technology that are already on campus may be pressed into service" (Yager, 2015, 308). Of course, UDL is a good idea in the abstract, but few instructors have the time and energy to reflect on, design, and implement multiform interactions with their learners. Further, when some faculty members or designers do take the initiative, as in the example that led off this chapter, they do so in a narrow way that requires significant work—and that only sometimes leads to better student engagement or performance.

The second constraint on awareness is the level of exposure that people have had to the concepts in UDL. "Almost by definition, successful academics thrived, as students, under traditional teaching methods. Thus, . . . faculty members will likely use teaching methods that worked well for them, although these methods may not work as well for a variety of students" (Yager, 2015, 309).

One of the barriers that new faculty members and course designers face is that they themselves were almost always "A" students, and they enter their teaching and support careers being asked to reach students across the ability and motivation spectrum. Add to this a disconnect between the study habits of low- and high-achieving learners, where low-achieving learners tend not to have learned how to learn and require more and different types of support from instructors (Credé, 2008, 431–32).

And then we throw in technology. The knowledge of technology and the range of different types of technology that both faculty and students own and use add more factors in thinking about how to increase access to courses for all. Few faculty members or support staffers have studied UDL in any depth, so they are susceptible to a more rigid application of a few concepts, as we saw with the faculty member in this chapter's opening example whose time and resources went into the creation of captions and transcripts for hours and hours of videos.

The third constraint on awareness is the structure of academe itself: "faculty often know little about student affairs or other offices that support students. . . . Who would seek out the office of disability resources if it is not necessary?" (Yager, 2015, 309). This is an especially challenging constraint, but it helps to explain how a professor like the one above could get so focused on making alternatives for all of her video content; it's a safe bet that she never talked with her disability support office people before embarking on what she thought was a legal requirement.

So, if UDL is not a set of legal requirements, and if it is actually a way that we can offer our learners more time for study and interaction when they are on their mobile devices, as you saw in chapter 3, how should we approach UDL so that it becomes a manageable way of creating interactions for our learners? How can we avoid doing lots of work and having almost no one benefit from that work? Start applying some plus-one thinking.

A Different UDL Story

Both Kirsten and Tom have worked with colleagues who end up reteaching certain concepts every time they teach certain courses; you can probably call to mind the one topic that everyone struggles with in your own teaching or design work. Picture a colleague who is a composite of many professors with whom we have worked. He teaches an introductory-level psychology course and notices that his students struggle with the same topic every time the course runs. The professor can't figure out what the problem is but is committed to supporting his students. He decides to experiment and provides his students with his PowerPoint slides before each class session; he also records his class lectures and posts the captioned videos as a study tool.

In order to gauge the effectiveness of these strategies, our colleague used his LMS reporting tools to track when and how often students accessed course materials. He found that students downloaded the PowerPoint slides and viewed the lecture videos more frequently in the days leading up to the midterm exam. In line with our conversations with other colleagues, our psychology colleague notes a number of students who used both the PowerPoint slides and the lecture content. Overall, student performance on his exams increased, whether learners chose one, the other, or both study aids. He asked some of his students why they chose the resources that they did.

Students studying in the library on their laptops said that they plugged in their headphones and listened to the video guides, taking notes on paper. Students with long commutes downloaded the audio and listened as they drove to and from home, school, and work. Students in the residence halls often printed the PowerPoint files and held small-group study sessions with classmates. It was so varied that the professor had a hard time finding a most-common study scenario at all.

UDL can seem like a lot of planning and work, especially when retrofitting existing course materials and interactions. It seems like it is almost easier to design from the ground up, creating brand-new materials and interactions that are not tied to how we used to work. What marks the difference between the UDL experiences of the history professor in this chapter's opening narrative and our composite psychology professor's experience?

First, our psychology colleague created his alternative formats to serve a specific (and measurable) purpose: helping learners to study for the midterm and final examinations. This is one of the keys to successful UDL implementation. UDL "is fundamentally about problem solving, [and] instructional design is about the efficacy of learning. Central to all of its constructs is evidence of intentionality and how problems can be solved through innovative design" (Edyburn, 2010, 37). The history professor, on the other hand, created captions and transcripts out of a sense of fulfilling a perceived requirement.

Second, and more crucially for the adoption of UDL, the psychology professor was not trying to respond to only a small slice of his learner population. The reason for creating the slide decks and video segments was to help everyone, regardless of how they chose to study. Contrarily, the history professor created alternatives for her videos to ensure that students with hearing challenges could still experience the content in her videos. Each professor perceived the alternatives differently, with the psychology professor talking about the benefit to the whole class and the history professor telling learners that those among them with disabilities could now use the captions and transcripts.

Reframing UDL: Plus-One

As a takeaway from this chapter, we want to show you how to think about UDL differently. Instead of adopting the mind-set that we must reactively address every access need, we can design our interactions so that the greatest number of people can take part in them without having to ask for specific accommodations. Fortunately for us, UDL doesn't require five different methods for each element in a course. Rather, it is an iterative process, where you and your colleagues create progressively more course content and interactions to be increasingly more accessible as you teach the course repeatedly. Instead of focusing on the three brain networks, think of UDL as merely plus-one thinking about the interactions in your course. Is there just one more way that you can help keep learners on task, just one more way that you could give them information, just one more way that they could demonstrate their skills?

This unlocks the plus-one mind-set. Having taught your existing courses repeatedly offers you one big advantage when it comes to adopting UDL methods: historical data. Think back and identify the places where your existing students bog down.

- Where do they always have questions?
- Where do they always get things wrong on tests or assignments?
- Where do they always ask for explanations in a different way from the one you provide?

Select these existing pinch points and adopt the plus-one approach at each point. Instead of providing all of the ways learners could get access to those materials, give just one more way to engage than exists now.

To add a plus-one approach to your day-to-day interactions within your class, think of the times where every class asks the same questions at the same point in the course. If you already have a text-based set of lecture notes, follow our psychology professor's example and record an audio podcast of the main content. For an existing video, provide captions or a transcript. Note that providing both captions and transcripts, while useful, might be overkill, especially as you start your UDL efforts.

To know whether to do captions or a transcript, think of whether viewers need to have the audio information at specific points of the video information. In a chemistry lab demonstration, viewers would definitely need to know when to add the chemical reagents and what the safety equipment looks like: since the audio and video content are linked, create captions. In a video interview with a colleague about the various types of banking models, the video content may not be tied logically to the audio, and so a transcript will suffice.

You can use plus-one thinking in assessments as well. For example, in addition to crafting a three-page written essay, you might also allow learners to record a video report, either for the final product of the assignment or as draft content (more on this distinction in the next chapter). Note that there is no requirement to allow students to create whatever they like and turn it in; just allowing them to have a choice about how they demonstrate the skill is enough to increase their sense of motivation in the course (Tobin, 2014, 20).

To keep learners engaged, your plus-one method might be providing breaks between parts of the course where they take in information and allowing learners to think, digest, and do. Schedule way-to-go or temperature-check messages to make sure communication keeps happening, not only about the content of the course but also about learners' progress and sense of accomplishment. It is likely that you are already interacting with your learners to keep them engaged, so offer them choices about how they stay engaged—they could watch your video recap of the unit's main ideas or read the e-mail message with the same content.

One caveat: some concepts and subject material are dependent on their format for understanding and application. For example, graphing the mean in a mathematical set allows researchers to display relationships among disparate data points in a way that allows for visual interpretation in various ways; changing the display conventions for such data actually changes how the data sets can be interpreted (cf. Schneider, 2014). No amount of text-based tables can replicate the procedure of visual inspection for such graphed data. In such cases, where the format is the message itself, we are under no requirement to try to create alternatives for everyone; indeed, even accommodations for individual learners may be challenging. However, don't be lulled into thinking that every problematic situation is impossible either; there are often creative and useful ways to apply plus-one thinking to the places in your courses where students need alternatives the most. In other words, format requirements can outweigh UDL practices, but only if the format is a part of the assignment that is *assessed.*

Concrete Benefits

By adopting this plus-one mind-set, UDL becomes a process of identifying the areas of greatest learner need, based on your previous experiences, and addressing those needs in order to keep students motivated, on task, and learning. Plus-one also works for new courses. When you develop new courses, consider areas, topics, and processes where you think students might get hung up. Offer one alternative method of presenting that information, engaging learners, or increasing their choices on assessments. Pay attention to these plus-one elements as you teach the course. Then, before you teach the course again, identify what worked and got used by your learners, tweak what didn't work out well, and begin identifying other pinch points as places to add new plus-one strategies too.

There are a few concrete benefits to taking the plus-one UDL approach. Learners are more likely to persist in your course: more of the students who begin the course take the final examination (Tobin, 2014, 21). More students are likely to be retained: more learners who finish one year of study will be back to begin the next (Ofiesh, Rojas, and Ward, 2006). Learners with options, choices, and a sense of control over their studies tend to rate their professor more highly in terms of satisfaction with the course, teaching methods, and instructor skill (Burgstahler, 2015b).

The real beauty of the plus-one UDL approach? Designers and professors don't have to throw all of their energy into cramming a few weeks' worth of effort into creating a perfectly UDL-ified course. In order to get started with UDL and then stay on a path of continuous improvement, "good enough" is good enough at the outset, and we can use our existing knowledge of our courses to pinpoint our efforts on the places where the application of a little UDL goes a long way toward providing access, motivation, and choices for our learners.

An important set of caveats is in order here as well. UDL is not simply another term for good teaching, and it "does not occur naturally" (Edyburn, 2010, 38). By simplifying our approach, we risk merely preserving the status quo of doing what we have always done when, in fact, a UDL approach is about purposely thinking differently about the interactions we create for our courses. UDL is a "learned skill, one that is refined over time, to produce high levels of performance" (Edyburn, 2010, 38).

Also, the law in the United States and in many Canadian provinces requires at least some methods in every instance, such as captioning or transcripts for instructor- or institution-created video content that is accessible on public web pages. There's also a plus-one way to approach those legal requirements. For example, when Harvard University was sued by the National Association of the Deaf in 2015 for not captioning its edX course videos (Lewin, 2015), the settlement outlined two things: (1) Harvard had to comply with the law and caption all of its video content, and (2) any content created after the settlement date must be captioned, and Harvard had to come up with a plan to caption the rest of its content within a reasonable time frame. That's plus-one thinking: otherwise, the resource drain in terms of people, time, and funds would have been crippling.

The Harvard case shows us two things that we can adopt (without having to be sued first): draw a line in the sand about doing what's legally necessary as of a certain date so you don't have to worry about your legal obligations going forward. Then adopt the plus-one approach to go back and create multiple access means for existing content, based on a needs list (e.g., for the most-enrolled courses first, or for the courses offered to the broadest spectrum of learners).

While the law is a good soapbox for faculty, designers, and disability providers to adopt accessibility, UDL goes beyond the law. Our legal requirements have a lot to do with multiple means of representing information, and not a lot to do with multiple means of demonstrating learners' skills and multiple means of learner engagement. Those other two parts of UDL often get short shrift when we think solely in terms of legal requirements, yet they are the parts of the equation that have the greatest impact on learner persistence, retention, satisfaction, and learning.

Conclusion

Remember the story at the beginning of this chapter, where Tom Tobin encountered a harried faculty colleague who had spent hours captioning and making transcripts for all of her lecture-capture videos? Kirsten Behling had what we might call the opposite experience. In her faculty-developer role, Kirsten worked one semester with a biology professor who had a student with low vision in his class. The student had the accommodation of a note-taker who was recruited from among students who had already taken and passed the course. The note-taker came to class sessions and lab periods along with the student with low vision, and they collaborated on what went into the notes. The professor redesigned his lab to be a bit friendlier to the student with low vision and to the note-taker: he explained the processes that he demonstrated using more descriptive language; he asked participants to explain their own work out loud; he asked various groups of students to work on different steps in a process and then hand off to the next group.

Some of the students in the class asked if they could also have access to the notes that the hired student had taken, either to compare against their own, as a study aid, or as a replacement for their own note-taking all together. By working closely with a student who needed a specific accommodation, the professor made changes where the benefits extended to all of his students.

As a postscript to this story, the role of note-taker is a good one to pass around a class of students; doing so allows learners to focus more on in-the-moment application and thinking, while still providing recall-and-practice study opportunities (Ahern, 2010, 111). Faculty members at the University of Colorado Boulder, Harvard University, and North Carolina Agricultural and Technical State University all upload student-generated notes, taken using the Cornell method, that are shared with the whole class (Maier, 2016). The added bonus of this method is that the uploaded notes can be mobile, which increases access even further for students.

That is what UDL is all about: proactively providing greater access and choices for every student. Whether the impetus is an accommodation, as in this instance, or a design process that tries to minimize accommodations in the first place, as with the psychology professor whom we met earlier in this chapter, the plus-one approach to UDL allows us to reach out to learners to help them be more successful.

In the next chapter, we will look at how UDL doesn't even have to be a lot of work all at once. We can apply UDL principles that require only modest effort on our part but that save us from having to answer the same questions again and again, provide students with better ways to find time for studying, and give professors a way to get back to the Socratic-dialogue ideal of what college- and graduate-level courses are meant to be in the first place.

A THOUGHT EXERCISE

This thought exercise is designed to help you take stock of a course you have taught or are considering teaching, or an interaction in which you support learners. Take a minute and, thinking about one of your own courses or student interactions, note your responses to the following questions in the worksheet below.

- What elements in your course or interaction rely on single-stream materials (i.e., content provided in only one format)?
- What assessments in your course or interaction require learners to demonstrate their skill in only one format?
- What are the points in your course or interaction where students always have difficulty with the same concepts or ideas, every time you teach the course or have the interaction?

Your responses will serve as a baseline for where to begin UDL implementation, as well as for thought exercises in later chapters, so keep them handy.

Course/Interaction: _____

	Pinch Point	Plus-One Strategy to Address Pinch Point	Needed Resources (Tools, Knowledge, Funds, Time)
Single-stream materials			
Means of interacting with learners (e.g., lecture, group discussion, hands-on)			
Assessments that require learners to demonstrate their skill in only one format			
Technologies you plan to use			

CHAPTER 6

Coach the Coaches and the Players

Meet Eileen

Eileen Bellmore is the director of Accessibility Resources at Stonehill College. Prior to her career in disability services, Bellmore worked as a school psychologist in the K–12 public school system and as a Section 504/ADA compliance officer. Bellmore understands Universal Design for Learning. She gets its impact on a variety of learners, and as a disability professional she felt it was a natural fit for higher education. The problem was how to get the message across to faculty members and support staff so that it had a lasting effect. When we spoke with Bellmore about her efforts, she talked about the "traditional" UDL presentations that she used to give to colleagues. There was some impact, but not nearly what she was hoping for. Recently, Bellmore collaborated with the college's educational technology team in hopes of having a more lasting effect, since their instructional technologist not only understands the benefits of UDL but can also provide colleagues with the tools and support to help them feel more comfortable with making changes.

While Bellmore continues to forge partnerships with colleagues across campus, she also notes that for many faculty members the impetus for adopting UDL methods is having had students with disabilities in their classes. Just one student with a disability, and the corresponding accommodation need, is often enough to bring about a UDL aha moment to instructors. Bellmore describes such an instance around the need to caption videos.

The professor with whom Bellmore eventually worked had chosen to show the TV program *Frontline: The Vaccine War* during one class period. A deaf student in her class had an accommodation: he needed captioned video content. Not knowing how to handle the access issue, the professor told the student that he did not have to watch the episode. The student felt excluded and went to Bellmore in the Accessibility Resources office. After consulting with the professor, Bellmore learned that she did not know how to obtain captioned videos. Further, once Bellmore found the video with captions on the PBS website, the professor explained that she did not know how to turn them on.

Bellmore's experience with this particular faculty member is a common one. Faculty members can be highly engaging and beloved professors, but for some, working with unfamiliar technology can be paralyzing. In this situation, the faculty member concluded that the easiest solution was for the student with a disability simply to be excluded from the experience that was expected of all of his peers.

This is the medical model of disability, where disability is seen as being part of the body of the person who has the barrier, instead of identifying the barrier where it actually is: in the environment. Change the environment (in this case, provide captions), and the barrier is removed. It is up to disability service providers like Bellmore to turn these frustrating moments into teachable ones, and she did just that. Drawing on her UDL experience, she sent the professor the following e-mail message: "Fingers crossed! I actually think many students in your class will benefit from the captions. Research shows that those with invisible disabilities such as ADHD, learning disabilities, and auditory processing disorders retain more information when written text is paired with spoken language" (Bellmore, personal communication, October 7, 2015). Bellmore's explanation that captioning is a teaching tool that has the potential to assist the rest of the professor's students helped her to think about providing accessible materials in the future.

Bellmore told us about a phone call that she received from the professor a few weeks later, thanking Bellmore for her help. The professor noted that other students in the class told her that they found it helpful to see and read unfamiliar terms, even though they were not deaf. The professor also confessed that she got a first-hand benefit from the captions as well. It turned out that the professor herself was struggling with age-related hearing loss.

Meet Jessica

Jessica Dzyak Morrison is the former learning differences specialist at Labouré College in Boston, a small college with a focus on health-care studies. Morrison, who has a counseling background, was the first person hired to serve as a disability specialist, and she was tasked to develop a one-person office and system that would ensure that the college considered the access needs of all students.

She was new to disability services, so Morrison attended the New England Association on Higher Education and Disability (AHEAD) conference and the Postsecondary Training Institute, two conferences focused on compliance, training, and support for students with disabilities in higher education. Following these conferences, Morrison returned to work excited, and with a plan. She focused on the first access point for any student considering Labouré College—its website.

Morrison spoke to her supervisor about the need to ensure that the college's website was accessible, especially since it was being redesigned. She had a dual focus: general website accessibility and a commitment to the entire school to purchase a mobile text-to-speech tool that could be used with the website. Morrison didn't foresee the uphill battle that ensued.

College administrators argued that they didn't have deaf students; therefore, website accessibility was a moot endeavor. Morrison argued that the website was considered a "place of public accommodation" under Title III of the Americans with Disabilities Act (U.S. Department of Justice Civil Rights Division, 2016). Her leadership team said that accessibility was not a college priority; Morrison countered that it should always be a priority. Fortunately, her supervisor agreed with her and asked Morrison to bring in a UDL speaker to whom the administration might listen, since her efforts were not getting a positive response.

Hoping to have more impact if the message came from an outside expert, Morrison and her supervisor brought in a consultant with UDL and website accessibility experience. The expert presented the legal reasons why website accessibility is important and then branched off into the positive impact it could have for all students, not only those with disabilities. A few campus leaders nodded in agreement and shared aha moments, which led Morrison to believe that change was possible.

Building on the moderate success of the outside expert's work, Morrison brought in a representative from a text-to-speech company as the second part of her two-pronged approach. She asked anyone whom she thought might see the benefit of this tool to attend, including all of the academic department chairs and the professionals from the Center for Student Success and the One-Stop student center. After the successful vendor presentation, all three groups independently concluded that the design step of adopting text-to-speech across campus resources would have a positive impact for the learners they served, whether they had disabilities or not. Labouré College adopted the text-to-speech tool under a sitewide license.

Did the success of the college-wide text-to-speech license and the nodding administrators at the UDL presentation mean that Morrison was successful and that website accessibility would be addressed fully? Not quite. Despite her efforts, and despite outreach from the marketing department asking what was needed to make the college website accessible, when the new college website rolled out, it was still largely inaccessible. Bringing in outside experts seemed not to work; the purchase of technology that could identify inaccessible content seemed not to work, and Jessica's hours of research about appropriate fonts, colors, and coding also seemed to have little effect. A universally designed website was just not a college priority. After months of effort above and beyond her role as a one-person disability service provider, Morrison ran out of steam. She had made small steps, but the bigger ones were just too complex for one person.

UDL Is Too Big to Do Alone

Simply put, UDL cannot be implemented effectively at a college or university by one person. UDL is not yet being widely adopted by institutions of higher education (Burgstahler, 2015a). Yes, one person can bring it to a campus and, yes, he or she may get a few people on board, but to have any lasting effect there must be a solid investment in the concept and its principles by a team of people at the college or university. We have learned a few things in our work in UDL adoption on our own campuses and working with other institutions over the years:

- UDL is too big an initiative for one person to roll out successfully.
- The institution's focus must be on learner variability generally, not solely on students with disabilities.
- The adoption program cannot come from an outsider. It must come from within the ranks of the faculty and staff.

A UDL movement needs to be led by a group of people invested in the effects that UDL can have on a campus. Asking one person who has another full-time position within the university to spearhead a UDL movement is seldom feasible. Ideally, a plan needs to be in place to identify

- which faculty members to target first,
- how to introduce them to the concept of UDL,
- how to support them as they adopt it, and
- how to showcase their efforts after they have been successful.

This alone could be a full-time job. As Morrison found out, you cannot associate UDL only with students with disabilities and expect a high level of faculty engagement.

Disability service providers, however, are often the first people on campus trying to bring the concept of UDL to life. To disability service providers, UDL removes barriers, benefiting those students with disabilities who have not yet sought out individual accommodations. It also reduces the need for accommodations, which makes the work of disability service offices easier. But, as Morrison learned, in order for the adoption of UDL to spread campuswide, the focus needs to be on how it can positively benefit a wider group of students.

In order for UDL to really take hold at a college or university, it must come from within. An outside expert may successfully introduce the topic but without an insider driving the next steps, asking people to participate and seeking out additional help, UDL will not implant itself on a campus. As with many higher education initiatives, the introduction of a good idea must be followed with next steps, persons responsible for implementing those steps, and a realistic timeline. An outside expert cannot effectively do these things in a one-shot presentation.

There is an African proverb that says it takes a village to raise a child, which resonates when we think about how to bring UDL to our colleges and universities. It takes a team of dedicated professionals, all of whom wear different hats, to bring UDL to a campus successfully. This chapter will walk through what that team should look like, provide goals and strategies the team can employ, and suggest how to begin the process.

The UDL Campus Team

The composition of a good UDL team models UDL in its own structure: just as UDL assumes learner variability, variety among the UDL team members is crucial as well. The most effective members and roles that we will recommend for the UDL campus team are based on years of grant-funded research projects about which stakeholders work best together to make a concept like UDL move through the compliance-commitment-culture stages of implementation that we discussed in the introduction.

A team approach to implementing UDL on campus allows for greater accountability, invites more creative problem solving, and creates in-house experts. Pulling together a group of diverse but invested professionals also increases access to resources across campus when the team supports faculty members. The UDL team model provides the time needed to develop the skill sets necessary to advise faculty members how to incorporate the principles and strategies of UDL into their courses.

The team first takes a semester to meet as a group. During this standing-up period, the team examines each member's professional responsibility to the institution, learns more about UDL together, and develops its approach to working with faculty members. Think of this first semester as a camping trip in which all the team members are dropped off on a metaphorical island to build trust and cohesion.

The second semester is when the team turns into advisors. Their job is to work with a small and selected group of faculty members to educate them about UDL through a practical, hands-on approach. The goal of most UDL teams is that, by the end of that second semester, at least 5 percent of faculty members have piloted at least one plus-one UDL strategy in their courses.

In the third semester, the team recruits new faculty members to join their group, repeating the same process from the second semester and relying on their existing faculty champions to mentor new participants, even if informally. The UDL team is a self-sustaining support structure for faculty members earnestly trying to learn about and incorporate UDL into their courses. Figure 6.1 outlines the three-phase model.

Who Is on the Team?

Team membership depends largely on the culture of the college or university and on who is generally invested in increasing access for all. Based on the authors' experiences, the following lists the key UDL team members.

- **Disability support personnel.** These professionals think primarily about UDL as it relates to the students they serve, particularly those who have yet to disclose disabilities or are hesitant about using the services provided by their offices.
- **Faculty development personnel.** These administrators are tasked with helping faculty members teach in a meaningful and constructive way that is aimed at transferring knowledge

to diverse learners. The UDL framework is often, but not always, part of their larger tool kit.

- **Instructional designers.** As colleges and universities have looked to the online environment either to supplement or replace the face-to-face classroom experience, instructional designers have become influential when working with faculty members. Designers think about how to create interactions to serve the needs of diverse learners, and the UDL framework is often a natural expression of their skills.

- **Librarians.** Beyond being the keepers of information, librarians are also concerned with teaching students and faculty colleagues how to be information-literate scholars. Librarians are advocates for open access to information, and UDL helps them provide information to the broadest possible audiences and reduce barriers to information access.

- **Instructional technologists.** These professionals are wonderful assets to UDL teams because they are aware of what technology tools are available on campus, and they have the capacity to help instructors use them. Further, many of these professionals have creative ideas for how to embrace the mobile technology through which students are interacting with materials, one another, instructors, and the wider world. This perspective is key to the reframing of UDL that we advocate in this book.

- **Faculty members.** The sooner faculty members from across the curriculum are engaged with the UDL team, the greater the scope and impact of the team.

These are the most common professionals who make up UDL teams, but they certainly are not the only possibilities. Depending on your campus culture, there may be others who would be assets to the team. We have seen UDL teams with campus ministry staff, budget professionals, veterans' affairs staffers, and people from the student affairs side of the administration (e.g., athletics, student life, performing arts). Any people who wish to expand access to their functional area's interactions with students are welcome on the team.

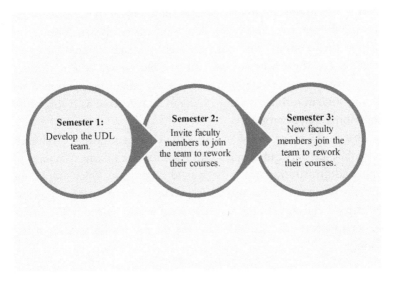

Figure 6.1: The UDL team time line (Behling and Linder, 2017)

The more people who can join the team and commit to monthly meetings the better. More voices add creativity to UDL solutions, share the workload, and keep the momentum going. To be as effective as possible, the composition of a UDL team should remain intact for at least a year. People cycling in and out of the team dilutes and delays the team's impact.

In order to get buy-in from potential team members, and to reduce the rate of attrition, it is critical to be up front about the time and work commitments involved. A solid team might meet at least once a month, for ninety minutes at a time. That gives the team three to four meetings each semester. Work performed in between the meetings usually consists of research, a reflection on how the team can be helpful to faculty members and how team members can implement UDL in their own work, and the piloting of those ideas. It is safe to say that membership in the UDL team will create an additional two hours of work a week.

It is also important to discuss who should not join the UDL team. Joining the team, especially for faculty members who are looking for help in their courses, can make the faculty member potentially vulnerable. For those who are not yet tenured, or for adjunct faculty members whose next appointment to teach might be predicated on strong student ratings, it can be risky to be perceived as trying to fix something that is wrong.

This is where our notion of reframing UDL as a means of outreach to mobile learners can create a safe space for risk taking. Members of upper administration or staff who hold supervisory roles should not initially be on the team. Instead, populate the team itself with operations-level colleagues and have the team report formally to senior-leader sponsors who can advocate for the needs and success of the team.

Time Frames for UDL Teams

The UDL team needs at least one semester to come together as a team. They must bond as a group, understand what their respective roles are at the institution, learn about UDL, and determine the best way to roll out their initiative to their campus. They will also need to recruit at least 5 percent of faculty members to join the group for the following semester. Some campuses can accomplish all of this in four meetings (once a month); some choose to have two meetings a month in order to begin working directly with faculty members in the following semester; and some campuses take an entire academic year to get the team established and trained.

Likewise, there is no set time frame for how long faculty members should be involved with the team. The norm is for faculty members to join the team for one semester to learn about UDL, try their hand at the plus-one approach, and then rotate off the team to become advocates or mentors. In this model, faculty members learn about UDL, know what and where their resources are on campus, and obtain some practical application experience. In other models, faculty members might remain on the team until they are comfortable on their own, or perhaps until they have redesigned an entire course to have multiple engagement points.

Either way, the UDL team continues to meet at least monthly. Unlike faculty participants, UDL team members are asked to commit to the team for at least a year. If they do leave, they are asked to find their replacements and help train them prior to their departure. This helps to ensure that the UDL team has longevity.

UDL Team Training Models

Prior to meeting as a group, one person on campus needs to drive the recruitment of the team itself. Most often, this person is someone in the disability services or faculty development office who has heard about UDL, much like Bellmore and Morrison above. They must use grassroots efforts to gather a group and charge them with developing a UDL team. When the first meeting occurs, one of the first things to determine is a stakeholder analysis: who is not at the table, but should be?

Once the team is established, decide the best way of learning about UDL. There are four models that in our experience offer the most success. Is there an in-house expert? In the absence of an in-house expert, how do the team members learn about UDL on their own? Is there an expert whom they can hire for a one-time training? Or do they have the resources to bring in a UDL consultant for the duration of the semester?

In-House Expertise

Often there are people at the institution—like Bellmore and Morrison—who have attended conferences, researched UDL, or have some prior positive experience with it. These people, while not experts in the subject matter per se, have enough knowledge to start the conversation with the team. They can point the team in the right direction when questions arise or additional resources are needed. The in-house expert model typically starts with the expert providing the team with an overview of UDL, their experience with it, and asking the team to research UDL on their own. Sometimes they are assigned research topics (e.g., how does UDL have an impact on instruction? What are the principles of UDL? What data show its effectiveness?).

At other times, in-house experts might ask the group to research how UDL might impact their specific career focus (e.g., how does UDL affect the library? The information technology department? Instructional design staff? The tutoring center?). Often, the in-house expert evolves into a UDL facilitator, setting meeting agendas and keeping the momentum going while allowing the team to learn organically about UDL through a process that works best for them.

In-House Teams

The in-house team approach is very similar to the in-house expert approach, except that the entire team is starting from scratch. Typically, there might be a few members on the team who are familiar with the concept of UDL but have not implemented it in their own work or guided others. In this scenario, the team must work together to determine how they can learn about UDL as a group and then translate their knowledge to faculty members.

Usually, the team will take the first meeting to look at UDL as a whole and then break the concept into smaller parts, tackling each part at a different meeting and assigning components within those parts to different members on the team. The goal is that by the end of the semester the team has taught itself UDL and become aware of a number of resources that it can refer to when meeting faculty.

One-Time Consultant

Some teams secure funds to bring in a consultant for an overview of UDL. The outside consultant may spend an hour to a full day with the team, introducing them to UDL and walking them through how they might guide faculty colleagues. In addition to that overview, the consultant should allow time for problem solving and provide a list of resources for the team to use when they begin working with faculty members. Hiring a one-time consultant is a nice way to introduce the concept to the team on equal grounds, where every member can be considered an expert. Funding for this workshop may come from one or all of the departmental budgets, or may be an institutional initiative.

A Consultant for the Entire Semester/Year

If a department, or the institution as a whole, has enough financial resources to invest in the UDL team approach, they may consider hiring a consultant to serve as the UDL educator for the first semester as the team settles into place. The consultant will introduce the team to UDL through theory, examples, and resources and then help them to figure out the best way to translate it to their institution.

Eventually the consultant's role should move from teacher to facilitator, simply guiding the process and answering questions as they come up. If the institution decides to contract with the consultant for the entire year, he or she can help the team introduce the concepts of UDL to faculty members and serve as a resource as the team works with faculty members incorporating UDL into their work. The consultant may be physically or virtually present at each team meeting, or a combination of both. Again, funding for this workshop may come from one or all of the departmental budgets, or may be an institutional initiative.

Sample UDL Team Agendas

We have seen each of these models work. Which model an institution chooses depends largely on the culture at the institution, its financial resources, and the level of expertise already on site. Below are examples of meeting agendas that the team might use for the first semester. Each institution should design an agenda that meets the needs of its team. Consultants will vary the agenda as well, according to their methods.

SAMPLE AGENDA A: IN-HOUSE EXPERT

Meeting 1: Welcome and introduction of the team

- Each member's role at the institution
- Experience with UDL
- What they hope to gain from this experience
- Outlining the role of the UDL team (led by expert)
  - o Goal and purpose
  - o Timeline
  - o Commitment needed
- Introduce UDL at the macro level (led by expert)
- Assign homework for each team member, which includes reading through examples of how UDL may affect their professional areas of expertise
- Set next meeting date

Meetings 2–5: Welcome and review of the last meeting

- Team members report back what they learned in terms of how UDL relates to their position
- Share student demographics with the team
- Brainstorm how UDL might help diverse learners (led by expert)
- Discuss UDL as it relates to curriculum design (led by expert)
- Using a course of their choice, each team member reviews the design of the course and identifies one area where UDL may be applied
- Homework: note what resources are needed to redesign that one component
- During meetings 4 and 5 the team should begin identifying faculty to join them the following semester
- Set next meeting date

SAMPLE AGENDA B: BUILDING UDL KNOWLEDGE FROM SCRATCH

Meeting 1: Welcome and introductions of the team

- Members' roles at the institution
- Their experience with UDL
- What they hope to gain from this experience
- Discussion of the structure of the team
- Goals and purpose
- Timeline
- Roles of team members (facilitator, organizer, note keeper)
- Commitment needed
- Introduction of UDL at the macro level—share websites, look over presentation materials, discuss resources
- Each team member should find three different UDL resources and relate them to their profession
- Set next meeting date

Meetings 2–5: Welcome and review of the last meeting

- Team members identify how UDL impacts their teaching and/or role at the university
- Brainstorm how UDL can be intertwined with the institution
- Mission
- Strategic plan
- Diversity of students
- Brainstorm what components of UDL the team should focus on first
- Homework: Begin researching those components, break down by task if necessary
- During meetings 4 and 5 the team should begin identifying faculty to join them the following semester
- Set next meeting date

SAMPLE AGENDA C: ONE-TIME CONSULTANT

Meeting 1: Welcome and introductions

- Members' roles at the institution
- Their experience with UDL
- What they hope to gain from this experience
- Introduction of UDL, including the institution's mission statement, strategic plan, and demographics of its students (led by consultant)
- Sampling of how UDL teams work (led by consultant)
- Brainstorm how this UDL team will work (led by consultant)
- Each team member should find three different UDL resources and relate them to their profession
- Set next meeting date

Meeting 2: Welcome and introductions

- Refer back to the consultant's talk—what questions remain?
- Referring back to the UDL team brainstorm, is the vision for the team still the same? If not, what needs to change?
- Discussion of the structure of the team
- Homework: Decide as a team where to start, what UDL topic should the team focus on first
- Set next meeting date

Meetings 3–5: Welcome and review of the last meeting

- Team members report back the information they gathered about UDL
- Continue the conversation about what aspects of UDL they think the institution should focus on, assign tasks for researching those further

- Homework: Gather at least three different course syllabi to begin practicing their UDL skills
- During meetings 4 and 5 the team should begin identifying faculty to join them the following semester
- Set next meeting date

SAMPLE AGENDA D: SEMESTER- OR YEAR-LONG CONSULTANT

Meeting 1: Welcome and introductions

- Members' roles at the institution
- Their experience with UDL
- What they hope to gain from this experience
- The consultant should discuss their role, time frame, and expectations of the group
- Discussion of the structure of the team
- Goals and purpose
- Timeline
- Roles of team members (facilitator, organizer, note keeper)
- Commitment needed
- Introduction of UDL, including the institution's mission statement, strategic plan, and demographics of its students (led by consultant)
- Each team member should find three different UDL resources and relate them to their profession
- Set next meeting date

Meetings 2–5: Welcome and review of the last meeting

- Team members report what they learned in terms of how UDL relates to their work within the university

- The consultant will choose which UDL principles the team should follow based on their conversations in the first meeting
- The first one or two principles will be introduced in this meeting (depending on the UDL model that the team has chosen to follow) (led by consultant)
- Using a course of their choice, each team member should focus how the UDL principle that was discussed can be infused into the course that they are working with
- Homework: Practice infusing the UDL principles into the course
- During meetings 4 and 5 the team should begin identifying faculty to join them the following semester
- Set next meeting date

Guidelines for All UDL Teams

No matter which approach the UDL team chooses for learning about UDL and preparing to work with colleagues, there are some common guidelines by which each should abide. These five topics need to be woven into the work done by the team prior to faculty members joining.

- Establish ground rules.
- Understand the initiatives at your institution.
- Describe your student body.
- Identify potential roadblocks.
- Be open to change; be flexible.

1. Establish Ground Rules

UDL aims to increase access to institutional interactions for a greater number of students, as well as to make course and service interactions more dynamic for the professors and staff members facilitating them. The process of rethinking course elements or service interactions can be difficult and, in some cases, can cause faculty members and staff members to feel vulnerable.

Likewise, through the process of learning about UDL, UDL team members may reflect on their own work and recognize areas that can be improved upon. For this reason, it is critical that the UDL team establishes ground rules, both at its first meeting as a team and then again when colleagues are invited to join. The ground rules can be quite simple, from "only one person talks at a time" and "it is important to hear everyone's opinion" to something more complex like "we will not judge methods; rather, we will consider them from different points of view." Ground rules allow for each person on the team to feel valued and provide all with the opportunity to participate fully. The team, as a whole, should respect the ground rules and enforce them.

2. Understand the Initiatives at Your Institution

Through the authors' experience, we have come to value the idea that anything done in higher education has a much better chance for success if it is closely tied to campus- or institution-wide initiatives. When you are selling the team's work or asking for financial resources, reviewing the strategic plan, mission statement, or some other recently created initiative at your institution—and finding a way to tie the UDL team's work into that plan—it will be far more effective than if your work is a stand-alone project.

Upper-level administrators are more appreciative of work that reflects their goals. It might be as simple as identifying a mission focused on diverse students' success to something more complicated such as a strategic plan designed to increase overall retention of the institution's students. In both of these examples, it is very easy to justify the foundation of the UDL team and a need for resources as a direct effort to support the mission or strategic plan.

3. Describe Your Student Body

One of the most effective arguments for UDL is the impact it can have on a broad range of learners. The key to a successful buy-in to a UDL team—by team members, faculty members, and administrators—is that the goal of the team is to create a more welcoming and inclusive collegiate environment for a diverse group of students. Saying this is one thing; backing it up with data is another. When the UDL team firsts meets, it is helpful to have a clear picture of who the students are at the institution. Many team members and faculty members have never seen demographic data about their students. Many also consider diversity to be defined largely by race and ethnicity, so adding other markers of individuality, such as socioeconomic status and the wide range across the ability spectrum, is instructive.

While this is true, it is also important to look at the number of students who attend full-time versus part-time, those who have financial aid, the number of international and nontraditional students, and the number of students registered with the disability services office. The team should appreciate some of the barriers that each of these groups may have to navigate to get access to their courses and in their other interactions with the college or university. The argument for UDL is that it has the potential to increase the ease of access for all students, thereby increasing their rate of institutional completion and increasing the alumni pool from which to draw donors in the future.

4. Identify Potential Roadblocks

Before a UDL team takes the time and actually spends resources on incorporating UDL into academic courses, it is important to identify potential roadblocks. Being aware of obstacles allows the UDL team to plan ahead, either to go around those roadblocks or to begin conversations about how to dismantle them. Members of the UDL team are dedicating valuable time away from their day-to-day work in order to increase access for all.

5. Be Open to Change; Be Flexible

If there is anything that the authors have learned when trying to introduce a new concept like UDL to our institutions, it is the need to be open to change and to remain flexible. Even the most well-thought-out plans are often interrupted by budget changes, staff changes, and new administrative initiatives. It is important for the UDL team to be flexible in terms of when and how faculty members are recruited and, once on board, how they translate the ideas of UDL into practice. Flexibility, after all, is a cornerstone of UDL.

Recruiting Faculty Members for the UDL Team

Just prior to the end of that first semester or year, the team should recruit faculty members to join them. The team needs to decide how many faculty members they want, and for what length of time they want the faculty members to be a part of the team—or to be on the receiving end of UDL scholarship and direct advice on their courses. Most UDL teams invite no more than seven new members to join them at any given time. More than this means less one-on-one focus and a lower likelihood that the faculty and staff members will successfully incorporate UDL into their work.

Conversely, having fewer than four new members can go either way in terms of its success rate. The smaller number of participants means more face time working on their courses and interactions. This could threaten those new team members who are not comfortable with constructive criticism. The key here is to find colleagues who are interested in trying to change their courses, even slightly, to better the learning outcomes for all students. If the number of faculty members participating is low, make sure that every suggestion is accompanied with a positive note about new participants' current methods.

The length of time that a team works with a group of faculty members also needs to be fleshed out prior to recruiting faculty. Ideally, it should be no shorter than one semester and no longer than one academic year. One semester gives the team three to six meetings (depending on the frequency of meetings) to introduce faculty members to the concept of UDL, to identify an area in their course where they are already doing inclusive work, and to incorporate UDL strategies into an area that has not been successful in the past, or that they are worried about teaching. Our research has shown that if faculty members add UDL strategies to just one component of their course, they often will be able to add it to other areas successfully without the UDL team guiding them.

Faculty members and support staff might avoid committing to new things because of their already busy schedules. Therefore, it is important to set their expectations in your first effort to recruit them. In your recruiting materials or elevator speech, do the following:

- Tell faculty members how they are likely already designing interactions that can be tied to the UDL framework (this may be in the form of an example specific to them or in general if you are recruiting in a wider format).
- Give them the exact dates and times for meetings (pick these out ahead of time).
- List the expectations of joining the group (attend all meetings, be willing to learn, rethink one aspect of their course).
- List the benefits of joining (examples might include better student engagement, increased retention, appreciation from their supervisor, ability to add this accomplishment to their tenure file).

In terms of how to recruit, we have found that the most successful start to adding faculty members to a UDL team is to ask each team member to invite one faculty member or staff colleague to join the team. It might be a close friend of the team member, a colleague whom he or she has watched excel with students, or someone with whom he or she has worked on a project and developed a trusting relationship.

No matter whom you choose, the personal invitation to the UDL team, especially within that first group of faculty members, has been the most successful approach for us. Going forward, encourage the faculty members on the team to recruit the next group of faculty. Many times, they may recruit from their departments, their friends, or colleagues with whom they have worked on committees. We have found that after you recruit that initial group, it is fairly easy to bring new faculty members into the team each semester going forward.

Many institutions choose to open up the invitation to the UDL team in a broader way. Often the faculty development office is a great resource in terms of hosting an introductory workshop for faculty members about UDL, the team, and the requirements of faculty participation. If there are team members from academic departments, they may have the ability to influence recruitment from within their departments, or the dean or provost may nominate faculty members to the team. These nominations should always be framed as rewards, highlighting the diverse teaching methods of faculty members, rather than punishments, remediation for those faculty members with poor student outcomes.

There are a lot of ways to recruit faculty members; the key is to understand the structure of your institution in terms of how faculty development is perceived and supported. Then you can decide what recruitment method is best to gather that first group, as well as subsequent groups.

The First Meeting with Faculty Members

There are a lot of different ways that a UDL team can introduce faculty members to UDL and to the goals of the team as a whole. Since the team is designed to support faculty members by incorporating UDL strategies into areas of their courses that have been troublesome in the past, we suggest an informal but structured conversation. The informal nature of the meeting will help to ease faculty members into the conversation as full partners in the effort.

The team is designed to deliver information in a workshop-type environment, not through a lecture experience. Conversation, stories of successes and failures, thoughts and ideas are welcomed. However, because of the team's limited time to work with faculty members, the conversations should have structure. We have included an agenda below describing how the first three meetings might run with the UDL team and faculty member participants. As always, this agenda is just a template. Adjust it based on the needs of your college or university.

MEETING 1: WELCOME TO THE TEAM!

- Introductions
  - What is each team member's role at the institution?
  - What is their role (if assigned) on the team?
  - What do the faculty members teach now and what are they planning to teach next semester?
- Develop ground rules as a group
- Gauge the UDL knowledge in the room
  - What do you know about UDL?
  - What are you hoping to learn?
  - What are your goals for this experience?
- Introduce UDL: make it as interactive as possible; use examples
  - UDL as a whole
  - The three brain networks associated with UDL
  - Ask faculty members to think of their course and identify areas that already might be UDL friendly
- Ask each faculty member to identify one area on which they might like to focus
  - Ask guiding questions, including what didn't work, what you are nervous about, what areas you would like to make better
- Prep for the next meeting
  - Assign a reading, video, or other example that helps faculty members to understand UDL better
  - Ask faculty members to focus on one area that they'd like to improve; ask them to come up with one strategy to use
  - Ask faculty members to reach out to team members for help if needed
  - Remind everyone of the next meeting time and location

MEETING 2: INTRODUCTIONS AGAIN AS A REMINDER

- Review the group's ground rules
- Review the one piece of course work/content on which each faculty member will focus
  - Ask them to present the area and describe the concern with that area
  - Initiate a group brainstorming session for UDL ways to help
  - Identify resources both within and outside of the team
  - Repeat the process with another faculty member (this might be ten to fifteen minutes per faculty member, depending on the time allocation and the number of faculty members on the team)
- Spend a few minutes sharing more information about UDL. Topics could include the following:
  - A more in-depth look at UDL
  - New data that someone found about UDL
  - A UDL resource (e.g., website, case study, journal article)
- Prep for the next meeting
  - Assign a reading, video, or other example that helps faculty members to understand UDL better
  - Ask each faculty members to rethink their one area of concern for the next meeting, using the strategies they gained at this meeting
  - Ask faculty members to reach out to team members for help if needed
  - Remind everyone of the next meeting time and location

MEETING 3: INTRODUCTIONS AGAIN AS A REMINDER

- Review the one piece of course work/content on which each faculty member chose to focus
    - Ask each faculty member to identify concerns and challenges with adding UDL strategies to that area of their course
    - Initiate a group brainstorming session for UDL ways to help
    - Identify resources both within and outside of the team that might help
    - Repeat the process with another faculty member (this might be ten to fifteen minutes per faculty member, depending on the time allocation and the number of faculty members on the team)
- Have a conversation about how to spread the word about UDL on campus
    - How can the team get their message across to a larger audience?
    - Begin thinking about recruiting faculty members for the next semester/year
- Prep for the next meeting
    - Assign a reading, video, or other example that helps faculty members to understand UDL better
    - Ask each faculty member to finalize the UDL strategy that he or she will add to a course
    - Ask faculty members to reach out to team members for help if needed
    - Remind everyone of the next meeting time and location

Acknowledging Those Who Participate

While most UDL teams start off small, the end goal is for a handful of faculty members to finish the semester or year with a solid knowledge of the UDL framework and ideas for how it can be incorporated into their work. Some UDL teams prefer to remain under the radar with their work, believing that the less attention the group is paid, the more likely faculty members will participate. Other institutions have cultures that respond positively to faculty members going above and beyond in their efforts to improve their teaching. At these institutions, the UDL team may hold an end-of-the-year lunch for their faculty participants, inviting their department chairs to celebrate their faculty members' success.

Some schools have held poster-session receptions for their faculty members, giving them the chance to highlight their work and the before-and-after effects of UDL incorporation. Other schools tend to be a bit lower key, asking their provost, dean, or department chair to write a letter of appreciation for the portfolios of faculty members who have completed the training. No matter what the approach, acknowledging the effort that faculty members have put forth to ensure that their classes are accessible to diverse learners is not only reaffirming to faculty members, but also to the team.

Shh! Don't Mention Disability

Have you ever hosted events with titles like

- "Disability 101,"
- "How to Support Students with Disabilities in Your Classroom,"
- "Faculty Responsibilities for Providing Accommodations," or
- "Legal Accommodation Requirements"?

If your campus is like the majority of colleges and universities in the United States and Canada, then if you get ten or fifteen colleagues to come, you are doing something right (perhaps the free lunch was a draw?). As we discussed in chapter 4, part of the challenge for faculty and staff development programming is that UDL can be perceived as extra work or as benefiting only students with disabilities. There's a bit more going on when we look at this challenge at the college or university level. There are ghosts on campus.

Now, we don't mean literal apparitions, spirits, or, in the words of the character Ray Stantz from *Ghostbusters*, "what we call a non-repeating phantasm, or a class-5 free roaming vapor" (Reitman, 1984). No, our ghosts are the students whose barriers are not visible to others, and there are a lot of them. This group includes not only students with invisible disabilities but also students with demanding family care commitments, mental health concerns both diagnosable and temporary (e.g., the loss of a loved one), challenging work schedules, or even long commutes. Although few studies have aggregated such data (cf. American Federation of Teachers, 2011), we are comfortable asserting that, taken together, more than half of our students are struggling at any time with barriers to putting their best effort into their studies, and their challenges are not visible to faculty members and staffers who support them.

Thus, invitations to Disability 101 events often meet with the response of "oh, I'm good" or "I don't have any students with disabilities in my class, so I don't need to attend." This is not because our colleagues are callous or unfeeling. In fact, cognitive science has a name for this phenomenon: it is called the What You See Is All There Is (WYSIATI) bias, wherein our thinking is biased by the assumption that our experience of the world is total, so we discount or ignore what we don't know or see (Kahneman, 2011, 86). Basically, our colleagues don't see students' disabilities, barriers, and struggles (many of which take place away from the classroom and away from campus), and thus they predict that they won't interact with any students with disabilities throughout the course of their careers. Fortunately, we can make some of these ghosts more visible by using another of our cognitive biases to work in our favor: the framing effect.

Daniel Kahneman coined the term *framing effect* to describe why our thinking is biased by how information is presented. For example, something advertised as being 90 percent fat free feels better than when the same product is described as containing 10 percent fat (Kahneman, 2011, 373). Change those workshop titles accordingly.

- "Diversity 101"
- "Support Diverse Learners in Your Classroom"
- "Teaching Diverse Students"
- "How to Reach Everyone and Teach Everyone"

Of course, we are partial to that last one. By framing workshops and other programming in terms of values that people tend to support, like diversity, inclusion, and time saving, you will draw more people in. The term *diversity* is broader than the word *disability*. It can be interpreted to include a wide range of learners, including those with disabilities. Terms like *diversity* also attract more faculty and staff because they experience interactions with students from diverse backgrounds in their classrooms. Diversity is visible and doesn't trigger people's WYSIATI bias.

In reframing UDL for your college or university, consider the people whom your faculty members teach and your support areas serve. Does your institution have many international, nontraditional, commuter, part-time, first-generation, or racially and culturally diverse students? Find out how many of your students own smart phones, have work and family responsibilities, and encounter other demands on their time.

The University of Massachusetts Boston used this approach to draw faculty members into a summer workshop series on inclusive design (they didn't even use the terms *UDL* or *disability* in their call for participants). Faculty members had been complaining about students failing to attend class or coming to class unprepared. The international student services office and the admissions office gathered statistics on the current class of students. Over 30 percent of the students were immigrants. Many of those were also working full-time jobs. When they realized that a large number of students were struggling to prioritize university work in their busy lives, these two offices got together with the faculty development office to offer the summer workshops on UDL.

Instead of presenting disability-focused strategies, the workshop focused on how to engage non-native speakers of English, those with poor executive functioning skills, and those who relied on their mobile devices during their busy commutes. This reframing contributed to a high adoption rate among the workshop participants, and—more importantly—among departments and programs across the institution that requested similar help after the workshop faculty members shared the positive results of less overall work for them and better outcomes for their students.

Conclusion

Like Bellmore and Morrison at their respective colleges, Kirsten Behling was the disability services coordinator at Suffolk University. Within the last few years, she saw a sharp increase in the number of students who depend on a screen reader for access to course materials. Screen readers are typically used by students with vision disabilities or those who process information better through auditory rather than visual inputs. Kirsten's office also received a lot of referrals from the international student office about students seeking testing to see whether they have learning disabilities or their difficulties with their courses are due more to their barriers as English-language learners. The increase in students seeking diagnostic referrals, temporary accommodations, and other disability support taxed the office staff and resources.

Kirsten decided to create a UDL solution to support international learners who may or may not have disabilities. Kirsten and her team, with the support of the Instructional Technology Department and chief information officer (CIO), purchased a university-wide license of Read and Write Gold, a text-to-speech software. The CIO strongly supported this purchase, not as an accommodation solution but as a tool from which the entire campus could benefit. When the license came up for renewal, the CIO paid for it out of the central technology budget.

The challenge, now that Suffolk University had the license, was how to roll it out so that everyone would benefit. Kirsten, the CIO, and the director of the Center for Teaching and Scholarly Excellence (a faculty development office) developed an implementation plan. If the disability services office maintained the site license and controlled who had access to it, then the only students who would use it were those with disabilities. The CIO suggested that all Suffolk community members have access to the software on their Blackboard home page. Because they were experienced with the software, staff at the disability office created short self-paced tutorials that were captioned and posted next to the links to the software, for ease of use. The team also offered workshops to all information technology staff through the faculty development center, uploaded the software on all of the library computers, and targeted outreach to the international student center and campus writing center.

The success of the adoption of this UDL tool was due to the teamwork among the disability services office, the CIO, and the faculty development office. Had just one of these offices pushed back against this initiative, it likely would not have been nearly as successful. By and large, faculty members and staffers who are aware of the UDL framework and its goals believe that it is a good practice and that designers and instructors should employ inclusive methods. The challenge comes in translating those beliefs into practice.

The UDL team is reflective of the individualized environments, politics, and key players at institutions of higher education. The UDL team creates a flexible, grassroots method to increase the active presence of UDL within college courses and service interactions. It is an approach to ingraining UDL into the college environment one course, one interaction at a time. Perhaps the most rewarding experience about the UDL team model is the collaborative efforts and relationships formed by individuals who might not otherwise meet or work together. This group increases awareness of the resources at the institution and leads to future collaborations beyond the UDL team.

Faculty members have an opportunity to sit with the experts on their campus, many of whom they may not have known existed, and receive directed group-on-one attention for their courses and their work. Through this process, they learn about UDL while also gaining the confidence to incorporate it in other areas of their courses. This grassroots approach to UDL has a lasting impact on a college campus. Before we move to the next chapter and break down UDL strategies for expanding access to just one assignment, take a few minutes to respond to a thought exercise about how you might put together a UDL team at your college or university.

A THOUGHT EXERCISE

One of the most successful paths toward sustained UDL implementation is to create a UDL team. Use this thought exercise to begin building your team. This exercise should be broken into two sections and filled out as the team is being established and after it is up and running. As a first step, predict how you and your colleagues might respond to each part.

Questions to consider when developing the UDL team

- What is your own experience with UDL?
- Who are your allies on campus (staff, faculty, administrators)?
- List three faculty members you know who teach in an inclusive manner.
- When is the first team meeting? Where?

Questions to ask during the first UDL team meeting, after the team has been established

- What is a problem that may unite the team initially to use UDL strategies?
- What is the college or university's mission or strategic plan?
- What resources do you have that support working as a team?
- What resources are missing?
- What is the overall experience of the team with UDL?
- Given the team's experience, draft (loosely) the team's goals.
- What are the team's immediate next steps?
- When is the next team meeting? Where?

PART 3

Adopt UDL on Your Campus

CHAPTER 7

—

Expand One Assignment

—

Meet Rachael

Rachael Cobb is a government studies professor at Suffolk University with a research interest in ensuring that all people have the opportunity to vote in elections. In 2010, Cobb and a graduate student collaborated with the City of Boston to create a supplemental training for Boston poll workers that focused on how to ensure that all people, regardless of ability or language preference, have the chance to vote. Their training encompassed the principles of Universal Design for Learning by highlighting the differences in voters and offering various ways for citizens to cast their ballots. Their training was so well received that those poll workers who went through it were designated as Disability Ambassadors and were assigned to various polling stations throughout the city.

Cobb's successful training with the City of Boston informed her Elections and Voting course, a combined undergraduate and graduate course designed to give students a detailed look at the history and politics of election administration in the United States. Traditionally, she explained the details of elections and the voting process through readings, lectures, and class discussions. While she found that her students grasped the material, they did not appear to appreciate the difficulties that voters from various subgroups often encounter.

As she considered how to engage her students more thoroughly with the election process, Cobb considered the poll-worker training that she and her graduate student had developed for the city. What if she asked her students to take the same training, assuming the role of poll workers and citizens with various ability profiles? How might a hands-on experience like that have an impact on her students' learning?

Her students learned to distinguish between pets and service animals. Using the AutoMark voting machine, students got a crash course in assistive technology for citizens who have vision disabilities, are non-native speakers, or who have a difficult time filling in the little ovals on a standard paper ballot. Some students played the role of citizens trying to communicate their needs to the poll workers, and found it frustrating if they were told that they had to follow the same process as everyone else, regardless of their ability to do so. Their hands-on experience enhanced the lectures and readings that Cobb had used in the past.

Cobb reports that as a result of the students' experience with the poll-worker training, some of her students actually went on to apply to be Disability Ambassadors during actual elections. Others reported a sense of joy at being able to support nontraditional voters. Perhaps most important for Cobb was the impact her course had on her students' awareness of voting and election issues. The fact that her students were driven to try to make a difference far outweighed her original goal of teaching them about the process. Cobb kept her students engaged in more than one way, gave them information in multiple ways, and let them demonstrate their various skills as well. This is what UDL is all about.

Meet Lisa

Lisa Bibeau is the assistant dean of disability services at Salem State University in Massachusetts. Because of her expertise, she was recently asked on short notice to develop and teach a senior-level course on disabilities for the university's Bachelor of Health Studies program. Bibeau, a UDL expert and someone consciously aware of the variability among all learners, decided to design a course that embraced the multiple-means approach of UDL.

Health and Disabilities across the Lifespan is a face-to-face course designed to help students move away from the medical model of disability and recognize societal barriers for people with disabilities. Bibeau decided to use this course as an opportunity to humanize the experiences of people with disabilities for future health professionals. The way in which she designed the course, her use of varied instructional approaches, and the many opportunities for students to show mastery of the course material reflect the principles of UDL.

The course explores a new disability every week. Bibeau begins by assigning reading and posting her lecture PowerPoint slides online ahead of class. She then asks her students to complete an online test to demonstrate that they have understood the material assigned. Bibeau stresses that these online tests are not about knowing how to test but, rather, knowing the material.

During the subsequent face-to-face class session, Bibeau goes over her slides in detail and then shows at least two videos of people sharing their personal accounts of living with their disabilities. She purposely chooses two videos with two different people—a male and female, people from different races and ethnic backgrounds. This conscious choice is an effort to help her students engage with and relate to the person on the screen. Once her students have taken in all of this information, she asks them to get into small groups for another test. This test is an extension of the one that they did online, but now they work on it in groups, discussing the possible answers and navigating different opinions and comprehensions of the materials together to come to one conclusion. Recognizing that some students work better alone and some better in groups, Bibeau then averages these two grades for each student.

Through reading about a specific disability, listening to a lecture, and then talking about it in groups, most students should be able to accurately demonstrate their comprehension. But not all will, and this is where Bibeau really excels. Following the two tests, she asks each group of students to apply what they have learned to a case study. This is an opportunity for the groups to work through a real-life scenario to solve a problem for people with that disability. The manner in which they solve the problem and share their solution with Bibeau is up to them (e.g., plus-one alternatives such as written papers and video responses). This final piece of the assessment process gives students one more way to engage with the content and show mastery of material through a means that works for them.

Health and Disabilities across the Lifespan is a successful course. It answers a need within the bachelor's degree program, and the way in which students are taught and assessed also answers a need within the larger university to engage students with a variety of learning preferences, styles, and barriers. Bibeau designed her assignments to recognize those needs and offer students options, and this is a productive way to begin applying plus-one design thinking.

UDL in Assessment

When academics consider UDL, most of us acknowledge that it is a good idea, and most of us think about multiple ways of giving information or motivating students. Captions and alternative formats for media? Yes, a great idea. Multiple ways of keeping learners engaged and on track? We'll give that a try.

However, we have found, over and over, that when we ask colleagues to consider incorporating UDL strategies into their assessment methods—allowing learners multiple ways to demonstrate their skills—the response is often "no way." In almost every presentation and workshop about UDL, at least one participant raises a question about offering learners choices in how they demonstrate their skills: assessment is frequently a sticking point. Some colleagues question whether offering alternative assessment formats will have a negative impact on the rigor of the course; others balk at the idea of having to do what they perceive as the extra work of designing multiple ways for students to demonstrate their knowledge. Some share a sense of fatigue at the idea of having to grade all of those different formats of learner responses, and others question whether one can grade a three-page essay in the same way as a five-minute video response. UDL and assessment can indeed be a challenging advocacy combination. Fortunately, UDL allows designers and instructors to narrow the scope of the work in order to see a positive impact.

Allowing students choices in how they demonstrate their knowledge and skills may be a contentious topic because few of us in higher education—support staffers and faculty members alike—have studied the underlying principles of assessment design. We are not like Cobb, with a subject matter that lends itself to multiple ways of practice, or like Bibeau, whose experience with educational theory helped her design multipart assessments that allowed learners to try different ways of showing their knowledge. Many of us design our assessments for the convenience of the grader (read also: us); we want all of our learners to show us a measurable indication of competence that can be compared simply against a standard and against the performance of other students. This makes grading quicker, simpler, and easier to administer.

UDL relies on the concept of *construct relevance* to ensure that we are actually testing students on only the skills that we want them to demonstrate—and that we aren't unknowingly testing learners' abilities in dimensions that are not related to the subjects we want them to learn. There are many ways to demonstrate skill, but when we ask learners to show their knowledge and skills in only one way, we are excluding a number of people from showing what they know. "Constructs are the knowledge, skills or abilities being measured by an assessment" (CAST, 2016a).

Construct relevance comes into play when we design assessments that require students to master skills on which we aren't ostensibly testing them.

[For a] math assessment that includes word problems to assess students' understanding of math concepts, the ability to read fluently is construct irrelevant. Even though it is an important skill, it is not part of the construct being measured. Learners who have difficulty with reading may miss certain items even though they may have a good grasp of the underlying math concepts.

[In an] essay exam in a biology class that is both timed and closed book, construct-irrelevant factors include motor coordination (handwriting or typing skills), short-term and working memory, organization and time management, attention, and the ability to work under pressure. The additional measurement of these many factors can prevent gaining an accurate picture of a student's biology content knowledge. (CAST, 2016a)

These examples provide compelling reasons for us to look critically at our assessments and ask what we are actually asking our learners to demonstrate. Learners can often seem weak in the knowledge we want them to show, not because they do not know it, but because we are asking them to shape their response in ways that cause some of them to struggle. This explains why Cobb noted that students seemed to be able to express themselves well during class discussions and their poll-worker training, but those skills did not always translate into exam performance. The flip side is also true for some learners: they are quiet in class and ace the exams and papers.

The question of how one can grade essays and multimedia responses consistently also brings up an area of assessment design that few higher education faculty members have studied formally, but almost every K–12 teacher knows: creating measurable objectives. The Every Student Succeeds Act, or ESSA (2015), encourages educators to design assessments with UDL principles as a method of accurately and broadly measuring students' knowledge (CAST, 2016b). Objectives are the skills or knowledge that students should demonstrate after experiencing a given part of a course, such as a lesson, module, or unit. In the K–12 world, teachers are trained to write assignment objectives from the point of view of the learner, using the shorthand acronym SWBAT, or "students will be able to . . . ," followed by measurable statements of the objectives for assignments.

Most college and university courses' course-level objectives are already stated; these have often been developed by department committees and get handed to instructors as-is. Based on those course-level objectives, the task is to make our unit-level and assignment-level objectives measurable. Without clear statements about what actions and skills earn them credit, students can get confused about what we want them to do and accomplish. Well-stated unit-level and assignment-level objectives help to ensure that all assessments guide students to achieve specific, behavior-based, measurable outcomes.

Objectives are defined by what students will know, do, demonstrate, or accomplish. Learners may take different amounts of time to master the materials or concepts, so we build that into our learning design with learning objectives that include behavior, measurement, and proficiency.

BEHAVIOR

The first part of defining an objective is to specify the behaviors that the learner must demonstrate. We talk about the desired behaviors as specifically as we can:

- Sequence the eight steps in the peptide chain.
- Write a three-page expository essay.
- Answer ten questions about the Civil War era.
- Juggle four one-inch wooden cubes.

MEASUREMENT

Next, we include the way we can measure the learners' level of mastery of the information or concept.

- Sequence all eight steps in the peptide chain **from memory.**
- Write a three-page expository essay **with a clear thesis, and using details, evidence, and examples to support the writing.**
- Answer ten **multiple-choice** questions about the Civil War era.
- Juggle four one-inch wooden cubes **for two minutes.**

PROFICIENCY

Finally, we add in the level of proficiency that separates learners who have mastered the objective from those who have not.

- Sequence all eight steps in the peptide chain from memory, **omitting or mis-sequencing no more than one step.**
- Write a three-page expository essay with a clear thesis and using details, evidence, and examples to support the writing. **The essay must contain fewer than four grammatical, usage, and syntax errors.**
- Answer ten multiple-choice questions about the Civil War era, **with at least 80 percent proficiency.**
- Juggle four one-inch wooden cubes for two minutes, **keeping all cubes in constant motion, and without dropping any cubes.**

Once we have created measurable objectives for our assessments and removed construct-irrelevant elements, applying the UDL framework becomes much easier. One reason that grading essays and video submissions in a similar way is often difficult is that we ask how we'll ensure that the video contains proper APA formatting, for example. That is the wrong question to ask. Instead, ask whether we are assessing our learners on how well they perform APA formatting. If that is not the primary reason for giving the assignment, then remove it as an objective, or restate the objective in a way that allows for variability (e.g., "students will be able to support their primary research assertion with at least three different professional resources") and that can be assessed whether one is reading or viewing the students' outputs.

If supported by construct-relevant elements and measurable objectives that are format-agnostic, UDL does not alter the rigor of course assessments (Harrison, 2006). Rather, the UDL framework ensures that students are able to demonstrate what they know to the fullest extent possible without being penalized by the method of demonstration. Some people are challenged by traditional test situations (statistically speaking, nearly a third of you reading this may count yourselves among them). Others struggle with presentations, and still others encounter barriers in the task of writing papers. If the end goal of the course is to make sure that students understand the material, we can review the construct relevance and objectives of our assignments in order not to pigeonhole learners into no-choice assessments that do not accurately reflect their learning.

A note about format is appropriate here. If the format is part of the learning, then do not offer students a choice about how they demonstrate the learning. For instance, in a writing course, one objective might be to learn how to format a written page using APA format. Since students are supposed to learn the written format, a video option would not allow them to demonstrate proper margins, spacing, and font sizes. However, as learners draft their work, offer them choices about how they create the content for their written work: on a lead-up assignment where learners are free-writing and learning how to support thesis statements with details, offer a choice of a written document or, say, an audio podcast file, and emphasize that the final product will have to be a written document. However, question whether all of the constraints of your assessment are truly related to the grading criteria: for example, many colleagues have stopped using time limits for testing because they are not testing whether students can show their knowledge quickly—just that they can demonstrate their knowledge.

Sometimes, though, we choose assessment methods based on time. What can we do quickly and effectively, especially if we are teaching large classes? The thought of adding even one assessment-method choice for learners can feel overwhelming.

- How can I possibly grade twelve different-format projects quickly?
- How will my students know how to select the best option?
- Does this mean that I need to develop a dozen different grading rubrics?

If the objectives are the same across all choices, then grading becomes easier, not more complicated. Having consistent objectives in assessments that offer learner choices allows us to develop one rubric that speaks to those common objectives. Such a rubric can expand across different assessment strategies, so that we can grade written work using the same set of criteria as our assessments for presentations, videos, or websites developed by students. And remember that you need not design for all possible options: just apply plus-one thinking and expand assessments by one method. UDL in assessments provides students with opportunities to engage with the course material in ways that are meaningful to them and that reflect their learning preferences. Figure 7.1 is an example of a rubric that Kirsten Behling uses in her Introduction to Disability Services course at Suffolk University; it is designed to be open to different types of assignment submissions and guides students in how they can mix from among those submission types in order to craft their entire response to the assignment.

Figure 7.1: Participant observation rubric

Student name:

Assignment: Participant Observation at a Disability Services Office

Goal for the assignment: Understand better how a disability office accommodates students.

Assignment value: 150 points

Assignment Options: For each objective, you may choose to create

- a website,
- a written response, or
- a video presentation.

You do not have to select one method for the entire assignment; if you do mix formats, indicate clearly which objectives you are addressing in each piece that you create.

Objective	Not Observed	Developing	Proficient	Excellent
Highlight the accommodations process	No accommodation process notes (0 pts.)	The accommodation process was mentioned (25 pts.)	The accommodations process was covered in some detail (33 pts.)	The accommodations process from pre-intake to accommodations fulfillment was covered (50 pts.)
Share possible accommodations	No accommodations shared (0 pts.)	Some academic accommodations shared (25 pts.)	Academic and some nonacademic accommodations shared (33 pts.)	All accommodations shared, including details of how to use them (50 pts.)
Identify a grievance process	No grievance process identified (0 pts.)	Grievance process alluded to (15 pts.)	Grievance process quoted in detail (22 pts.)	Grievance process identified, rationale given for why it is used (30 pts.)
Highlight the programs offered through the DS office.	No programs highlighted (0 pts.)	Programs listed (10 pts.)	Programs listed with descriptions (15 pts.)	Programs listed with descriptions and targeted audiences identified (20 pts.)
Earned (out of 150)				

Another approach to UDL in assessment comes from the Disabilities, Opportunities, Internetworking, and Technology (DO-IT) Center at the University of Washington. DO-IT advises faculty members to offer multiple methods of assessment throughout the semester—and not just choices on the midterm, course papers, and final exam.

- **Set clear expectations.** Use one rubric for each assignment, even if there is learner choice in that assignment. Make sure due dates are clear on the syllabus, and reinforce those dates through the course.
- **Provide multiple ways to demonstrate knowledge.** Use a combination of individual assessment, group work, and entire class participation. Change the format of the tests used (some multiple-choice questions, some essay, some short answer). Ask students to do a combination of papers, presentations, role-playing, video/website making, and so on.
- **Be willing to adjust your assessment plan.** Based on the learning styles/strengths of the students and their progress throughout the semester, be willing to adjust the type of assessment planned.
- **Provide examples of good work.** Give students study guides or access to previous good work, removing the guessing game and anxiety for many students.
- **Use assessment methods that mirror instructional methods.** Assess student's knowledge of the content, not their ability to adapt to a different format of presentation.
- **Allow opportunity for students to check in by minimizing time constraints.** Make due dates clear, scaffolded assignments encouraging students to check in throughout the process of getting to that final assignment. Allow all students to have extra time on the tests, not just those with approved accommodations. (Burgstahler, 2012)

Like the DO-IT Center, the Neag School of Education at the University of Connecticut has a Postsecondary Education and Disability program that supports faculty members who teach using digital tools. In response to the mobile learners they serve, more and more faculty members are using online surveys, quizzes, and exams to assess informally how their students are progressing in their courses. Brief, one-to-five-question surveys can help to gauge understanding and reset the focus of the course.

By allowing students to do brief, frequent knowledge checks online and in the comfort of their homes or dorm rooms, faculty members can assess student's knowledge of the material instead of their ability to memorize facts or test in potentially stressful environments. It may seem counterintuitive, but adjusting course practices to respond to learner variability also enhances academic honesty: the high-stakes assessments can be designed as timed and/or video-proctored exams because students get frequent practice and feedback about their work well before the situations where they must demonstrate their skills under constrained circumstances.

The work of CAST, the DO-IT Center, and the University of Connecticut shows us that UDL strategies increase the effectiveness of assessments when we build in learner choices about how they demonstrate their knowledge and skills, without sacrificing the overall academic integrity of assessments. We will now examine some specific strategies for UDL in assessment.

Back to Plus-One

Adding flexibility to assessment is a challenging task for many faculty members and course designers. We may vary our instructional methods based on the topics we cover. We may vary our course texts and readings as new ones are published or we find new resources. Our assessment methods and instruments tend to change much less frequently. Adding to the complexity is the fact that some course assessments cannot be flexible. They must be done in a specific way, either because the format is one of the grading criteria, or because the format is required by a future professional exam.

For example, a significant part of the accounting licensure exam is multiple-choice; therefore, many accounting professors give multiple-choice exams to help students prepare under conditions similar to the licensure exam. Nursing courses, too, include assessments that mirror the practicum that students must demonstrate for licensure, so that courses include evidence-based practices as part of their exams—demonstrating a student's ability to administer medication, for example. Even within such courses, though, there is opportunity for variability, and it begins at the level of the course interactions.

The rule of thumb is to design courses at a conceptual level first, and then to design the interactions within them using the UDL framework. The idea is that the goals, objectives, and content for any interactions need to be developed and clearly specified before any plus-one options are introduced. According to the Center for Teaching and Scholarly Excellence at Suffolk University, course goals should reflect the essential questions of the course, and the learning objectives should reflect what students should be able to do (remember SWBAT?). Look at the goals of a sample college writing course, for instance:

- Goal 1: Become critical thinkers
- Goal 2: Be able to consider plural perspectives
- Goal 3: Be able to self-reflect on one's learning

The objectives are:

- Objective 1: Write for a variety of purposes, audiences, and contexts
- Objective 2: Identify audience expectations and textual conventions
- Objective 3: Use the writing process, especially peer review and revision, to re-see and extend your thinking

In order to assess these objectives, instructors might ask their students to write a course paper. This will indicate whether or not a student can write well (Objective 1), reflect on the work or topic about which they are writing (Objective 2), and engage their peers in evaluating their work (Objective 3). This could take the form of one paper or multiple related papers, each of which measures a different combination of objectives. However, not all students can demonstrate their knowledge effectively by writing to specific paper topics. Is there room within the course to offer flexibility when assessing students?

On the surface, this might seem like a disingenuous question. Since this is a writing course, shouldn't students have to write in all of their course work? A closer look at the goals and objectives reveals some ways to offer learners choices.

The goals of the course are for students to become critical thinkers, to consider multiple perspectives, and to become self-reflective in their learning. There is no stated goal that a student must learn how to write, say, a fifteen-page paper. Instructors can implement the plus-one approach and ask their students to give presentations, create self-reflection videos that discuss a particular book and the audience expectations, create podcasts, or, yes, write papers. Each of these options allows learners to demonstrate those course objectives as they build toward the final course project, where there is no choice: for a writing course, the final assessment is a written paper (see "When the Format Is the Assignment" below).

The bottom line is that UDL strategies can be implemented more seamlessly when goals and objectives are clearly defined, measurable, and not tied to irrelevant constructs. We can get creative in how to offer choices in assessing our students' knowledge and honoring the variability among them.

Choosing What Types of Assessments to Use

Once the goals and objectives are clearly stated, the engaging task of designing assessments that are outside of the traditional exam/paper/presentation pattern can begin. In our workshops, we love seeing the moment when colleagues start exploring what is possible. People usually start out with some trepidation. What kinds of assessments should they offer? How many? And what if they don't work or there are no student takers for an option?

Our response is always to dream big. We ask colleagues, "What would excite you? How might you yourself demonstrate your knowledge of this topic?," and, finally, "Thinking about this course as a stepping stone to a profession, what skills are needed to be successful?" In accounting courses, for instance, students might choose to take an exam about personal taxes, based on various forms that people receive (e.g., W-2 wage forms, 1099 interest income forms), or choose to prepare a tax return using the same forms as inputs. In biology courses, students might write a paper about invertebrate anatomy or record a video of themselves dissecting a worm and identifying its primary parts. For a pre-law course, students could choose to participate in a mock trial or write a dissenting opinion. Note that constraining students to a choice between two options provides freedom and flexibility without overwhelming them (and the instructors) with too many options: this is the power of plus-one thinking.

Through a grant from the U.S. Department of Education Office of Postsecondary Education, Kirsten worked with a number of different schools across New England, helping professors adopt UDL strategies. One professor involved with the grant was teaching a course on survey methods. After learning about UDL, he expanded his final assignment. Initially, students needed to develop a survey on the experiences of college freshmen with the dining hall. The professor added choices to the assignment, broadening the scope but not the format; now, students survey any population at the university—faculty members, staff, students, athletes, those involved in Greek life—about a topic important to the students. Initially, the students struggled to get their final projects off the ground because the professor gave them only the rubric with the assessment objectives and some minimal directions. Some students worried that it was a trick: how could a professor let them choose what was important to them? How would they be graded, if everyone chose a unique topic and methodology? As we see in this example, faculty colleagues are not the only ones who can be skeptical about choices in assessment. With a bit of reassurance from the professor that the assignment was not a trick, and after the professor answered the questions below, his students were off and running.

- How many survey questions should we use? *Whatever it takes to get the answers you want.*
- How should we share the results with you? *In the fashion that best fits the data that you have collected.*
- When is it due? *May 1st.*

The results were wonderful. The professor reported that the students displayed a level of engagement with survey methods that he had not seen for years. Some students were so engaged that they needed to be guided to think a bit smaller: surveying the entire campus is not realistic in only a few weeks. Others were able to use the data that they collected for projects in other courses, and one group was able to use their data to advocate for a gluten-free dining station.

This level of engagement motivated the students, while also helping them to understand how to do surveys and how the process will benefit their future careers. This professor might benefit in the future by narrowing the format options for what the students eventually create to, say, a written or video output; especially where the assessment provides maximum choice of topic or approach, using plus-one design helps to guide students to think in a more focused way while still tying the assessment to course objectives.

Offering Flexibility in Assessments

Many faculty members and course designers choose first to offer flexibility in their final assessment. The thinking is that by the end of the course, students should have the foundation to be able to run with the final assignment and make it their own. Leading up to that assignment are smaller, more structured assignments that faculty members have created to give the students the tools they will need in order to be creative in their final work.

Other faculty members begin offering flexibility from the start. It might start with subtle things, such as choices in an essay topic, a choice among which ten of fifteen possible multiple-choice questions students answer, or a choice in what presentation topic they pick. Students are still required to complete the assignment in the format that the faculty member wants—but within that format, plus-one design gives learners choice. This type of plus-one design provides learners with the feeling of having control and options.

Flexibility in assessments (for example, by scaffolding the stages of an assignment) also extends to the concept of providing students with multiple opportunities to practice their new skills and multiple opportunities to receive feedback. The most common example of this is breaking a larger assignment (e.g., paper, presentation, wiki development) into smaller steps (e.g., choose a topic, review your outline, submit a first draft, submit your references, submit your final draft).

Building up to the finished product using a scaffolded structure in which each completed stage feeds information and skills into the next stage of the project, creates opportunities to provide feedback that is not graded, and allows learners to take risks or repeat parts of the process without fear of losing credit or points.

Mandatory-but-ungraded parts within assessments give learners the freedom to relax, play, experiment, and try new approaches and ideas before they are called on to demonstrate their skills and knowledge when it counts for points. This promotes a collaborative relationship between faculty members and students, and it encourages students to seek out the expertise of their instructors.

A great example of supporting students in their efforts to learn new content comes from Anne de Laire Mulgrew, a Spanish professor at Tufts University. De Laire Mulgrew teaches a chapter on travel in her intermediate Spanish course. The lesson for this class includes the traditional aspects of a Spanish course: vocabulary, grammar practice, and pronunciation with peers in class. But during one of her classes, de Laire Mulgrew changed the traditional assignment to give students the opportunity to really engage with the idea of traveling in Spanish-speaking countries. She asked them all to choose a Spanish-speaking country and do the following: research the country, identify the capital, note important tourist attractions, and find different aspects of the country and culture that are not well known. She then asked them to create a travel brochure using their research. For this brochure, Anne gave the students a lot of choice in how they presented the information, whether it was a traditional paper-based brochure or a web page or video brochure—she just said it needed to be persuasive.

The results were exciting. Students liked the assignment because it allowed them to bring out their artistic side and create a brochure that was engaging based on what they found out in their research. Some students were excited to explain artwork they had created; others worked with maps; one was eager to discuss the culture of his chosen country through film clips. The students presented their research to their classmates, who found it interesting to learn something new about countries that they might not have known otherwise. By allowing her learners to own the decisions about how to format this project, Anne helped her students engage with the Spanish language well beyond just reciting vocabulary words.

When the Format Is the Assignment

Sometimes, as stated earlier, certain courses lead to licensure or are part of a series of classes required for advancement in a profession. In such cases, faculty members often prefer to evaluate their students in the same way they will be evaluated in their profession so that they can give the students a chance to practice test taking. We have explored how to incorporate UDL strategies through the scaffolding approach. For practical, goal-oriented courses and interactions, keep those high-stakes exam simulations and employ UDL choices and plus-one thinking in the lead-up to the skill demonstrations that students must execute in a particular format.

Incorporate UDL strategies in creating review materials that can be used in preparation for those career exams. For example, another professor associated with the UDL grant from the U.S. Department of Education had taught an occupational therapy (OT) course for three years and noticed that many of her students struggled in their homework assignments when learning new OT therapeutic physical positions for patients. However, when she taught the positions in class by demonstrating on students and then asking the students to practice on one another, they were able to grasp the finer points of the positioning more quickly. She came to realize that even though the textbook had both words and pictures (plus-one UDL thinking), the two-dimensional aspect of the text was not effective for all of her learners.

Toward the middle of the semester, she asked the class to break up into groups of three and added her own plus-one approach. She made sure that at least one member in each group had a cell phone with a video camera in it. She then asked two of the students to demonstrate the positioning (one played the role of the patient and one was the OT). The third student filmed the positioning from the perspective of the OT, creating a video of the view that an OT would have when working with a patient. Each group had a different position to work through. At the end of class, she asked those who had filmed the movements to send them to her electronically. She then posted them to her course website. The next week, she asked the students to demonstrate those positions. Compared to the class whose models were only in the textbook, the accuracy of the students who had seen the videos increased by 75 percent, and they excitedly reported that this was due to the more realistic movements-in-time experience that the videos provided, instead of the static two-dimensional textbook pictures.

At the end of the semester, the instructor gave a combination exam that mirrored the one these future occupational therapists would have to take for licensure. Part of the exam was multiple choice—something familiar to the students, since they had already taken five multiple-choice quizzes throughout the semester—and the other part was demonstration of technique. The year that she had the students create videos, the final exam grades increased by 18 percent. Both the students and the professor attribute this to the availability of the videos for studying throughout the semester. This leads us to another good practice for reframing UDL: to reduce cognitive load and new-tool learning curves, let learners use technology with which they are already familiar.

Using Technology in Assessments

The multitude of technology tools available to faculty members, course designers, and students encourages flexibility in assessments. Whether instructors are aware of it or not, students are already using technology in class. They might be recording the lecture on their phones, taking pictures of the notes written on the board, or researching content on their laptops. Textbook publishers have also expanded beyond hard-copy books to include software packages tied to book topics. Students can review materials after hours via electronic flashcards, quizzes, and simulations of the content covered in class. Recall the mobile phone frame that we set up in previous chapters. We can embrace technology and anytime-anyplace learning when we assess students' knowledge of the material as well.

Perhaps the easiest way to embrace technology is to use your college or university's learning management system (LMS). Many faculty members use it as a course document repository (recall the filing cabinet metaphor we used in chapter 3), storing electronic copies of their syllabi, course assignments, and handouts.

A UDL approach to using technology tools continues the plus-one mind-set for assignments. Use the electronic discussion board to extend conversations beyond the classroom and make responses searchable for repeated viewing and study. Use the LMS to quiz students (an opportunity for ungraded practice) or require students to submit their assignments via the Dropbox feature: students can easily manipulate their work prior to turning it in, and faculty members can provide feedback electronically in multiple formats, such as text and audio.

Encourage students to use the technology that is familiar to them as well: websites, cell phone videos, and social media posts. Everyday technology gives students options to demonstrate their knowledge in media and ways with which they are familiar.

One of the best examples of encouraging students to use technology to demonstrate their knowledge comes from another colleague involved in Kirsten's UDL grant. An agricultural science instructor wanted his students to advise local farmers on how to replant crops in a manner that would increase their harvest by 10 percent. He had spent the semester teaching students many methods to do this, depending on the different qualities of the soil, climate, and the crop plant itself. He asked the students to create a guide for farmers that could be used independently of the university, something the farmers could refer to later on. He also asked that it live someplace electronically. He did not say what form of technology the students were to use but did insist that it should be accessible to all viewers (i.e., be compliant with the Americans with Disabilities Act, or ADA).

His students ran with this assignment and created projects based on the technologies with which they were most comfortable. He received a handful of captioned time-sequencing videos about what to do first and how best to tend to the soil. He received a few slide shows with audio commentary, for which the students provided transcripts. Two students created wikis with step-by-step guidelines and links to resources should farmers encounter problems. And he received one video in which a student created a computer-generated step-by-step look at how seeds react to different types of soil. He asked that the assignments be turned in a week early so that students could review one another's work and provide peer-to-peer feedback. Based on the feedback, the assignments were edited and then released to the local farmers.

Benefits of UDL in Assessment

UDL in assessments offers benefits to both students and instructors. Students are able to demonstrate what they have learned in a manner that reflects their learning preferences or circumstances. This means that students can spend more time learning course content than learning how to succeed in a particular type of assessment. Flexibility in assessment also creates a greater level of learner ownership of knowledge. By being invested in a project's outcome, by being able to choose topics that are interesting or have meaning to their future careers, students will often go beyond the requirements of the project to really try to understand what they are learning. This quest for knowledge is one of the keys to successful future professionals.

Instructors, too, benefit from incorporating UDL into their assessments. UDL strategies require faculty members and course designers to think concretely about their course goals and objectives and to consider what students should be able to demonstrate as they move through the course. It also creates a greater level of freedom in design and implementation of course interactions.

Perhaps the biggest reward for faculty members comes in watching their students' excitement and creativity with the material. Students long for the opportunity to show what they know in real-life settings. That level of excitement extends to faculty members when they are faced with grading the assignments. Rather than grade forty

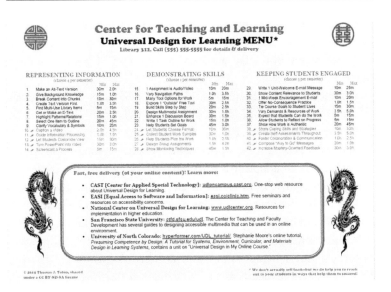

Figure 7.2: The UDL "Chinese menu"

three-page papers, faculty members enjoy the variety by which students demonstrate their knowledge. UDL strategies in assessment can reduce grading fatigue. Another benefit is the ability to use multivariate student work as examples and teaching tools in future classes. UDL in assessment draws out creativity and can improve the experience of all involved in multiple ways.

A Chinese Menu

When Tom Tobin was at Northeastern Illinois University, he was talking with the LMS administrator about the ways faculty members could apply the three parts of the UDL framework as outlined by CAST. The conversation turned to ways that faculty developers could simplify the range of options among multiple ways to keep learners engaged, provide information, and demonstrate learner skills. In an offhand remark, the system administrator said, "Yeah, it's kind of like a Chinese menu—you know, choose one from Column A and one from Column B." The result of the conversation is figure 7.2, a literal "Chinese menu" for UDL adoption at the level of a single college course.

The menu allows designers and faculty members to see specific examples of engagement, access, and choice techniques that fall under each of the three areas of UDL. Note how the Chinese menu document does not contain the word *disability*; rather, it focuses on attainable strategies for adopting a plus-one mind-set within the context of a single course. Each of the bite-sized practices listed on the menu is backed up by the neuroscience as an effective way to keep students motivated and help them to learn and show what they know.

We are sensitive about the possibility of cultural appropriation with the Chinese menu format, and we were pleasantly surprised to learn that Chinese menus as we know them in North America are an invention of Chinese-American immigrants (Li, 2017). During the gold rush years in the nineteenth century, Chinese immigrants who opened restaurants began to cook dishes with ingredients more familiar to their customers from all ethnic backgrounds, and hung out slates with pictures of the dishes, which did double duty as advertising and a menu. Customers could order by number or just point to what they wanted. These early versions evolved into the menu style that we associate with Chinese restaurants today. This was pretty UDL, for its day: multiple means of representing information, multiple ways for customers to indicate what they wanted, and multiple ways to stay engaged (i.e., order more dishes).

Conclusion

UDL in higher education represents best practices for reaching out to our increasingly diverse college student population. While it can be incorporated into many different aspects of college courses and interactions, assessment is often the last area in which faculty and staff members are willing to consider UDL. Many faculty members use just a handful of ways to assess student knowledge and skills: papers, exams, and presentations. These methods reflect how many faculty members were themselves assessed as students, and with which they are comfortable. Because many of us were never formally trained to teach, we tend to fall back on teaching in the ways in which we were taught.

It is also important to remember that faculty members are experts in their fields. That means that, as students, they were probably at the head of their class in their content matter, which means that they responded well to the assessment methods used by their own professors. Single-stream assignments like papers, exams, and presentations are, for many instructors, comfortable, easy, familiar, and nonthreatening.

UDL in assessment can seem threatening to that comfort, at least initially. It means changing the ways we think about measuring knowledge. For some, a UDL approach asks them to take a huge leap of faith. This chapter breaks down that leap into small steps. UDL can be incorporated into assessments successfully and with care.

Cobb and Bibeau are perfect examples of this. They each took traditional courses with tests and papers and added UDL strategies to the original assessments. They did this because their end goal was to make sure that their students understood the content that they wanted to impart. By providing students with the opportunities to practice skill sets needed for the content of their courses (role playing poll workers and citizens coming to vote, working in teams to develop strategies for how to support people with disabilities), they empowered their students beyond the scope of their courses. Their students will now forever be influenced when they go to vote or encounter people with disabilities out in the community. The lessons of their courses do not end with the semester.

One might argue that Cobb and Bibeau went above and beyond, and we would agree—and we would argue that the UDL changes that they enacted did not make their courses easier or provide students with ways to avoid demonstrating all the course objectives. The first, and perhaps most important, outcome of adopting plus-one UDL to share with faculty colleagues is that flexible assessments do not alter the rigor of our courses. It doesn't matter whether students take an exam or create videos, so long as the evaluation rubric criteria are consistent and the assignment reflects the goals and objectives of the course. From there, we encourage faculty members to consider making small changes to their courses, things like offering choices about which essay prompts to respond to, choices of topics on papers, and choices in how to present student work (e.g., in a group, alone, with a video, via a PowerPoint presentation, as a poster).

As in the examples in this chapter, once faculty members take that leap and offer small choices, the reward is observable and measurable: instructors can see and decide for themselves whether the experiment of offering choices is worth doing. Students begin to own their learning, rather than rely on faculty members to spoon-feed it to them. UDL in assessment is a positive response to meeting the needs of all learners while increasing knowledge attainment of the content being taught.

A THOUGHT EXERCISE

Use this worksheet to redesign and include UDL strategies in one assessment activity in a course or interaction that you have with learners. It can be as small as a quiz or reflection, or as large as the final project or examination.

Course/Interaction: _____

Next semester to be taught: _____

List the goals of the course: _____

_____

_____

List the course objectives: _____

_____

	Example	Your Assessment
Assessment	*Five quizzes*	
Point value	*50 points each*	
Description of the assessment	*Biweekly quizzes to evaluate learner knowledge of material covered in those two weeks*	
What worked?	*Students knew that they were coming. Low point value*	
What didn't work?	*They are all in essay format*	
What UDL strategies can be built in?	*Substitute two of the quizzes for reflection exercises with their peers (same point value)*	

Once you have rethought your assignments, follow these next steps to implement UDL.

Next Steps

- Update the rubrics for each assessment in your course to reflect the UDL strategies you chose to use. Attach both the old rubric and the new one to this worksheet. Consider using and editing the rubric found here to fit your purposes.
- Ask a colleague to review your material and provide feedback.
- Adjust based on your colleague's feedback and your experience with the assignment.
- Implement the changes and observe changes.

Student name: _____

Assignment: _____

Goal for the assignment: _____

_____

Assignment value: _____

Objective: *Describe the steps in the accommodation process (50 points)*

Not Observed	Developing	Proficient	Excellent	Demonstration Method
No process notes (0 pts.)	*The process was mentioned (20 pts.)*	*The process was covered in some detail (40 pts.)*	*The process from pre-intaking to accommodations fulfillment was covered (50 pts.)*	*Website, paper, or video presentation*

Objective: (maximum points)

CHAPTER 8

Enhance One Program: UDL across the Curriculum

Meet Beth

In 2016, we spoke to Beth Harrison of the University of Dayton about how she and her colleagues created a curriculum-wide adoption of UDL principles. Harrison's story exemplifies one path that readers can emulate for moving along the knowledge-need-advocacy-action continuum. Harrison came to Dayton in 2008, after seventeen years at the University of Arizona. One of the first things she heard from colleagues was that "the ADA doesn't apply to us" because Dayton was a nonpublic institution. "Even if ADA wasn't directly applicable—which is debatable," Harrison told us, "Sections 504 and 508 of the Rehabilitation Act definitely do apply to Catholic higher education institutions."

Part of the initial challenge for Harrison and her colleagues in the Office of Learning Resources (which included the university's disability services staff, as well) was just "getting the knowledge about inclusive design into the right heads." Harrison has been doing accessibility workshops around the United States since 2001, and she encouraged her colleagues in the staff and the administration to pay attention to access issues through attendance at trainings and information sessions. For example, Harrison sent the university's head programmer for the learning management system (LMS) to a workshop on inclusive design from WebAIM: "He came back ready to spread the word to faculty members that inclusion is not just about students with disabilities, and he's been a key trusted voice on campus advocating for the benefits of UDL to faculty members themselves. He also ensures that the learning management system is accessible on the back end. That is a huge piece that I don't have to think about, because I know he's taking care of it" (Harrison, 2016).

Harrison then worked with her colleagues to simplify the message that the Office of Learning Resources was sharing with the campus. "The Ivy Access Initiative on Universal Instructional Design [see chapter 1] at Brown University focused on just two concepts: instructor flexibility and multiplicity of access methods. That was something that faculty members could wrap their heads around, and makes a good starting point for the campus conversation."

In order to help the campus work systematically instead of in the typical silos, Harrison and her colleagues purchased two pieces of software for use by the entire campus, "and these weren't just for use in disability support, either": WYNN literacy software, which performs advanced text-to-speech functions (see Freedom Scientific, 2015), and SensusAccess, which converts electronic files into formats such as accessible pdf, audiobooks, e-books, and digital Braille (see Sensus ApS, 2017).

Harrison and her team quickly saw that faculty members and students were using these applications as self-serve tools to help them interact with materials in ways that made the most sense in the moment. By allowing anyone at the university to convert content on the spot to formats more useful for individual needs, these two programs lowered barriers not only for learners with disabilities (for whom they were nominally created), but also for learners who wanted to study in settings where the original format of the content would be intrusive, such as converting text files to spoken audio for in-car studying during student commutes, or turning off the sound on video files and using text transcripts while studying in places like laundromats and public libraries.

Harrison says that "it took almost seven years to convince our administrators that we should caption all of our video content," but that it was well worth the effort. To make sure captioning became just part of what the University of Dayton did, Harrison and a small cross-university team proposed a four-tiered system that supported a policy requiring captions for all video content after a certain target date:

- The university contracts with a third-party vendor for captions (department pays for captions).
- The Office of Learning Resources and E-Learning staff trains student captioners to staff an in-house service (department pays less but turnaround time is greater).
- Do it yourself—the Office of Learning Resources and E-Learning staff trains faculty members and department staff members to do captioning.
- Adopt a hybrid model of captioning using YouTube's auto-recognition followed by manual text correction and clean-up.

The four-tiered approach offered departments a range of options, from most convenient and most expensive to least expensive and most labor-intensive. In a 2017 follow-up conversation, Harrison noted that the University of Dayton had found a champion for UDL among their senior campus leaders. "The Provost objected to having departments pay for captioning and to putting the burden of captioning on faculty members (because it's more work and there's really no way to ensure that it gets done), so he asked for another committee to explore other ways to make the captioning happen. . . . Captions will be done through our learning management system in conjunction with two third-party companies: one hosts videos, the other captions. And our legal department has agreed to start the long process of creating an accessibility policy to govern everything" (Harrison, 2017). To continue the department-level adoption process for UDL principles, Harrison is now identifying accessibility representatives throughout campus from academic departments and support areas. Her next step, now that the tools, processes, and workflows are in place, is to educate everyone about how and why to use them, as well as to create policy collaboratively with all of the involved stakeholders. In order to make visible the university's commitment to diversity of all kinds, the administration recently hired a vice president for diversity and inclusion, and Harrison is looking forward to moving departmental mind-sets along the path from thinking about accessibility to access to inclusion.

Talking to Administrators Like Administrators, Part 1

UDL advocates can take advantage of their positions within the political hierarchy of their colleges and universities. Often, the people pushing for inclusive-design techniques like UDL have one foot metaphorically in their institution's daily operations and the other foot in the strategic planning for broader and longer-term outcomes. Such people often have titles like coordinator, director, and technologist, and they are used to working directly with faculty members and support staffers in order to effect programmatic changes. We have spent a number of chapters offering suggestions about how to get those primary audiences—faculty members and support staff—to buy into and apply best practices that fall within the UDL framework.

However, when we talk with senior leaders at colleges and universities—chancellors, presidents, provosts, and deans—we speak very differently. At the level of courses and faculty interactions, we always prefer to listen to the instructors' and designers' own experiences and work on plus-one techniques that help to reduce workload for instructors and learners alike. At the level of program and curriculum development, we adopt the language of senior campus leaders and talk in terms of student retention, persistence, and satisfaction.

Mathew Ouellett and Sara Kacin of Wayne State University, along with Shaun Longstreet of Marquette University, presented a model for "Accessible Campuses: Partnering with Teaching Centers" at the 2016 Professional and Organizational Development (POD) Network conference. Their framework for organizational development is a model for how to structure and conduct UDL-adoption conversations with campus leaders. Many such leaders often adopt a crisis-driven approach, moving from one possible lawsuit to another, with a focus on individual behavior change: the institution asks one instructor to create one accommodation for one student with a barrier to learning.

We've seen in chapter 2 how appealing to the law and a sense of compliance is perhaps the least effective way to adopt accessibility as a college- or university-wide practice.

Instead, Ouellett and his colleagues adopted a narrative in which they talked about UDL as a component of multicultural organizational development (MCOD), weaving a social justice argument together with a vision-driven set of goals that could be championed by senior campus leaders who would agree to partner across all executive areas in order to infuse accessibility into the mission, vision, strategic plan, curriculum, and faculty reward structures. The goal is to change policies, practices, and the culture of the institution by moving through three distinct phases of multicultural organizational development (Jackson, 2005):

- **Monocultural.** This phase is marked by exclusion and an in-club atmosphere: "you can join us if you become us."
- **Nondiscriminating.** This phase is marked by compliance and affirmative reaction, a desire to change the social diversity profile by openness to token nonmajority people.
- **Multicultural.** This phase is marked by redefinition of cultural norms, not satisfied with being merely socially just or nonoppressive.

Ouellett cited Wayne State University in 2014 as an example of an institution moving along the MCOD process. The university was generally, at the time, at the nondiscriminating stage, where students would make specific accommodation requests and individual faculty members would respond. As might be anticipated, some faculty members were still in the in-club mind-set where compliance with accessibility laws might still be seen as coddling or providing an unfair advantage to learners with barriers. Ouellett and his colleagues in the Office for Teaching and Learning (OTL) were invited to facilitate the strategic conversation to help the leadership task force to define a good means of demonstrating legal compliance for accessibility, especially in response to the rising awareness of recent lawsuits brought against other universities.

In their POD Network workshop, they mapped out a four-square depiction of selected campuswide efforts that were or could be undertaken (see Henderson, Beach, and Finkelstein, 2012 for more about four-squares). We re-create the model in figure 8.1, below.

The four-square chart has two axes: the vertical axis represents at one end changes that apply to individuals and at the other changes that apply to environments and structures. The horizontal axis moves from changes that are prescribed (top down) to changes that are emergent (bottom up). This creates four squares: changes that are emergent and apply to individuals help to develop reflective teachers, emergent changes to the environment help to develop shared vision, prescribed changes to the environment help to develop policy, and prescribed changes for individuals help to develop curriculum. The various inclusivity projects that the campus wanted to enact are placed on the four-square matrix, and the team strived to ensure that projects would help with change in all four of the chart's quadrants.

By focusing on the larger campus goals and outcomes, the Wayne State University OTL and Student Disabilities Services Office were able to get better buy-in and support from their senior academic leaders to create the campuswide Provost's Committee on Accessibility; divide up responsibility for UDL and accessibility training; and expand on existing efforts, such as an inclusive procurement process for all areas of the university (e.g., athletics, general purchasing, web services) that requires vendors to meet accessibility requirements. With the support of senior leadership, the OTL "overlaid UDL into everything that we do: faculty consultations, templates, speakers we invite to campus, the OTL web-site re-design, and workshops on syllabus and document accessibility" (Ouellett et al., 2016).

Both in our own experiences and in those of colleagues across North America, we have found that UDL adoption at the level of the curriculum is founded on three key areas of college or university programming: faculty development programming, staff development programming, and visibility during major technological changes. We will share strategies for holding UDL conversations with people in specific leadership roles in chapter 10, but we want to encourage

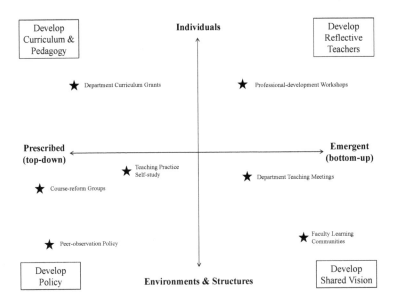

Figure 8.1: Four-square model for institutional impact

readers to use one concept in every UDL conversation with campus higher-ups: retention.

Retention, Retention, Retention

Student retention numbers drive university officials, boards of trustees, and admissions officers every day. Especially at the level of senior college and university leaders, the business aspect of higher education weighs in campuswide decision-making at least as much as its societal and knowledge-promotion missions. Institutions thrive when greater numbers of students come back to continue their educations. A truism in admissions offices is that it costs far less to keep students than to find and recruit new ones. Because retention rates also closely parallel graduation rates, increases in student retention translate later into more alumni, more donations, and a greater network of connections on which colleges and universities rely in order to find new students and to leverage the social and financial capital of their alumni networks.

Retention (students come back for more courses) and persistence (students in courses on day one are still there at the end of the term) are equally important to faculty members. Supporting students through their courses in a manner that helps the greatest number of students to demonstrate mastery of the course concepts reflects positively on faculty. High student-persistence rates in courses and high retention rates from term to term correlate strongly to higher faculty evaluation scores when faculty are observed by administrators and to higher student rating values at the end of the term as well (Braxton et al., 2013).

Retention is a value-positive topic through which to engage faculty members and staff into campuswide conversations about UDL, especially in terms of increasing access for the broadest range of learners. When we build learner choice and ease of access into course content, teaching interactions, skill assessment, support interactions, and the technology used across the institution, such actions contribute measurably and directly to student retention and persistence rates (Braxton et al., 2013, 87–88). The positive frames that we are suggesting throughout this book—mobile-friendly learning, advantages for faculty workload—are especially useful for those readers who work in environments where colleagues are resistant or seem unready to be open to UDL as a concept. Of course, when all else fails (and despite what we said in chapter 2), legal compliance can be a way to compel colleagues to begin with accessible design, or at least scare them straight.

Faculty Development Programming

Most colleges and universities have a program for faculty development, ranging from new faculty orientation efforts to ongoing efforts such as teaching workshops, faculty learning communities, and professional development book study groups. Whether or not your institution has a formal teaching and learning center, adopting UDL principles should move beyond the realm of the disability services office.

For example, at Northeastern Illinois University, Tom Tobin worked with his team in the Center for Teaching and Learning (CTL) to incorporate UDL principles in all of the programming offered by the CTL. Workshop materials were provided in multiple formats, and assignments in the courses on how to teach hybrid classes and how to teach online classes asked faculty participants to create their deliverables in the formats that matched best with their needs and preferences. Individual and departmental consultations always contained plus-one options for finding information and demonstrating skills.

The breakthrough usually comes when other faculty support areas adopt UDL practices as well. Beyond the teaching center's programming, when the information technology (IT) area conducts training for faculty members, plus-one design ensures that, curriculum-wide, the assumption is that's just the way we do business at your college or university. CAST recently tweeted that the "expectation at @TowsonU [Towson University in Maryland] is that if you are faculty at the College of Education, you are implementing #UDL" (CAST, 2017). It's just the way they do things.

Faculty development conferences are a leading indicator of the next big topics in the field, and for a few years accessibility and UDL presentations, workshops, and keynote speeches became increasingly common at the Distance Teaching and Learning, Online Learning Consortium, EDUCAUSE, POD Network, and other major conferences in the field. Initially, interest in accessible design was fed by lawsuits about accessibility, and faculty development centers are leading the push to move the narrative away from a narrow focus on legal compliance and into a broader narrative about reaching learners where they are. This book is an extension of this desire to adopt good teaching and design practices across our institutions.

Staff Development Programming

UDL is sometimes viewed through a teaching-only lens. In fact, any interactions in which people learn new skills or encounter new information is fertile ground for UDL application. This has two benefits, one for faculty members and a second for students. When faculty-facing support areas offer support for faculty members, using plus-one inclusive design provides a consistent message and structure for faculty colleagues, and the likelihood that faculty-produced materials and interactions across the curriculum will follow best UDL practices goes up in direct proportion to the number of support areas that model inclusive design in their interactions with faculty members.

Likewise, student-facing areas of the college or university can benefit from UDL principles when they think about the desired outcomes of student interactions with their areas. If we think of the curriculum as extending beyond the courses that students take—out into the advising, registration, and student support processes—then the more we apply plus-one design thinking to those interactions, the more we are able to lower barriers to entry or continuation.

For example, offering tutoring services face-to-face, via telephone, and via online synchronous meeting, during as many hours of the day and week as possible, allows learners to choose their preferred method for reaching out for assistance. Likewise, expanding student choice for receiving advising help beyond in-person real-time sessions to e-mail and text message asynchronous sessions allows learners with nontraditional schedules to receive good advice for planning their next steps for study. The more students we bring in the front door, so to speak, the more we can work with course-based curricular access to keep them with us.

Showcase Effective Work

Another visibility problem about UDL can be addressed at a program level as well. Often, campus leaders do not know who among their faculty and staff are already using inclusive techniques, and some of those faculty members and staffers don't yet have language for claiming their good practices. We do not believe in accidental UDL; the framework requires purposeful planning and introspection. However, because the mind-set behind UDL is deliberately simple (consider from the beginning the need of a broad range of people in the interactions you have with them), it allows for numerous responses to learner variability to fall under its umbrella. The key to using this strategy is to find examples of good UDL and then reward and highlight them at the institutional level.

Lance Hidy is a professor of art and design at Northern Essex Community College (NECC). In 2007, a colleague from the college's Learning Accommodations Center called to tell him that he would have a student in his upcoming Photoshop course who would need large, 16-point type on any printed course materials as an accommodation for the student's vision impairment. Hidy looked at a handout he planned to use—and with which his students had struggled in the past. The handout, reproduced in figure 8.2, covers the process by which Photoshop users can trace photographs. The directions fill two columns on one page of 12-point text. Students often struggled with this version of the directions and took, on average, three weeks to demonstrate all of the steps in the process.

Hidy redesigned the handout, as seen in figure 8.3, with 16-point type. He also added twenty new illustrations, including screen captures of the Photoshop interface, to guide his students through each step, utilizing the UDL plus-one approach to provide students with two paths through the handout, which expanded to four pages.

Although Hidy had designed the new handout with only one student in mind, he gave the revised version to everyone in the course. What he describes as his "UDL awakening" occurred as he watched the class complete the assignment in only two weeks. Hidy used the extra week for scaffolding, allowing his students to use the time to refine their projects even further—another welcome, if unexpected, effect of applying UDL.

Hidy's UDL awakening set him on a quest that aligned with his expertise. A graphic artist by trade, he understood the value of multiple modes of expression and quickly became a UDL advocate. At NECC, the directors of the Learning Accommodations Center and the Center for Instructional Technology and Online Learning (Susan Martin and Melba Acevedo, respectively), were already positioning the college as an early leader in accessible media and UDL, and Hidy gradually became involved with both teams.

Photograph tracing process

Digital Imaging, Lance Hidy, © 2007
Northern Essex Community College

1. Select a photograph that has qualities such as these—
   a. Some significant emotional content for you.
   b. Clear, sharp details, especially in important areas such as face and hands.
   c. Good exposure, so you can see necessary details in highlight and shadow areas.
   d. For animals and people, choose expressive gestures.

2. Scan the photograph
   a. Make a preview scan.
   b. Click and drag a cropping marquee around the part of the photograph you need.
   c. Adjust the resolution of the RGB scan so that you obtain a file size in the range of five to ten Mb.
   d. Keep a permanent copy of your untouched scan in case you need to refer to it in the future.

3. Make a version of the image for tracing.
   a. In Hue/Saturation (command-U) choose colorize.
   b. Change Hue and Saturation to obtain a bright, pure blue.
   c. Increase Lightness to roughly +60 to eliminate the dark blues without losing important highlight details.
   d. Using Print with Preview scale the image to fit the whole page and send it to the color printer.

4. Trace
   a. Using the Ultra-fine Sharpie pen, slowly, SLOWLY, trace the important contours.
   b. Use medium-light, even pressure to create a clear line of uniform thickness.
   c. Make a single line, like a thin wire, for the whole outline—not sketchy, rough lines.
   d. Make sure the lines that enclose an area to be filled with color have no breaks, or leaks.

5. Scan the tracing
   a. This will be your final document, so set the resolution to obtain an RGB file size of ten to fifteen Mb.
   b. In Image/Adjustments/Threshold move the pointer so that you eliminate the blue tones and are

left only with a clear black line. (Check this at 100% on your display to be sure you have a clear, unbroken line.)
   c. If your tracing did not scan well, then you may find it is faster to start over and make a new tracing than trying to doctor it up in Photoshop.
   d. Check the outlines again for leaks.
   e. To repair leaks, choose a pencil (not brush) the same thickness as your outlines, and fill in the gaps.
   f. It is important that the lines be sharp, stair-stepped, and solid black for this entire project.
   g. Go to Preferences/General and change Image Interpolation to Nearest Neighbor.
   h. Whenever using Paint Bucket and Magic Wand, be certain, CERTAIN, that you **TURN OFF ANTI-ALIASING** at the top of the window. That prevents the hard edges from becoming blurred.

6. Preserve a mask of the outlines
   a. Use Magic Wand (*no anti-alias, no contiguous*) click on the black line. You may need to zoom in to be sure you are actually on the line, and not the white background.
   b. In Select menu choose Save Selection, and title the selection Outlines. This will create a new channel that appears in the Channel palette. If your outlines become damaged during the work, you can restore them using this channel mask. It is your safety net.

7. Preserve your background layer with the drawing.
   a. Click on the pointer in the upper right corner of your Layers palette, select Duplicate Layer.
   b. Hide your original background layer, and work only on the duplicate. You can make additional duplicate layers if you want to try different versions of the colors in your artwork.

8. Backup
   a. Keep a duplicate of your scan and artwork on the classroom workstation, and on your home computer.

Figure 8.2: Photograph tracing process handout: Before. © Lance Hidy. Used with permission.

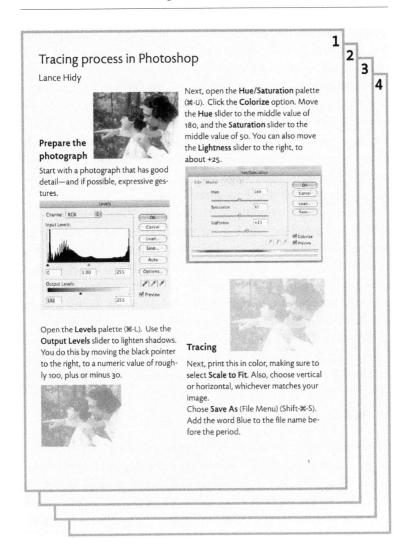

Figure 8.3: Photograph tracing process handout: After. © Lance Hidy.
Used with permission.

Martin and Acevedo welcomed Hidy into their Accessible Media Committee to help coordinate and facilitate the growth of UDL across campus. The committee recruited people from the library, management information systems (MIS), audio/visual, and marketing and communications areas, as well as faculty members—people with and without disabilities. They built their campaign for accessible digital media, building on NECC's mission and strategic goals, which focused on inclusion and diversity. To widen the scope of the committee to the entire college, they tapped the expertise of campus allies with shared values about social justice.

To increase the visibility of UDL efforts, Hidy and other colleagues led workshops during the college's recurring professional development days, and he added his voice to theirs in standing committees, faculty meetings, and at conferences. He and his teammates worked with faculty members one-on-one to demystify UDL and to show the positive effects of engaging in UDL work. When Martin and Acevedo obtained funding for a half-time accessible media specialist position, Hidy applied and was hired. He now divides his time between teaching graphic design and campaigning for UDL and inclusive design—a job he fell into naturally and loves.

Conclusion

Harrison and Hidy are not the only people who saw UDL opportunities in campuswide changes. When big technological changes come to your campus, it is an opportunity to incorporate inclusive-design elements into the processes that surround such changes. For example, when Northeastern Illinois University switched to a new learning management system in 2012, several testing and advisory groups were created, including student, faculty, IT, and financial groups that evaluated each candidate LMS. In the design of the tests conducted by each group, the university included UDL criteria such as checking for alternative text for visual elements, testing whether tools within the LMS supported multiple ways of interacting (e.g., ability to post text, audio, and video in the discussion tool), and requesting the vendor's Voluntary Product Accessibility Template (VPAT).

Further, the visibility that technology change affords to support areas like teaching centers creates an opportunity to examine the design of interactions in courses and support areas generally. During technology changes on campus, faculty colleagues are often more receptive to thinking about how their courses take advantage of skills from previous courses and prepare learners for future courses across the curriculum. In chapter 9, we will examine how the transition from face-to-face to blended and online teaching modes is a special subset of technological change that allows us to incorporate UDL principles throughout the curriculum.

A THOUGHT EXERCISE

Think about the ways in which faculty and staff members receive professional development at your college or university. Using the plus-one approach, think of how such programming can be expanded in two different ways:

- Make the professional development an exemplar of UDL by providing multiple means of engaging learners, representing information, and demonstrating skills and knowledge.
- Make the learning takeaways UDL friendly by offering participants models for adapting their own contexts to expand the ways in which they engage, inform, and assess the interactions they have with others.

Professional development opportunity	Plus-one faculty/staff engagement	Plus-one method of representing information	Plus-one method of demonstrating content knowledge
Course design institute	*Ask faculty members to film one of their lectures*	*Provide student feedback on the use of a specific course text*	*Ask participating faculty to add two different types of media to their course*

Once you have a list of specific plus-one techniques in each area, think of the campus champions who can push for adoption of the strategies in the four quadrant areas of the four-square model:

- Develop shared vision
- Develop reflective teaching
- Develop policy
- Develop curriculum and pedagogy

CHAPTER 9

Extend to One Modality: The Online Environment

Meet Scott

Scott Ready is the director of customer relations and accessibility strategist for Blackboard, the learning management system (LMS) company. He presented on "Accessibility; eLearning Environments for All" at the 2016 annual Online Learning Consortium (OLC) conference, where he showcased the ways in which Blackboard designed its systems to nudge users toward UDL techniques. This is in line with our overall aim of making UDL how we do business at our colleges and universities. Although technology tools are not required in order to implement UDL strategies, such tools make the multiplicity inherent in good UDL much easier to achieve.

Part of Ready's story shows how a failure to think small about accessibility can lead to big headaches for colleges and universities. For example, Ready says that "academia oftentimes sees accessibility as an additional step that 'someone else,' such as the Office of Disability Services, takes care of when specific students need accommodations." Ready met recently with the leadership of a large for-profit online university, and they stated that they had a hard time getting the executive team to recognize accessibility as a pressing issue and allocate funds and resources to it, until one student in one course couldn't use a screen reader to get access to one PDF file. Instead of disclosing a disability and requesting an accommodation, the student went to the U.S. Department of Education Office of Civil Rights (OCR) and filed a complaint. OCR verified that the complaint was valid and then investigated the entire university's curriculum for accessibility.

Ready noted in his presentation that between 60 and 80 percent of undergraduate students with disabilities choose not to disclose them. As we saw in chapter 2, access to education and information is increasingly seen in North American courts as a broad civil right, as opposed to a niche request from a small group of people with barriers. These trends have helped Ready and his team at Blackboard to work on solutions in their LMS that incorporate UDL's multiple means of engaging learners, representing information, and allowing choices for learners in demonstrating their skill. Further, the company recently purchased the Ally accessibility review product from its developer, Fronteer Software (Fronteer, 2016). Instead of making the Ally tool proprietary software that works only with Blackboard, the company is integrating it, freely shares it, and has developed it to work with all major LMS products—seeing access as a critical need that crosses even corporate lines.

The company is committed to making UDL and accessibility a core part of their consultation with all of their new and existing clients. They develop custom e-learning accessibility plans for individual client colleges and universities, providing sample online content that follows UDL principles, feedback on existing materials and interaction design, recommendations on removing barriers in existing systems, and on-site training for client campuses.

This focus is not unique to Blackboard. Other LMS and technology providers design their products with accessibility in mind, both because it's a legal requirement and because it makes good business sense (cf. D2L, 2017). In this chapter, we'll advance the idea that online components of courses—whether they support a face-to-face curriculum or are used as elements in blended and fully online courses—are a natural place for adopting UDL principles because of the ease with which we can transform them using the plus-one approach.

You'll Go Online, and Like It!

In 2012, when Kirsten Behling was the director for the Office of Disability Services (ODS) at Suffolk University, the incoming university president made an announcement at a university-wide town hall meeting that he intended to transform the university's course delivery method from primarily face-to-face to at least 20 percent online and hybrid courses within the next two years. You could have heard a pin drop in the audience. The silence was due to a few things:

- the audience was mostly made up of faculty members and staff;
- this was the third university president in as many years; and
- the initiative suggested instability in terms of which programs and departments would thrive during (or even survive) the presidential transition.

Given the uncertainty at the university, the directive to move traditionally face-to-face courses to an online environment was met with anxious hesitation. The president's announcement was short on details. There was a timeline, but there was no further direction about which programs should consider doing this, who should teach online, what experience might be necessary to get ready to teach online, and what resources were available to support this initiative. The lack of information caused quiet chaos among the faculty members and staff at the meeting: no one wanted to admit their fears with the president standing in front of them.

The response, as you might imagine, was mixed. Some faculty members were familiar with the online environment, having either taught online before or having taken online courses at some point in their own student experience. These faculty members embraced the challenge, grew excited at the opportunity to try something new, and tended to welcome the technology challenge. Others, perhaps fearing for their jobs, decided to move their courses online but had little to no experience with the online world. Still others begrudgingly complied with the initiative by copying and pasting their existing face-to-face course materials into the university's LMS and wiping their hands of any additional work.

On the staff side, there was more concern and angst than excitement. Who would support the faculty members and the students? Would there be a committee who decided which courses went forward with new offering modes? Would course-design training be required? In her role as ODS director, Kirsten wondered how accessibility would be considered for students with disabilities. These questions lingered as the town hall meeting ended and people walked out, unsure how to proceed.

In the coming months, the university responded to the initiative. The faculty development center was tasked with putting together strongly encouraged—but not required—training sessions for faculty members. The tutoring center drafted an online-readiness survey for students to take when considering online courses. The ODS partnered with the faculty development center to incorporate accessibility awareness into their training. The provost's office wrestled with whether to require in-house training before anyone could teach online, and whether course materials needed to be reviewed before courses could be offered online. At the beginning of the project, neither training nor course review was mandated. Faculty members who were excited about the initiative and those worried about their jobs jumped in, but sometimes blindly.

The initial results were mixed. In the first months, a few programs went completely online, some had a course or two online, some followed a more hybrid model, and some faculty members chose to ignore the initiative all together. Students reported excitement when taking classes where faculty members were engaged, familiar with the technology, and up for trying new things, generally. Conversely, courses in which faculty members simply audio recorded their face-to-face PowerPoint slide decks and monitored the in-course discussion boards received lower student ratings than courses where faculty members tried new things to engage and assess their students.

Especially at first, a significant number of students failed their online courses, realizing the hard way that the online environment required different skills of self-motivation and time management than they were used to in the face-to-face classroom. Others excelled with the flexibility of being able to participate in their courses when and where it was convenient for them. One crucial correlation came to the fore: online courses that offered multiple ways for students to interact with content, each other, and their instructors saw better outcomes over all.

Staff members scrambled to anticipate the needs of faculty members and students, and to fix issues as they occurred, including accessibility issues that had not been considered at the start. The university did a great job observing and evaluating the programs that had previously moved online. The leadership team took the lessons learned into consideration, making changes in between semesters and working to improve the resources needed by both faculty members and staff.

But this ad hoc process was not an ideal method for rolling out online courses in higher education. The online environment presents a unique opportunity to embrace UDL—due to the diversity of student learners, the relative newness of the format to many instructors, and all of the educational technologies available at one's fingertips. To avoid the filing-cabinet approach to online course design that we talked about in chapter 3, the transition to the online environment requires a strong partnership between faculty members and campus technology experts to develop courses that are both engaging and accessible. UDL makes online learning less scary for colleagues who have never taught with technology: it helps faculty members and campus support units to move gradually and smoothly along a path from fully face-to-face to hybrid to wholly online interactions. The principles of UDL lend themselves to this idea very nicely, targeting variability in both learners and faculty members.

The Online Learning Continuum

Online learning and in-person learning can combine in many ways: tech-enhanced face-to-face instructions, flipped classrooms, hybrid instruction, and fully online instruction. Figure 9.1 details the progression of online presence in each of these models, with face-to-face having the least presence and online having the most. Even institutions that do not offer online courses typically employ an online environment to supplement the face-to-face classroom experience, so even web-enhanced courses contain some online learning elements.

Online learning as an educational option has exploded in the last fifteen years. As of 2015, more than six million students in U.S. higher education have taken at least one fully online course (Allen and

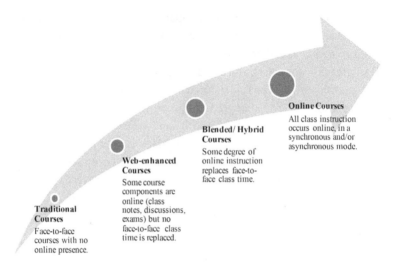

Figure 9.1: The range of technology-enhanced courses (Behling and Linder, 2017)

Seaman, 2017). Online enrollments as a percentage of total enrollments have risen from 9.6 percent in 2002 to 32 percent in 2012. And 94.5 percent of higher education institutions have some form of online offering for students (Allen and Seaman, 2013). Most faculty members now have, or are required to have, some degree of online presence, whether through course websites or the use of digital materials.

The population of students enrolling in college courses that have at least some online learning components has increased drastically since 2000 (Wang, 2007; Venable, 2011). UDL strategies increase persistence and retention especially for nontraditional learners, those who

- attend school part-time,
- work full- or part-time,
- have family responsibilities (many are single parents),
- are first-generation college students,

- are older than twenty-five,
- speak a language other than English (15 percent of the college population),
- are minority students (33 percent), and
- have disabilities (11 percent) (Wilson, 2004).

The label of "nontraditional" has recently begun to be a misnomer. Beginning in the 2011–12 academic year, "74% of all undergrads . . . had at least one nontraditional characteristic and about one-third had two or three" (U.S. Department of Education, 2015). In other words, treating all learners as though they were nontraditional students is a safe bet as we design our course interactions, and UDL helps us to respond to the increasing variability in our students' life circumstances.

But faculty members are not required to use UDL strategies to design their online content. Most do not know about UDL or even consider it as a guiding framework when converting their courses to the online environment. Faculty members and course designers should consider learner variability when developing online courses or using an online environment to supplement their classroom experiences. Many students enrolled in courses with online components are poorly prepared for the self-regulation that is needed in virtual environments. Many others do not have the technical skills to navigate websites that were designed quickly or in a complex or confusing way. The diversity in which students learn best, combined with their ability to navigate the online classroom environment, are potentially insurmountable hurdles for some students. UDL helps to lower those hurdles considerably when it is integrated into the design, instruction, and assessment of courses, and online tools help to increase the reach of well-designed interactions.

Online Barriers

Faculty members are not solely responsible for students' inability to access all aspects of their course materials online. However, faculty members are often the easiest and best-defined campus group to work with, which is why many institutions have chosen to focus their resources first on faculty development. As figure 9.2 shows, there are actually three main areas where barriers to online courses can occur: the LMS, publisher-created content, and locally created content.

Learning Management Systems

Online learning includes any aspects of courses that are housed online. Many institutions are moving toward requiring all faculty members to have some minimal degree of online presence in their courses. The easiest way to do this is by posting course content to the institution's LMS. The LMS itself can be hit or miss in terms of its accessibility for diverse learners. While some learning management systems were designed with inclusive accessibility in mind (as you read about in Ready's story), others were not; instead, they were designed to help instructors host course information and facilitate conversations using technology mediation. These online classroom spaces provide places for designers and instructors to add information about courses, to encourage student discussion, and for students to submit assessments.

Instructors often see the LMS as an organizational tool that enhances their courses, and they are surprised when they receive student complaints about barriers that the LMS places in their way. For example, Tom Tobin worked with a professor who received several late-night e-mail messages from a particular student, asking about due dates and questioning how to take part in the online discussion. After a little investigation, Tom and the instructor discovered that the student had a visual disability that made it challenging to understand the screen layout and use the tools within the LMS.

Many instructors use the LMS to conduct quizzes and tests under secure conditions, which can create its own barriers, such as for students trying to take tests on their mobile devices in locations with spotty internet connections, who often complain that they are unable to finish timed assignments due to poorly designed mobile interfaces or the inability to save and return to assessment work within the time limit. Of course, not every barrier in the LMS is due to the software design itself. For example, a faculty member posts a study guide online

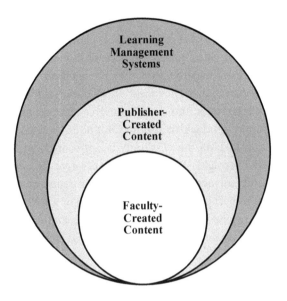

Figure 9.2: Barriers to online courses (Linder, Fountaine-Rainen, and Behling, 2015)

but students continue to ask when it will be available. It turns out the faculty member posted it the week before in an out-of-the-way sub-folder in the LMS and expected everyone to find it. Both inaccessible features of the LMS and inaccessible ways that instructors use it become wearying because faculty members are often called on to put together fixes for barriers that they may not have initially considered or created. The end result is often that instructors post only the obligatory minimum in the LMS and seldom refer to their course websites again.

The National Federation of the Blind (NFB) has taken LMS companies to task for their products not being accessible to users with visual disabilities, based on whether users are able to get access to all areas and tools within the software. The NFB issues Gold Stars to those LMS providers that incorporate accessibility and UDL principles into their overall design (Zou, 2011). Many LMS providers are not there yet. They may recognize the need for accessibility but are not yet able to ensure that their entire product is accessible. Faculty members are at a further disadvantage because they do not have a choice about which LMS system to use. They must either use what they have available to them, or go rogue and choose resources that are not supported by the institution—and which also may not be accessible.

The solution to LMS inaccessibility is not something that can be accomplished overnight. Rather, it is imperative that institutions, driven by faculty advocacy and student-access issues, push LMS providers to design their platforms to be accessible by all. The more pressure that they receive from their client colleges and universities, the more likely changes will occur. But, what should faculty members do in the meantime?

Since institutions have various LMS providers and vary in how they use such systems, the best solution is to determine, through testing, which components of the LMS are inaccessible, and then provide institutionally supported accessible alternatives. Faculty members should be encouraged to be creative about using other resources that are usable to a wide range of learners. Finally, to help students avoid confusion as to where content is or how they should navigate the online environment, faculty members should work with instructional designers to design courses that make sense and are intuitively navigable. In other words, UDL works best when the tool set supports learner variability and multiple ways of engagement, information presentation, and skill demonstration.

Publisher-Generated Content

Another area where we should insist on UDL and inclusive design is in publisher-created resources. Since 2004, Part B of the Individuals with Disabilities Education Act (IDEA) requires publishers to make electronic copies of the books they produce available to students with disabilities (U.S. Department of Education, 2004), according to the National Instructional Materials Accessibility Standard (NIMAS). When they produce new texts, many publishers now also create electronic files that can be converted into specialized formats. While adherence to NIMAS has pushed publishers to consider accessibility, it has its limitations.

NIMAS applies only to materials designed for elementary and secondary education; it does not cover textbooks and content used in higher education. It also applies only to students who need alternative material formats based on their disabilities, leaving outside the standard students who are English-language learners using screen readers or the busy moms listening to their textbooks from the carpool lane.

NIMAS also does not cover supplemental materials, such as videos, quizzes, interactive questions, additional readings, charts, graphs, interactive simulations, and flash-card study aids—all of which give students resources to reinforce course concepts. We support the creation of such ways to interact with publisher materials since they give students multiple ways to interact with the material. Further, because these materials are often bundled with textbooks on CD or via website access codes, they are available to students twenty-four hours a day, seven days a week.

Many faculty members specifically adopt textbooks that are supported by multimedia supplemental materials, using the supplements to reinforce course concepts in multiple ways. However, merely requiring students to use a variety of tools in multiple formats is not in line with the UDL framework. Instead of forcing all learners first to read a text chapter, then listen to an audio guide, and then watch an overview video (as many publisher packages would have them do), learners should have choices for how they experience *each* of these resources. Each should demonstrate multiplicity. The text chapter should have an audio alternative. The audio guide should have a text transcript. The video should have captions or a text transcript. It is at this level of providing choice for every item, what we term *plus-one design*, that publisher content often falls flat.

As staff members and faculty members, we should pressure publishers to make all of their content accessible, and we should also learn how to recognize accessibility features ourselves, since some publisher materials that are touted as being accessible are multiple-format only for the primary resources, such as the textbook itself.

Institution-Generated Content

Faculty and staff members are the final barriers in the online learning usability dilemma. But, of the three barriers, they are the most easily influenced. Before we can influence change, it is important to recognize how faculty members often create online content in the absence of assistance or training. In the early days of online courses at Suffolk University, most faculty members simply cut and pasted their lecture notes, narrated PowerPoint slides, and image-only PDF documents into the university's LMS and called it a day. A few who had taught online before began exploring the tools within the LMS to see how they could teach differently from their face-to-face interactions, and a few who had never taught online but were excited to try contacted the faculty development office.

Those faculty members who had taught online previously found the switch from face-to-face to online courses smoothest. They had an idea of how to structure their courses in an online environment, and they knew what kinds of tools they wanted to use. Their very experience with technology was problematic, however. Their desire to incorporate shiny new mobile devices and apps—without first considering their accessibility and usability—got a few of them into individual-accommodation trouble when they began to teach online. The experience reminded them of the need to design a course first and then select a few pieces of technology to incorporate, in the plus-one model, later on.

Those who sought assistance were excited to try new things but naïve about the amount of work it took to get courses in reasonable shape, especially for the first time they were taught. They also struggled conceptually, trying to figure out how to engage learners remotely. Largely, their enthusiasm and willingness to try new things led to success and a reframing of their mind-set. They started to look at courses as a series of interactions rather than series of content items. The UDL plus-one mind-set helped them to make their interactions as open and easy to use as possible.

Finally, the cut-and-pasters had the least initial success. Their courses tended to look like online hoarding environments, in which course materials seemed to be dumped in with little rhyme or reason. Once these faculty members sought help from the teaching and learning center, they, too, were able to get the hang of designing their course interactions with UDL quickly. Kirsten Behling created the "Best Practices for Ensuring Accessibility in Courses with Online Components" worksheet (below) to offer faculty members a fast and easy way to check whether their materials are accessible.

BEST PRACTICES FOR ENSURING ACCESSIBILITY IN COURSES WITH ONLINE COMPONENTS

Instructor: _____

Department: _____

Course: _____

The following should be present in all hybrid and online courses. Answer yes or no to each criterion, and provide comments for all "no" responses.

BEFORE THE COURSE BEGINS

- Students have been provided with your course textbook/ media requirements before the class starts.
- You have contacted the Office of Disability Services to discuss your use of multimedia tools before you decide to use them.
- You have listed a statement about disability services on your syllabus.
- You have provided students with the URL for accommodations in the learning management system your institution uses.

- Course textbooks were selected at least six weeks prior to the start of the semester and posted online for students to see.
- Textbook information includes the correct ISBN numbers and editions to be used. If electronic copies are mentioned, they correspond to the paper versions.
- When possible, you have chosen materials from publishers and journals that provide electronic content.
- Textbooks have been made available at the library's reserve desk.

Learning Management System (LMS)

- The syllabus is provided in a Microsoft Word format.
- If you include links on your LMS pages, they have accompanying text that has a meaningful description.
- Buttons in your LMS menu have descriptive text alternatives.
- If your LMS page includes redirects or timed actions (such as clicking OK to continue), provide adequate response time for users to navigate the page.
- If your LMS site includes timed actions (such as quizzes), ensure that you can adjust response time, if needed.
- Type styles, sizes, and orientations are consistent throughout the LMS (consider using the preset *Styles* function).
- Color combinations are used that provide sufficient contrast between foreground and background.
- You have avoided flickering texts or animations.
- For HTML table-based layouts, provide appropriate headers and data call designations.
- Acronyms and abbreviations are spelled out (screen readers pronounce these as single words).
  o Auditory and Visual Content

Microsoft Word Documents

- The preset *Styles* feature in Word has been used to apply headers to all documents.
- There are no ornate fonts (use standard fonts such as Arial or Times New Roman).
- Headers are larger font sizes than the body of the text.
- No fonts smaller than 10-point type.
- 1.5 line spacing should be used, when possible.
- For documents over six pages in length, a table of contents has been created (use the *References* tab in Word).
- All images, graphs, and figures have ALT-text (alternative text) tags (right-click on image, select *Format Picture*, and click *ALT Text*).
- All tables have clear labels for rows and columns and no empty cells.
- No documents have been *Saved as Web*.
- All hyperlinks have been added using the *Insert Hyperlink* feature, and all hyperlinks are spelled out in the text.

Microsoft Excel Spreadsheets

- All tables have row and column headings.
- All graphs have ALT-text tags (right-click on image, select *Format Picture*, and click *ALT Text*).
- All hyperlinks have been added using the *Insert Hyperlink* feature, and all hyperlinks are spelled out in the text.
- Color and highlighting are not the only means of providing information.
- Each worksheet is labeled appropriately (not just *Sheet 1* and *Sheet 2*).

PDF Files

- All words can be individually highlighted with your cursor (i.e., the text will not be read as a picture; when in doubt, create a text-only HTML version of the content).
- All Word documents have been made accessible before conversion to PDF.
- Tag PDF documents whenever possible. For specific instructions, visit the Pennsylvania State University's AccessAbility site: http://accessibility.psu.edu/pdf.
- PDFs that cannot be made accessible have been provided in an alternative format.
- No text files with multiple columns have been converted to PDFs (screen readers might still read the text across columns).

Images

- ALT-text tags have been used on all visual elements, including charts, graphs, mathematical/scientific notation, and photos (right-click on image, select *Format Picture*, and click *ALT Text*).
- Extended text descriptions are provided for all complex images, including charts, graphs, mathematical/scientific notation, and photos.

Microsoft PowerPoint Files

- All slides have simple layouts and avoid busy, themed backgrounds.
- Content is organized in a logical structure.
- Fonts are larger than 14-point type, and a sans serif font is used.
- Color combinations provide sufficient contrast between foreground and background.
- Ample white space is provided on each slide.

- ALT-text tags have been used on all visual elements, including charts, graphs, mathematical/scientific notation, and photos (right-click on image, select *Format Picture*, and click *ALT Text*).
- All audio narration discusses slide contents in relation to the larger themes or ideas of the course.
- A transcript of narration for each slide has been added to the Notes section of that slide.
- All hyperlinks have meaningful descriptions.
- No slide transitions or automatic timing functions are used.
- Slides have been designed with a slide layout format provided in the software.

Video and Audio

- Captioning or written transcripts have been provided for all video or audio files.
- Video files are embedded into one of the following players: QuickTime, RealPlayer, iTunes, YouTube.
- Videos with visual information critical to comprehension include a description of events or images.

Flash

- Written descriptions are provided for all content offered in Flash files.
- Ensure that all Flash content is accessible. For more information, see https://www.adobe.com/accessibility/products/flash/author/html.

Conferencing Tools

- All content in web conferencing tools is typed and selectable by a cursor and adheres to the guidelines above for Word, PDF, PowerPoint, and Excel.

There is further opportunity to influence the usability of self-created course materials. Consider the web-based materials and technologies that we are asking students to use. Is the website accessible? Can students access that journal article at 2:00 a.m. on their own? Does the survey app work with a screen reader? Are the podcasts transcribed? By encouraging faculty members to give thought to how users from all walks of life will access the content that they select for their course, you are empowering them to create universally designed courses for all.

The Elephant in the Room

Who, specifically, should encourage faculty members to adopt UDL thinking for their online courses or course components, ask usability questions, and hold publishers and LMS developers accountable? A recent study of who is responsible for online learning and accessibility (Linder, Fountaine-Rainen, and Behling, 2015) looked at over 190 colleges and universities across the United States, trying to figure out how many institutions are bringing awareness to this issue, and who is doing the asking. The results suggest that while there is widespread awareness of the need for interactions to be usable and accessible, few campuses are taking actions. The largest reason that the issue is not receiving more attention falls to the lack of time, expertise, and resources that higher education institutions have at their disposal.

So who asks questions about online learning and accessibility? Largely, it is the professionals in the disability services office. They are asking questions, often retroactively, about access when student clients come to them complaining that they cannot get onto the LMS, can't access electronic textbooks, or their screen readers cannot read the PDF files due for the next class. Disability service professionals are often the front line for online learning and access. They then scramble to educate faculty, instructional technologists, and instructional designers about the problem, with the intention of creating long-term solutions, but often settling for short-term responses to immediate problems.

Ideally, the responsibility of online access belongs to many on campus. Disability-service providers should be included in the conversation and are often responsible for bringing attention to the problem, but they are not content developers. They are also not technologists trained in coding and writing websites. A team of people needs to focus on this issue, like the UDL team referenced in chapter 6. The team should include an instructional technologist or designer, a web developer, a representative from faculty development, and the librarian. Instructional technologists and designers can bring to the conversation their knowledge about the online environment, tools used to create online courses and content, and best practices for organizing online courses. A faculty development professional will have access to best practices for increasing faculty members' engagement and knowledge of effectively teaching online. Librarians are starting to join this conversation, as more and more resources are available electronically. They have a responsibility to push back with publishers to ensure that the resources they house in their libraries are accessible.

This team of people can tackle each of the barriers to online learning more effectively than one person or one office retroactively addressing the problem. The team approach also helps to navigate the shortage of resources, time, and expertise by distributing the workload across many offices. In many instances, the work that this team does is groundbreaking. It is important for the team to be recognized for its work by the college and university administration, as well as to ensure that its work is publicized across the institution to encourage greater buy-in and long-lasting effect. The case studies below are examples of how UDL has been applied in the online environment to reduce access barriers for diverse learners.

A Math Department's Decision

A few years ago, Jan, a student who uses a screen reader as a primary method of accessing her course materials, came into Kirsten Behling's office at Suffolk University, crying. She had just attended her first class of a required math course and couldn't do the online homework. Kirsten was astounded, since she had spent the better part of her summer translating the math textbook for this course into an accessible electronic format. Kirsten had communicated with the professor throughout the summer, working to ensure that the class was accessible for this student. Both the professor and Kirsten had been optimistic that Jan would be successful in the course. However, on day one of the fall semester, Jan was visibly upset because she could not access her homework online.

Part of the student's frustration could be explained by an accident of timing. In late August, just before the beginning of the course, the professor was told by her department chair that the department would be using the textbook publisher's new product: an online self-paced assessment tool. Students would be required to go online before each class and complete ten math problems that the department chose. The new tool was designed to support students while also reducing the grading time of professors. The problem was that Jan could not see the problems with her screen reader because the problems were displayed as pictures in the Flash-based application.

At this point, Kirsten and Jan had few options. Kirsten could read the problems to Jan and enter her answers into the online system. But that required Jan to make appointments during weekday business hours. Jan would not have the same 24/7 access as her peers and the same right to complete these problems any time before midnight on the day before they were due. About a week later, when Kirsten was still trying to figure out what the best solution might be, the professor called to report that three other students were also struggling to access the system. The students said that they did not know how to get to the questions, or that the system did not give them enough time to work through the problems. The professor wondered if the three students were registered with the disability services office as students with disabilities. When Kirsten told the instructor that they were not, the professor went to her department chair.

The department chair, the professor, and Kirsten all sat down to discuss the problem. The chair shared that students were complaining about the practice-problem system as a whole. It was not user friendly, not helpful, and professors were being asked to review each homework question in class, which was taking up valuable class time. Kirsten then demonstrated Jan's inability to "see" the questions with a screen reader. At that meeting, the math department chair did something unprecedented at this small university. She declared that from that moment on, they would no longer use this tool. If one student could not see it, then she considered it a failure for all students.

The excitement of her decision was tempered by the publisher's response when the school asked for a refund for the system. The publisher argued that the benefits of a self-paced tool for the majority of students far outweighed the inaccessibility barriers "for a few students." The math department invited the publisher to come to campus and discuss the situation. The department chair, not Kirsten, demonstrated how the tool was inaccessible to Jan, and had other students describe their inability to work in the system. Again, the publisher argued that these things, while valid, were not enough to terminate the contract. Kirsten then cited the law. The publisher quickly responded that within a year they would be compliant. The math department held strong and refused to use the software, and the publisher was eventually obliged to refund the contract.

The most exciting part of this story is the enthusiasm of the math department to do right by all of their students. A few faculty members partnered with Kirsten and with colleagues in the computer science department to create a homegrown study tool for students. This tool performed many of the same functions as the publisher's software, but it was less polished. More importantly, it was designed from the beginning with learner variability in mind. The math department reframed its idea of what they wanted, from a tool for practice questions to a tool that allowed math students to practice anywhere, any time, on any device. They applied a plus-one approach to UDL and reframed their desired outcomes away from just disability accommodations outward to access for learners across access methods.

Word of their work got out on campus, and their stand was praised by the president. They eventually went on to present their story and their new tool at a local math conference. Today, they continue to refine the tool with access and usability in mind, on both the faculty and the student sides of the interface.

Meet Colin

Colin Hesse exemplifies the type of instructor with whom Ready, the Blackboard accessibility strategist, loves to work. Hesse teaches in the Speech Communication Department at Oregon State University. He was asked to convert his Advanced Interpersonal Communication course for online delivery. New to online teaching and design, Hesse sought guidance from the faculty development office. When he met with an instructional designer, he confessed to some uncertainty about using technology with which he wasn't yet familiar. Hesse also had difficulty envisioning how the varied abilities he observed in his face-to-face students would translate to what he perceived as a single-stream online environment.

Together, Hesse and the instructional designer talked through his entire course. He shared his course goals and objectives, how he usually introduced new material in the classroom, and how he assessed his students. They decided to create a plan for how interactions would take place in each course unit. The pattern would repeat throughout the term, giving students confidence to know how the course would be taught, where to look for information, and what to do next at any point in the course. Each unit would focus on one topic as the focal point of the assigned readings, lecture materials, course discussions, and assessment activities.

When students logged into Hesse's course in the LMS, they were greeted with an introduction to online learning in the form of a PowerPoint presentation marked *Start Here*. Hesse included screenshots of how to navigate each unit's folder, how to post to the discussion board, and how to submit assignments. He reminded his students that the PowerPoint presentation would remain available for the length of the course, so that they could refer back to it as often as they liked. In the spirit of plus-one UDL, Hesse also provided a text-only version of the information in the PowerPoint presentation.

Hesse started each unit with a short, two-to-three-minute video of himself discussing what the week would cover and how students should navigate the materials. The idea behind these videos was to increase the connection between him and the students. He wanted the students to see him as they might in the classroom. These captioned videos also increased ways that students could stay engaged with the course—one of the three core UDL framework elements—by helping them with self-regulation, time management, and expectation setting. Each unit also contained a minilecture using PowerPoint slides with audio voice-overs. Students then read a specific resource and responded to a prompt on the discussion board. Each of these requirements was clearly labeled and listed in the order in which students were supposed to proceed, and Hesse and the instructional designer tested each interaction ahead of time, making sure that students could apply plus-one access methods, such as using their mobile phones to take part in the course's online discussion boards.

When asked to reflect on his first online-teaching experience, Hesse found that he was pleasantly surprised with the detail and depth of the conversations occurring on the discussion board. He felt that some students who may hesitate to participate actively in the face-to-face environment were very vocal and shared detailed ideas and experiences in the online environment. That level of participation helped to create a better learning environment for his students. He also noted a greater diversity in his students' assessment responses, even though the assignments were the same as in the face-to-face course. It was almost as if because the class was online, students felt greater freedom to refer to online resources and bring videos, podcasts, and websites into the conversation.

While the class was largely a success, Hesse has already identified areas on which he intends to improve next time. He wants to set expectations a bit more clearly in the online environment than he typically does in the face-to-face one. For the group project, for example, one group was stumped about how to communicate effectively online. Another group had some active participants and some who chose not to help their group. He plans to create group roles next time and give a clear rubric of what is expected in the group. He will also give examples of places and methods by which students can work together virtually. He also hopes to add more pictures and animations to the course. He feels that students will benefit from a multisensory approach to his content—plus-one thinking, again. Hesse recognizes the need for his content and interactions to be accessible, and he is working with Oregon State's disability services office to determine how best to do that.

Hesse's overall impressions of the online experience mirror those of his students. The online environment, to the extent that its interactions are designed compellingly and inclusively, provides a rich and engaging experience for his students. It requires significant work and planning to transition from a face-to-face class model to online delivery. Hesse is grateful for the support from the faculty development office; without the assistance of the instructional designer, he feels that he would have been lost.

Hesse's experience embodies Ready's call for institutions to think small. Ready, a leader at one of the largest LMS companies, recognizes that faculty members like Hesse are the key to getting larger institutional buy-in. The partnership between Hesse and Oregon State's instructional design department exemplifies Ready's point that the push to adopt UDL cannot come from just one office. Further, the success that Hesse had and the positive feedback from the variety of learners in his class may be what will ultimately drive Oregon State University's larger adoption of UDL principles.

Conclusion

As we've tried to emphasize throughout this book, UDL is a framework for approaching interactions to make them as easy to take part in as possible, for everyone, and such design should not be solely the responsibility of instructors. In the development of online courses, especially, the principles of UDL help us to approach courses through their component interactions. It is with online course development that many institutions bring UDL into their curricula, since team-based approaches, new theoretical lenses, and different ways of approaching teaching and learning are already part of faculty expectations. We certainly won't tell your faculty colleagues that your online teaching secrets are really just UDL applications.

A THOUGHT EXERCISE

Use the criteria below to design plus-one elements for common areas in online courses. For each criterion, respond with the current method of interaction, one additional possible method (plus-one), and the name of a resource who can help create the additional interaction method. A sample is provided for the first criterion.

Common Area	Current Method	Plus-One Method	Helpful Resource
Professor contact information	E-mail	Skype	Sally in Media Services
Professor contact information			
Course logistics			
Goals			
Objectives			
Course materials			
Course technology			
Assessments			
Other			

After you have filled out this form, use the best-practice checklist as a self-assessment to determine what other accessibility considerations you need to make.

CHAPTER 10

———

Embrace One Mind-Set: Campuswide UDL

———

Meet Bruce, Angela, Ryan, Darin, and Eric

In a 2016 conference presentation, Bruce Kelley, Angela Jackson, Ryan Los, and Darin Jerke from the Center for Teaching and Learning (CTL) at the University of South Dakota (USD) presented on "Developers' Response to the Redefined ADA: Leading from the Middle," in which they related how their university looked proactively at a big question: what was the difference between accessibility and accommodation? In light of the high-profile lawsuits against other institutions, USD paid attention when, in early 2016, the U.S. Access Board proposed an update to portions of the Americans with Disabilities Act and Section 508 of the Rehabilitation Act, to adopt into the law the until-then voluntary Web Content Accessibility Group (WCAG) web-accessibility standards and the ISO 32000-1 standard (PDF Association, 2012) for accessible PDF files. As we saw in chapter 2, these proposed updates—known as the Information and Communication Technology (ICT) Refresh—have since become law in the United States.

In October 2016, thirteen higher education institutions commented on the proposed standards in order to determine whether the new standards would, in the language of the statutes, "impose an undue burden" on colleges and universities to comply. Kelley and his colleagues, realizing the importance of this issue, began developing a "visible, transparent road map or plan toward adopting inclusive-design practices and policies" (Kelley, Jackson, Los, and Jerke, 2016).

The University of South Dakota also reviewed other universities that had been sued as models for what proactive steps to take in order to avoid similar challenges. For instance, they examined the University of Cincinnati's consent decree with the Department of Justice (see chapter 11) to put together teams around the processes of information technology (IT) audits, captioning, training/awareness, technology migration, and communication. On a limited budget, they initiated UDL discussions with representatives from the library, IT, marketing, and Continuing and Distance Education. Internally, they supported Jackson's efforts to become well versed in issues related to ADA, accessibility, and UDL. They did that by underwriting training, supporting travel to relevant conferences, and funding Jackson's participation in several certificate programs. From there, USD created accessibility and UDL workshops, explored the accessibility of commonly used software applications at the university, and—key to this book's purposes—put a greater emphasis on UDL in their course design quality assurance processes and the campuswide course review processes as well.

In addition to the internally facing efforts, the USD team set up an information session for senior campus leaders so that they could develop a shared understanding of the scope of the challenge and discuss possible solutions. Continuing and Distance Education began their own UDL and accessibility-review process as a result of these conversations. The CTL team also implemented a software review protocol with their colleagues in IT, so that both purchased and free software went through an accessibility check.

We conducted a follow-up interview with Kelley, Jackson, and their CTL assistant director, Eric Mosterd, in which they provided more details about the role of UDL specifically in their accessibility program for the University of South Dakota (Kelley, Mosterd, and Jackson, 2016). The seeds of adopting UDL principles developed from questions that the team initially asked. They saw an unstated UDL component in the Section 508 and Quality Matters training that Jackson attended, as well as in the Quality Matters–based rubric used by the institution, per South Dakota Board of Regents guidelines, especially the first standard in Quality Matters Standard 8. The team could not recall a specific origin for their interest in adopting UDL; as Mosterd mentioned, it was "always part of it, from [Section] 508 web compliance to quality review for online course design." One of the challenges for the university is the fact that accessibility policies are set by the board of regents. Fortunately, they are carefully examining this issue, and one member of the CTL staff, Eric Mosterd, is also the Regents Fellow for e-Education Initiatives. This allows for an unusually direct line of communication between the CTL and the board of regents' vice president for academic affairs (VPAA) on this issue.

One Size Does Not Fit All

When institutions of higher education are considering how best to apply the principles of UDL to their work, they must do so with an eye toward the mission of the school; the culture of the faculty, staff, and students; and the available time, funds, technology, and staff resources. This is good news. At the level of the entire college or university, there is enormous flexibility in how we can use the UDL framework to move toward the goals that most of us espouse: greater student persistence, retention, and satisfaction.

During her work as a universal design specialist in the university's Institute for Community Inclusion, Kirsten witnessed firsthand how the University of Massachusetts Boston expanded its UDL approach from the department level to the entire university. The university sits in an urban location and serves large populations of commuter students, nontraditional students, and students working to supplement their professions by going back to school part-time. Beginning in 2006, the president and university trustees took a hard look at the school's retention numbers. While they were not bad compared to other schools in the state system, they were not good, either. Too many students would come, take a few classes, and leave. Some left for other institutions. Some left because their work-life-school balance was too demanding, and others left because they did not feel that their professors really understood the ways in which today's students learn (as we've seen in chapter 2).

This last reason sparked an initiative by the university president to support diverse learners better (University of Massachusetts, 2006). Around the same time, a professor in the education department proposed a partnership with a professor of architecture to develop an instructional design course that would focus on how to weave UDL throughout instruction.

The two professors read in the university's newspaper about the president's push for increasing access for diverse learners. They quickly assembled a team of colleagues with whom they had worked closely over the years supporting student diversity, including Kirsten, the director of the Office of Diversity Services, a university librarian, a representative from the admissions office, and someone from the provost's office. This group discussed how they could individually and collectively support the president's mission. The two professors shared the course they were building, citing increasing learner variability at the University of Massachusetts Boston and its largest feeder high schools. They framed their project as a way to go beyond educating future high-school educators who would then practice with their own learners more inclusive course interactions and teaching. The goal for the university was to create an entire curriculum that would be welcoming to the broadest spectrum of learners and that would be effective in educating them as well. Everyone at the table agreed to meet regularly in order to determine the most effective approach to bringing UDL to the university.

Since the president's diversity support initiative promoted student retention, the group focused their work on faculty development. They asked the director of the faculty development office how to make faculty members aware most effectively and what training platforms they responded to the best. They planned to educate a small group of faculty members from different academic departments, who in turn would educate their departments and then publish their work to the university as a whole. By helping a few departments increase their retention rates and student rating numbers through UDL, they would create evidence to use when spreading the word about UDL's effectiveness.

However, when they sought faculty colleagues to join their bimonthly conversations, few people came forward. The group largely heard a litany of excuses and predictions that the project wouldn't work. In late spring 2006, the group asked the president for his support, directly, and adopted a more formal structure and name: the UDL Working Group (UDLWG). They felt that if the UDL initiative came from the president, perhaps more faculty members would find time to commit to the regular meetings. The president was highly supportive, to the point of offering up to five faculty members a teaching-load reduction for one semester if they participated in bimonthly meetings and reworked one of their courses to include UDL strategies. He also agreed to host an exhibition of the faculty members' work at the end of the summer to use as a recruiting tool for the next semester. Within a week, the UDLWG had eight faculty volunteers (three of whom joined the group on top of teaching a full load) and full commitments from the original group members.

At the end of the semester, the president hosted a lunch during which the faculty participants were asked to summarize their experience and explain at least one UDL change that they had made. The president awarded each faculty member with a certificate of completion. The lunch was open to all faculty members within the university and served as a recruiting opportunity for the fall semester.

The UDLWG is still operating in a similar fashion, and it has graduated sixty-three faculty members, covering almost all of the academic departments. As an added bonus, those who have completed the UDLWG program are now in-house experts to their colleagues in their departments. A few have even presented at national conferences about their experiences. The UDLWG worked at the University of Massachusetts Boston because there was a top-down need to support diverse learners. A vital group of people who work with these students every day was able to harness this enthusiasm and build upon it. The key to figuring out how to expand UDL to become a pillar of your institutional mission is to figure out where that entry point is.

Get UDL Attention at Your Institution

Once you have identified an access point around which others can create their own efforts, make a purposeful plan for getting your institution to adopt the UDL framework for all of its learner interactions. Ask mission-critical questions that get the attention of campus leaders as well as those at the operational level of your college or university.

- Is your institution generally aware of UDL?
- Do your mission, vision, and goals include resources for and outreach to diverse learners?
- Are there populations of students whose retention rates could be higher?
- Does your institution serve students who have time-management concerns, such as returning learners with work and family responsibilities and military service members?
- Are you currently undergoing a lawsuit or investigation where a UDL response would address the concern?

Strategic Partnerships

When she worked in Suffolk University's Office of Disability Services, Kirsten Behling and her assistant director, Andrew Cioffi, encountered a barrier in the university's student services interactions, and they applied plus-one UDL principles to help overcome it—with help from their colleagues around the university. Students who used screen readers to interact with online systems were unable to register for courses using the school's new web-based interface, which relied on frames-within-frames and image maps: two design features that made it impossible for screen-reader software to make sense of the information being displayed. Students using screen readers complained that their peers could register online for courses starting at 1:30 a.m. on the first day of registration, but they had to wait for the disability services office to open for the morning, and then register with assistance from staff members. The students feared that they might not get the classes that they wanted, and they thought that the accommodation of waiting for the disability services office to open was unfair.

Across campus, the registrar's office was fielding numerous calls from other students upset that they could not log in to the registration system to register for classes. Students cited issues with the technology and the interface itself. Some had slow Internet connections; some found that the registration system wasn't mobile-device friendly; others weren't sure what to do, based on the minimal text-only instructions on the registration site. The registrar and her staff spent the better part of the day calming students down and registering them manually. A system designed to save effort had instead created barriers.

A few weeks later, Cioffi and the registrar arrived early for a meeting regarding another university initiative. They exchanged pleasantries and shared their different frustrations with the new online registration system, and quickly recognized that the collective impact on students (and on their offices) was significant enough to warrant its own conversation. As two relatively small offices within the larger university system, they reframed the narrative regarding the new online registration system. It wasn't a barrier to students with disabilities. It wasn't a source of glitches only for students using certain access methods. The disability services office and the registrar's office framed their argument in terms of the negative impact to overall student enrollment—in a software system that had been sold to the university as convenient and easy to navigate. Further, they used patterns in student enrollment data to suggest that the online system was creating a degree of unintended discrimination. The argument was sound, and the registrar was used to being able to call issues into question at a high level. Because she oversaw course listings, classroom scheduling, and transcript requirements, she had access to a wide array of functional areas across the institutional hierarchy.

Cioffi and the registrar decided to build strategic partnerships in their effort to provide choices to learners interacting with the registration system. They began with the facilities management area. Facilities management staff adjusted classroom assignments on the fly every semester, depending on the needs of both students and faculty members. In the past, facilities management staff had grumbled about all of the last-minute changes that needed to be done because students with disabilities couldn't register in time, or when faculty members needed better access options for their rooms.

The team went next to the IT area because they had to rewire or add equipment to rooms based on student and faculty needs. When students with hearing impairments couldn't register until late in the process, their classroom assignments were also not known until the last minute, sending IT staff scrambling to install special FM-radio transmitters in the rooms, often after classes had begun. The IT area also fielded the help desk, who, the team discovered, had noted a huge increase in the number of student calls during open registration about how to navigate the registration system. The majority of calls came during overnight hours, and the IT director added staff capacity temporarily, which strained an already tight budget, after noting a number of dropped and hang-up call attempts. Both the facilities management and IT departments backed the initiative to create a more inclusive registration system.

The full team then went to the academic affairs dean about the lack of equal access in the registration process. The dean listened to the registrar about the increase in complaint calls. She already knew about IT's increase in technical support calls, and she watched as Cioffi failed to navigate the registration system using a screen reader. The dean, too, agreed that a new system had to be developed. She championed the idea with the provost, who found the finances to develop a new system, augment the existing one, or purchase a more accessible solution.

This story of strategic partnerships is a success in many ways. The original two offices were able to secure a new universally designed registration system that allowed any students to register for classes at any time of day and on any type of technology, including mobile devices. By approaching the problem as a series of interactions, the team developed more robust, multiformat guidance for their website, allowing students choices in how they learned to use the registration system. Because the team's scope was the entire university, they adopted a "build once, use many times and ways" UDL approach to the students' interactions with the registration system and with registrar's office staff as well. The number of confused and angry student calls to the various offices dropped.

What could have been seen as a problem only for the registrar's office—after all, they were the ones with the less-than-optimal software—was instead framed as an opportunity for the entire institution to save effort, time, and money through the up-front investment of energy and inclusive UDL thinking. The various campus areas learned a great deal about one another and brought in others who were dealing with similar issues that had been caused by this one trigger point: the registration software. The people involved walked away with a new level of respect for what each office contributes, an increased awareness around access as a core business driver, and a sense of shared advocacy for collective needs.

Perhaps the biggest and most wide-ranging result from these strategic partnerships came from the provost. When he was made aware of the issues that students were facing with the registration software, he began poking into what other college-supported technologies students also struggled with. He brought the chief information officer (CIO) into the conversation and asked Kirsten and her colleagues in ODS to test a variety of the technologies that the university required students to use. The results were disheartening; almost no technology systems were broadly accessible to learners using assistive technology or mobile devices, which left everyone concerned. As a result, the CIO, provost, and Cioffi updated the university's procurement policy to require future technology purchases to be evaluated for accessibility. This was a groundbreaking and forward-thinking result, all because of what the CIO referred to as "a little old gripe fest" at the start of a meeting.

This is perhaps the most challenging aspect of adopting UDL principles at the level of your college or university. In higher education, it seems rare to find functional areas working outside of their own silos, and even rarer to see campus leaders adopting the argument that a small investment of time, people, and funds in broader access and learner choice today can save many multiples of those resources later on. This is why we advocate reframing UDL away from disability access stories alone, and toward mobile access narratives where making changes has a direct impact on student retention, persistence, and satisfaction, as the people at Suffolk University discovered. The push for campuswide access doesn't need to be precipitated by a crisis or urgent situation, however. Strategic partnerships for campuswide UDL adoption can start with something as narrowly defined as good web design.

Start with the Institutional Website

When we think about UDL and institutions of higher education, we typically think of the interactions among those who are already enrolled, teaching, and working at the institution. There are clear U.S. laws and industry standards regarding web accessibility (we talked about WCAG and legal requirements in chapters 2 and 4), and the outward-facing nature of institutions' public websites are a natural place to start moving from compliance to campuswide best practices, using the frame of mobile device access as an emotionally neutral carrier that underscores the positive impact of inclusive design.

College and university websites are great entry points into larger UDL conversations. Picture an admissions counselor at a rural community college receiving a phone call from a prospective student asking how he can schedule a tour. The counselor suggests that he use the online calendaring system on the college's website. The prospective student says that he cannot see the system because he is blind. The counselor refers the student to the disability services office ("they handle this kind of thing") and calls the IT help desk to complain that the website is broken. As you're well aware by now, the website is not broken; rather, it is inaccessibly built.

Imagine that the community college is in the process of hiring a firm to redesign its website, as Tom Tobin has experienced three times in his career. The procurement team uses the counselor's call with the blind student as an interview question with every candidate firm. The initial complaint leads to a campuswide resolve to hire web designers who have the UDL chops to be able to broaden prospective students' choices, but it also opens the door to more.

Both Tom and Kirsten have seen a process like this one play out at various colleges and universities. A faculty member who teaches, say, communication hears what is going on and wonders about other aspects of the college's web presence. Are all of the videos captioned? Do hyperlinks use text-based descriptors? Are college calendars in table format? Can students navigate the website without the use of a mouse? All of these are access issues, broadly speaking, rather than accessibility issues only for students with disabilities.

Given his background, the communication instructor wants to know if the website is inviting and usable. Can prospective students get the information they want quickly? Is the font friendly to users with dyslexia and other processing barriers? Does the site use in-house acronyms and jargon that might confuse visitors? Are the colors user friendly and, further, inviting? This professor begins asking people across campus what they think. He seeks out the experiences of those working to support students and staff with disabilities. These conversations turn into a research project.

Over the course of a semester, the communication professor turns his quest to figure out how to create an accessible and usable college website into a course project for his Introduction to Social Media class. He asks his students to interview various people at the college about their experiences with the website. He surveys the first-year class about their demographics and their familiarity with technology. He asks them how hard it is to find specific things on the school website, and he asks his students to come up with alternative designs for the website that reflect the data collected and aim to be more accessible and usable.

Over time, he asks his colleagues in disability services, admissions, IT, and web design to come in and explain to the class their own experiences with the website. At the end of the semester, the communications instructor gives a formal proposal to the website development search committee, based on solid research and student input that takes into account both access and general usability. Even after the community college hires a web design firm, he continues his effort each semester by focusing on a different component of the website (subpages for the different academic departments, course selections, athletics, student activities, and so on).

Eventually, a group of campus access and usability advocates decides that the communication professor's work reflects a need to carve out a professional position to monitor the website, faculty posts on their course websites, and the new online systems that the college plans to purchase. This is underlined by the fact that the college's web presence is no longer static, or even relatively stable from day to day. There is now a consistent flux, with social media and other real-time information sources that need to follow the law and industry best practices for accessibility and UDL.

Expand to Student Activities

Another space in which to focus your UDL efforts is in the student activities area, specifically student organizations and clubs. These groups do not often think about access needs, even though they frequently engage in the programming of events that are designed to attract diverse groups of students. This a great space in which to insert the concept of UDL, since it helps student leaders become more familiar with how to create a welcoming environment and also creates allies among students who advocate for attention to be paid to other areas of the campus that may need UDL strategies.

We have seen students who are trained to incorporate UDL strategies in their work call out other organizations on campus who do not do so. For example, a student club focused on cultural explorations of food called out the dining service office at their institution for not placing ingredient cards next to each food offering, leading to a discussion of the benefits of access to information for all diners, not just for students with food allergies. Student leaders are often the most open to applying the UDL framework to the interactions in which their organizations engage, viewing access and choice as part of a social justice mind-set.

The best way to get student activity leaders involved in UDL is to hold a workshop for them, sponsored by the main student activity office. Create an alliance with the staff members who oversee these organizations and offer a training session to their leaders. Demonstrate how to consider the needs of all group members. Topics within the training might include how to choose and create inclusive and accessible

- meeting spaces (physical room access, ease of access routes, ease of parking);
- advertising materials (paper and digital, color contrasts, legibility of poster information);
- online sign-up forms;
- activities hosted within the club (cultural diversity, transportation requirements, participation fees); and
- choices of activity topics (how to be sensitive and yet informative).

Most student leaders who participate in these types of trainings say that they are more aware of the needs of their members, even when club members haven't expressed particular needs. The leaders also report that this training bleeds into other areas of their life, whether in the dorm, in class, or attending campus events.

Working with student clubs is an ongoing process, thanks to the transient nature of their leaders and members. To bring UDL to your campus, revisit it with student groups annually. Connect with clubs' faculty sponsors and ask to be a part of their agenda each year during the club leadership training. Ask the group's student directors to participate in their first year, with the idea that they oversee and mentor new student leaders in future trainings. Beyond student activities are the electronic information touchpoints with which all students engage.

Include Information and Communication Technology Touchpoints

The information and communication technology (ICT) that students must use to navigate campus requirements has been the subject of many recent U.S. Department of Justice and Office of Civil Rights investigations and settlements—at Miami University of Ohio, Florida State University, Harvard University, and Massachusetts Institute of Technology, to name a few (Carlson, 2017). Because they perceive ICT as being easier for students and staff to use, as well as more flexible, many institutions of higher education now require or prefer that many interactions take place online, such as

- course registration,
- sign-up for student events,
- filling out financial aid forms,
- booking appointments with advisors, and
- reserving library books.

Other types of ICT are not online, like library copy machines, video display monitors in the student lounge, and the ID-card-swipe access system at the residence halls. All of these items were designed to make things run more smoothly on campus, but few were designed with access in mind. Colleges and universities have been navigating lawsuits or federal complaints made by people with (and without) disabilities who have struggled to get access to information or interact with their schools via ICTs. The way we advocate reframing UDL for mobile device users is especially relevant for making ICTs serve their intended purpose of increasing convenience and access.

As you saw in chapter 2, we seldom advise using legal requirements as a strategy for initiating campuswide collaborations with other service areas. "Guns blazing" usually turns people off, or at least scares them—and we've demonstrated how far things get when actions are based on negative emotions. With regard to ICT, however, "it's the law" might be an appropriate starting point. Because the topic of ICT accessibility is fairly new to higher education, there is still little information or research about how to ensure that such resources are usable by all.

This is where the UDL framework comes into play. By adopting the mind-set of offering at least plus-one choices for users of ICT, many institutions are using recent legal settlements as a call to proactive action. Some are creating procurement policies that ask the vendors who supply ICT resources to prove, through a Voluntary Product Accessibility Template (VPAT), how usable their technologies are for diverse populations (spoiler alert: even when vendors have VPATs and claim their products are widely accessible, test anyway, because there is not yet a centralized authority that checks the validity of VPATs). As more institutions ask vendors about usability and inclusive design as a routine part of their procurement processes, vendors are taking a harder look at incorporating UDL into their products.

Because ICT products are not yet routinely inclusively designed, approach your college or university's implementation of ICT in two different ways. You can choose not to implement, or stop using, products with access barriers until they are usable by all. This approach puts the pressure back on vendors to come to a solution sooner rather than later. In some instances, ICT products are necessary immediately, such as photocopy machines: few institutions could operate without photocopiers. In such an example, imagine a vendor brainstorming how to make the digital dashboard on its photocopy machines usable by all. Such a process might take weeks or months and entail significant retooling. In the meantime, institutions must come up with creative workarounds. Some have installed screen-reading software directly onto the copy machines; others have educated their library staff members on how to work with students who have problems using the digital dashboard; still others have posted directions in different languages above the machine. Immediate solutions should apply to the needs of the specific study body at your institution.

In order to use ICT as an accessibility selling point, the key is to be aware of which ICTs are problematic for students and staff members. Once you hear of issues with specific touchpoint devices, contact the company and offer to demonstrate the problem. Encourage your colleagues in the service area using the ICT to request a solution from the vendor that incorporates plus-one UDL choices and multiplicity. Simultaneously, work with your colleagues to figure out a workaround until a permanent solution is put into place. Pretty soon, you might find yourself sitting in a meeting about a new course registration system and wondering if it is accessible.

Talking to Administrators Like Administrators, Part 2

In order to effect campuswide UDL adoption, we need to reframe our conversations, pitching them differently to audiences at the strategic and operational levels of our colleges and universities. Several scripts and stories about how best to conduct UDL conversations with your colleagues follow.

The Technology Experts

The director of your campus technology group or the chief information officer (CIO) is often a strong advocate for UDL, although he or she might use a completely different vocabulary to describe it. Those in the technology realm support a wide variety of products: the learning management system, the college or university website, online communication platforms, and academic technology used in the classroom. In their world, inclusive design is measured in terms of usability, a concept that predates UDL and partially overlaps it.

Usable software, interfaces, and tools are designed to allow the greatest number of people to be successful in using the broadest set of the product's features. Interfaces and interactions are designed for maximum usability and then tested with the most variable group of user testers that can be found. In the tech world, products are deemed worthy of adoption only after people try to break them (through many cycles of testing), identify flaws, and subsequently design the flaws out of the products.

This suggests strongly that your CIO is an advocate for inclusively designed software, hardware, and tools. A good crosswalk conversation often helps, in which you share how UDL is about designing interactions to be more accessible, to offer learners choice and control, and to keep learners engaged. Show your tech leaders how UDL does for interactions what usability testing does for tools. This is especially useful because usability is seldom an issue at the top of campus technology leaders' minds. Often, just demonstrating how tools are not usable for everyone can lead to UDL support and advocacy from your technology support colleagues.

When Kirsten Behling was the director of disability services at Suffolk University, she took part in a conversation that helped the university lay the groundwork for UDL by adopting a more accessible set of technology tools, all through the lens of usability. After the university unveiled its brand-new website, a prospective student called the admissions office because he could not get access to the online application. The director of the admissions office called both the director of the website team and the disability services office, seeking an immediate solution from the disability services office and a long-term solution for the website itself.

The director of the website support team argued that the website and all of its forms must already be usable because the vendor with whom the university contracted to build the website had assured the university that the site and forms met accessibility guidelines. Based on this feedback, the admissions office director assumed that the prospective student was just struggling and ultimately assigned his complaint back to the operations-level staff in the admissions office.

Two weeks later, however, they got another call with the same issue. This time, the admissions director set up a meeting with Kirsten to review the website. Kirsten approached the meeting from a usability standpoint and acted like a typical beta tester who is trying to uncover flaws in a product that is almost ready to be released. Using a screen reader, they found that the website and admission forms were indeed not accessible at all. Further, the forms did not scale down when viewed on mobile devices. The interactions that the website and forms were supposed to facilitate were prevented by the single-stream design of the content and materials.

They called the website vendor again, who told them once more that the site and forms were accessible, and that if students were "still stuck, just ask them to use paper forms." This was hardly UDL. Kirsten and the admissions director decided to take the issue to the CIO, whom they knew had dealt with website access concerns at her previous institution.

The university team set up a meeting with the website vendor and invited the university's legal counsel to join them. They began that meeting by demonstrating the inaccessibility of the website. The vendor continued to argue that it was fine and that students could just apply to the university in a different way. The lawyer put his foot down and said that it was a compliance issue and needed to be fixed immediately. The CIO agreed, and the vendor was tasked with fixing the website and adding a layer of usability access checks to any new pages before they would be published. This institutional change was due in large part to being able to demonstrate the issue and back it up with legal arguments, all in the service of usability.

The Academic Side of the House

The people involved in the research and teaching at your institution are often the first audience for UDL campaign conversations. Start with a small, targeted group—whether a department, a group of department chairs, or an education committee—to keep the scope manageable initially. If you can convince a department to incorporate UDL strategies into its courses and then measure the effectiveness, you will have data to create greater impact for your later conversations with the provost to broaden the project into a university-wide initiative.

Think back to the occupational therapy (OT) professor from the University of New Hampshire, whom you met in chapter 7. After seeing such promising results from her initial experiment, the professor expanded her plus-one use of videos into a full-blown research project. She taught two sections of the same introductory course and changed the method of instruction and studying in only one of them. In the traditionally designed control course, the instructor showed the class the movements to perform with patients once and then referred students to the pictures and descriptions in their textbook for more information. In the experimental course section, the instructor showed the students the movements once and then asked them to break into groups of three: patient, occupational therapist, and videographer.

As the professor had seen with her ad hoc changes in previous courses, this addition of another choice or channel for studying improved students' overall ability to understand and practice their patient-practice movements, especially in comparison with the single-choice method of looking only at the static images in the textbook. The professor calculated that those who used videos performed, on average, 10 percent better on their final examinations.

With the professor's data in hand, the department created a video-based plus-one initiative across all OT courses. Within two years, they had substantial data and were writing journal articles about their collective success. The dean of the graduate school was not aware of their work—until she happened to read about it in a scholarly journal. She was so impressed that she asked all of the graduate schools in the University of New Hampshire to begin implementing UDL the following year.

The Policy Makers

When your college or university purchases tools that have accessibility built in, you are better able to implement UDL practices in your interactions. In recent years, institutions have begun to look at usability in much the same way they look at security. Most institutions have a security policy: no technology tools can be purchased until they have undergone extensive security tests to ensure that sensitive data will be protected.

Colleges and universities rely increasingly on an ever-widening array of digital tools—websites, online forms, e-mail and calendaring systems, course registration interfaces, ICTs, and learning management systems. We can now perform usability and accessibility testing to ensure that these purchases, many of them mission-critical and concomitantly expensive, are checked for accessibility, which can save hundreds of thousands of dollars in potential lawsuit settlements.

Institutions of higher education are wrestling with this idea, though, since it appears that a significant portion of the technology we currently use is not accessible. Vendors are slowly becoming aware of the need for their products to be universally designed, but many are not there yet.

In response, start by creating a procurement policy that allows for exceptions while still requiring follow-ups for vendors not yet in compliance with accessibility requirements. This allows universities to ask questions about accessibility, to push back against vendors whose products aren't accessible, and to demand better services and products.

To draft or update your procurement policy, meet with those on your campus who created your data security policy and work to understand and mirror their reasoning in your work on procurement. Present it to the chief financial officer and your college or university counsel. Share any legal requirements, explain how you'd like your institution to be forward thinking, and review the policy details.

The Dean of Student Affairs

At most institutions, the dean of student affairs oversees all those departments that do not directly involve the teaching and research aspect of the school. The dean might oversee the student activities, athletics, residence life, health services, and diversity services areas of the college or university. There is a wealth of opportunity to infuse the principles of UDL into the work done by these offices.

Perhaps the easiest entry point is to focus on the number of programming events that these offices put together annually. A large part of many of their jobs is to provide activities in which students participate outside of the classroom. For example, the student activities office might run a robotics club or sponsor the choir; residence life might offer floor programming around Halloween; health services might provide a flu-shot clinic; diversity services might program events to celebrate Black History Month; and the athletics department might advertise intramural sports for students. As we shared in chapter 2, activities outside of the classroom are opportunities to apply UDL strategies in order to increase awareness and attendance for students with diverse needs.

As you work to make allies in these offices, remember that the resources in many such areas are overextended. Adding UDL, no matter how simply or in how limited a way, may not be a welcome addition. This is why you need the support and advocacy of the dean of student affairs. The dean can mandate that the directors and staff in student service areas attend workshops on how to apply UDL strategies to welcome more students.

It is common for disability services professionals to be the point people for event-access questions. In her role as a disability services office director, Kirsten has heard many such questions, such as the orientation office staffer who wondered how to make a visit to a local museum accessible to a student in a wheelchair; or the residence life director who wanted to know what food they should offer at floor meetings since one of their residents had a gluten allergy; or the drama club advisor who called to ask how to make their playbills accessible to a student with a vision disability. All of these examples were reactions to specific situations, and the staff members who raised the questions were still in the "make accommodations" mind-set.

Kirsten remembers more such calls. The athletics department asked what to do about a transgender student who wanted to use a specific locker room. The debate club called, asking how to help a student whose first language was not English participate more fully. Again, the questions were reactive, what-do-we-do-now concerns. Eventually, Kirsten took all of these issues to the dean of student affairs and asked for help in managing them. She proposed a UDL program for the student affairs division to increase awareness and empower other offices to adopt UDL strategies proactively and broadly. The dean was thrilled to support the idea, infusing the presentation into her annual departmental retreat. The materials from that workshop were also made available to each director for use later on. Each of these target points and methods of getting the message across about the benefits of UDL for everyone can be customized to a specific campus, department, or group.

Be a Leader

Most institutions of higher education want to be recognized for being leaders in their field. Whether it is having the best law school, the highest career placement rates, the best sports team, the most diverse campus, the largest number of student activists, or the university with the most research grant dollars, being the best is an attractive vision for administrators.

UDL and "most accessible" are not typically at the top of administrators' lists of categories in which they want their colleges and universities to be the best. UDL makes good sense, they concede. There is wide support for creating an inclusive environment, but it does not seem to draw in more funding, more research opportunities, or more prospective-student interest like other big-ticket items. One way to reframe UDL is to use it as a driver for best-of categories that are on many administrators' minds: "mobile friendly" and "best fit for time-strapped students."

Shortly after the voluntary resolution agreement between the Pennsylvania State University and the National Federation for the Blind, in which the NFB sued the university on behalf of students with disabilities because they were unable to access the online systems of the school, other universities began to take notice (Carlson, 2017). In 2016, we spoke with Aaron Spector, the director of Disability Resources and Services at Temple University in Philadelphia.

Spector and his colleagues used the Penn State settlement as an opportunity to examine and rethink their online presence proactively in terms of UDL. An initial conversation between Disability Resources and the instructional technology department led to the establishment of a much larger university-wide Accessible Technology Initiative. Temple University has taken a number of proactive steps in establishing itself as a leader in the field of online access.

They established an Accessible Technology Compliance Committee—made up of a mix of staff, faculty members, and administrators—that looked at how to approach online access to interactions throughout the university from a UDL standpoint. They began with a university-wide audit of all things online (websites, the LMS, the e-mail system, online forms), recognizing quickly that they were not in compliance with U.S. law. They then set a list of priorities for how to resolve the issues found in the audit. They established an accessibility liaison at each of their schools to make sure that the work of online access did not fall to just one person.

They created a procurement process that requires any vendor with whom they might do business to provide a VPAT (see chapter 4), and adopted policy that gives Temple the right to refuse to work with vendors whose products are inaccessible. And, perhaps most importantly, Temple is committed to reevaluating their work on a regular basis, understanding that even though they addressed barriers once, development is an iterative process. Spector notes that the changes they adopted have had the greatest positive impact for one of Temple's largest group of learners: people who commute into Philadelphia's Center City for work and who take courses in addition to their family and work responsibilities.

Since Temple adopted their proactive stance toward online accessibility, many other institutions of higher education across North America have looked to them for guidance about how to engage their own colleagues in the conversation about inclusive design and UDL. Temple staff members frequently give presentations at national conferences and are often the subject of articles citing their forward thinking. Temple is the example you can use when you approach your administrators with solutions to problems that may not be at the top of their mind. Turn your UDL conversations into a race to be the best.

Conclusion

The catalyst for the University of South Dakota's current efforts came in July 2015, when the university's director of student disability services heard a Department of Justice presentation at an industry conference and reached out to Bruce Kelley and his team. The collaboration "really helped us to shift gears," Jackson noted. "We invited senior leaders to attend an information session about the lawsuits that were in process with other universities. The former president at the University of Montana, which was one of the places that was sued, used to be our provost at USD, and we realized that if it could happen to Royce [Engstrom], it could happen to us" (Kelley, Mosterd, and Jackson, 2016).

Once USD sent Jackson to workshops, conferences, and courses in order to become their in-house expert (she is now certified in UDL by

Rutgers University), she brought back UDL as a framework for making changes to interactions with learners across campus. "We amended our online-faculty orientation to model UDL practices, using our own materials, tutorials from Desire2Learn, and presentations from the university's student disability services director." The team also reached out to faculty members with existing courses not scheduled for review by changing their popular Designing for Impact workshop to be structured around UDL principles. As we are doing in this book, the team also reframed accessibility in terms of benefit for broad audiences, such as playing up the advantage of captions for video-search studying and English-language learners.

The University of South Dakota team is careful to say that their efforts are, as they are at most other institutions, a work in progress. Because their team has limited resources, they have focused on those areas over which they have direct control: faculty training and development. They are now refocusing training to address accessibility in online and face-to-face courses, have created a Statement of Achievement in Accessibility program (which debuted in fall 2017), and are working closely with their Continuing and Distance Education colleagues to develop a comprehensive plan for accessibility. Senior leadership at USD is supporting the CTL's efforts and is engaging in conversations with the board of regents to determine specific policies. The CTL is adopting a circle-of-influence approach. Their greatest focus is on faculty members themselves, while also positioning themselves to be able to hold key conversations with those entities that set specific policies for the entire university and regents' system.

They proceed by making the argument for a step-by-step process emphasizing the benefits of UDL. We ended our conversation with Kelley saying that "students want multimedia and access. They are coming to us from high schools where the interactions were designed to be inclusive, and we're stronger to the extent that we can reach out to them where they are, which is on their phone, on their iPads, on their laptops, when they have a few spare minutes" (Kelley, Mosterd, and Jackson, 2016).

To ensure the success of UDL initiatives, you must know the culture of your institution. What are its goals and mission? Who are its students? What is the overall balance between teaching and research among faculty members? Do you have resources to solve potential problems proactively? Have you come under investigation about inaccessible interactions? What is important to the history of the college or university and to the administrators who run it?

When you are able to answer some of these questions, you can then find ways to infuse your UDL initiative into the bigger institutional picture. Understanding campus culture is key to the successful broad implementation of UDL through ownership of the concept by more than one person, program, department, college, and service area. Such understanding generates the commitment to incorporate UDL strategies into all of the work done on campus, as well as the desire and the patience to build up to long-term positive effects.

Prove that UDL increases access for everyone by measuring the impact of your work in terms of improved retention rates, financial savings, increased website traffic, and better student-ratings data. And then, when you have success at one level with one audience, feed your results forward into a broader and more comprehensive program of UDL adoption. One phrase that we associate with UDL throughout this book applies equally well to its own implementation: think in terms of plus-one.

A THOUGHT EXERCISE

Use the worksheet below to plan your institution's UDL life cycle. You may choose to do this alone or with your UDL team, if you have established one.

What is your UDL focus area?	
List the steps you need to take to bring UDL to the attention of an institution (five steps minimum).	
Who can influence change for you?	
List five points you need to cover in your meetings with the people who can influence change.	
Describe the proactive approach you will take when sharing your UDL idea with your influential colleagues.	

CHAPTER 11

Engage! The UDL Life Cycle

Meet Heidi and Kimber

In a 2016 interview, we talked with Heidi Pettyjohn and Kimber Andrews at the University of Cincinnati and heard how they helped to move their institution toward a campuswide UDL and accessibility culture. It all started when, under a resolution with the U.S. Department of Justice's Office of Civil Rights (OCR), a proactive accessibility audit of the university's website in 2014 found several gaps in general accessibility, such as finding that site visitors could not complete the full application and class registration process using some types of assistive technology, or control videos unless they were using a mouse—a significant drawback. As you are seeing in this book, this is also a barrier that excludes learners who are on their mobile devices as well.

Pettyjohn says that "we were aware that new web-accessibility regulations were coming," referring to the Information and Communication Technology (ICT) Refresh to adopt the Web Content Accessibility Group (WCAG) standards as the legal requirements for the accessibility of public-facing web content (you may remember this from chapter 2). "We hired an EIT [electronic information technology] accessibility expert for our Disability Services Office to focus on helping the campus ensure accessibility with its electronic information."

The University of Cincinnati program grew when senior campus leaders charged the entire university to go beyond compliance. The senior vice president for academic affairs and provost, vice president for student affairs, vice president of information technology and CIO, vice president of government relations and university communications, senior vice president for administration and finance, and faculty senate chair all signed on to the three-phase plan that we discussed in the introduction, which we will paraphrase here.

- **Compliance.** The university focused on its Office of Civil Rights (OCR) resolution and applied an audit tool to its publicly available web content to identify gaps in accessibility, upgraded its web infrastructure to support accessibility, built awareness across campus about access challenges for all types of learners, and provided training for faculty members and support staff in good interaction design techniques.
- **Commitment.** The university gears up for making needed changes. All areas of the institution identify the resources they will need in order to equip their staff to be able to remedy challenges as they are found.
- **Culture.** The university adopts UDL principles in the design of all interactions between learners and materials, each other, instructors, support staff, and the wider world. UDL becomes just a part of what we do here. (Andrews and Pettyjohn, 2016)

Pettyjohn is grateful for the backing of her senior leaders: "Administrative support for broad campus change can be rare. They often don't have the deeper expertise in the accessibility field to be able to fold accessibility or UDL into their broader vision for the institution." The senior leaders at the University of Cincinnati, however, are executive sponsors of the Accessibility Network, a cross-functional team of staff and faculty with expertise in web and e-learning accessibility. The university committed a significant financial investment in the program, including the creation of eighteen new-to-the-university positions to help move the entire campus in the direction of inclusive design.

One of those new hires was Andrews, with the Center for the Enhancement of Teaching and Learning (CET&L). In their initial conversations with the provost, CET&L made the case for adopting UDL in terms of return on investment. Andrews explains that "CET&L saw many similarities between the Center's work in building a culture of continuous growth and a focus on evidence-based practices. UDL is an umbrella that embraces all aspects of teaching from course design to active learning and the scholarship of teaching and learning."

As they began to work toward moving the campus from compliance to commitment to culture, Pettyjohn explained that supporting UDL and accessibility didn't suffer from a common challenge: "it was refreshing to work on [UDL], because the hardest thing to communicate about adopting any change is the 'why' of it. With UDL, people already understand that it's important, so we were able to start from a place of common purpose."

CET&L began by offering workshops on UDL and creating a faculty learning community around UDL. The faculty learning community had an especially positive impact: faculty members often didn't know about UDL and were intrigued to learn more about how they could offer choices for learners (and save themselves effort and time over the long run as well). Members of the faculty learning community have been actively engaged in supporting efforts to make the university more accessible by being part of university-wide focus groups on electronic accessibility and starting discussions about UDL in their own departments as well as providing teaching demonstrations on how to incorporate UDL principles into their curriculum and syllabi.

The commitment of the university to creating an inclusive and accessible environment has encouraged faculty to embrace UDL principles. Pettyjohn notes that "we were really trying to coincide education for faculty and staff with the implementation of additional resources. With our updated content-management system (CMS), we made sure that accessibility is now built in and have invested in an audit tool to ensure that content owners know which aspects of their websites are accessible. We pulled together a strong team, and our success is and will continue to be dependent largely on concentric circles with a shared vision." At the time of our conversation, the University of Cincinnati was getting ready to move toward the next phases in its plan. Andrews mentioned that listening to faculty needs is shaping the resources and workshops CET&L is offering as well as many other departments including the Disability Service Office and the Center for Excellence in eLearning.

In 2017, we want to increase the campus's general awareness around accessibility. We want to

- make faculty members aware of things that perhaps they didn't realize before,
- provide just-in-time knowledge through consultations and Lynda.com mini-courses,
- encourage the community to incorporate accessibility into all new materials they create, and
- focus on connecting principles of UDL to creating learning materials that are accessible for all students. (Pettyjohn and Andrews, 2016)

To foster greater ownership of the initiative, the university ran a naming contest, coming up with the Accessibility Network at the University of Cincinnati. CET&L and their colleagues plan their next push to focus on communication to all affected audiences. Pettyjohn emphasizes that "our goal is to empower and motivate. We hold a diversity conference every Spring semester, and we hope to work with our conference organizers to do a UDL theme while the program is happening across campus."

They have created an online course titled eAccessibility: An Introduction, available to all faculty members and staff, which aims to bring a general awareness about the importance of accessibility, and which will eventually become a mandatory training. The final goal for the University of Cincinnati is to create a true network of interested faculty members and staff, so that each area of the university will have one or more members who can act as champions to train their colleagues in accessibility and UDL basics.

Becoming Subtle Evangelists

Many readers will remember Patrick Stewart as Captain Jean-Luc Picard in the television series *Star Trek: The Next Generation* bravely pointing a finger in the direction of danger and issuing the one-word command, "Engage!" The word could mean anything from "increase the engine thrust" to "fire the weapons" to "open a communication channel." We want to help you to engage with your colleagues, campus leaders, and students in order to change their way of thinking about UDL.

Throughout this book, we've shown why UDL can be a tough sell for faculty members, support staff, and institutional leaders who can seem content to wait for something drastic to happen before they take action. You've read of colleges and universities that were prompted to act only after being sued. Atul Gawande, a noted surgeon and author, suggests in an article entitled "Tell Me Where It Hurts" why adopting an incremental approach, such as the one for which we advocate in this book, can be a struggle:

> The only visible part of investment in incremental care is the perennial costs. There is generally little certainty about how much spending will really be needed or how effective it will be. Rescue work delivers much more certainty. There is a beginning and an end to the effort. And you know what all the money and effort is (and is not) accomplishing. We don't like to address problems until they are well upon us and unavoidable, and we don't trust solutions that promise benefits only down the road.
>
> Incrementalists nonetheless want us to take a longer view. They want us to believe that they can recognize problems before they happen, and that, with steady, iterative effort over years, they can reduce, delay, or eliminate them. Yet incrementalists also want us to accept that they will never be able to fully anticipate or prevent all problems. This makes for a hard sell. (Gawande, 2017, 43)

Gawande is talking about preventive health care and the importance of primary care physicians to people's overall health and the efficiency of the health-care system as well. His point is that people tend to wait until they must take action, rather than seek out maintenance-level care, whether the subject is keeping our roads and bridges safe (we tend to raid maintenance budgets and then get stuck with huge bills when catastrophic failures happen), our medical care (we tend to pay doctors more who specialize in heroic life-saving measures than those who help keep people healthy over the span of their lives), or educational practices (we tend to fund technology and materials at the expense of human resources and long-term practices).

The UDL framework is definitely in the category of maintenance practices, and we are most certainly what Gawande calls "incrementalists." We believe strongly that taking proactive measures now, even though it entails effort and thought, produces lasting benefits and savings in terms of time and effort that allow practitioners—faculty members, support staff, and campus leaders—to spend far less of their time repeating themselves or putting out fires when individual needs come up, and more time where it matters most: interacting with learners.

UDL is not a magic wand that makes the need to provide accommodations go away entirely. We will always encounter situations where we still have to make one change, in one course, for one person, one time. But with UDL practices in place, we will have to make far fewer of those, and we will have designed our interactions so that they fit better with our students' busy, tech-enabled lives. That's a win for everybody, and it all starts with a little plus-one thinking.

Positive Impact for Students

We want to close our book with a story from a student perspective. James Lang from Assumption College recently wrote a moving opinion piece about the need to treat all learners as capable and valuable members of our colleges and universities:

> The teaching center I direct teamed up with our office of accessibility services to host an event earlier this fall for faculty. The idea was to invite students who have received accommodations to share their experiences—what helped and what didn't—with professors. . . .
>
> The student with a visual impairment, for example, noted as particularly beneficial for her something all of us would probably recognize as a good teaching practice: writing in black marker on the white board, and doing so in large and legible

letters. She said she found herself shut out of a course whenever a faculty member wrote hastily in crabbed script all over the board, or used green markers that were barely legible, even to the fully sighted students. . . . In example after example, she and the other students described teaching practices that would have universal benefit in the classroom and that could be adopted without putting a spotlight on students with disabilities. . . .

A student who had described her need for accommodations in response to multiple challenging conditions explained that what she really wanted was for her instructors to see her as a valued member of the course. "What we don't want," she said, "is to be made to feel like we are a burden to you because we have requested accommodations. Many of us already have this feeling that we're burdening you, and it really helps if you can treat us like you want us to be in your course. We're not asking for accommodations to make your life difficult, or because we're trying to get away with something. We want to be in your course. We just need your help learning the best we can."

UDL can seem like one more buzzword to college faculty members who already have an earful of them. And the case for its positive effects can also be overstated: Not every design principle has a positive impact on every learner. We can argue about those cases that seem to create conflicts between the needs of the individual and the welfare of the group.

But I hope we can agree—as a universal principle in the creation of college courses—that we want all students to feel welcomed and to have equal opportunities to succeed in our courses. If we begin our course design with that simple plea in mind, and keep it at the forefront of our deliberations and debates about accessibility, we can help lift the weight of requesting accommodations from the backs of students who already have been asked to bear significant burdens in the pursuit of learning. In so doing, we are more likely to help all students succeed. (Lang, 2017)

The Whole Book in One Section

Think about the faculty and staff members at your college or university, and chances are the same 10 percent of them attend professional-development workshops and get engaged in campus governance and committee work. To get the other 90 percent of people involved requires a motivator that goes beyond avoiding lawsuits (compliance) and fixing something—making one change, in one course, one time, for one person—when requests are heard (accommodations). The process of shifting those motivators has five big pieces.

1. IDENTIFY THE GAPS

This is the polite way of asking "what are the things that bother us or create more work for us?" When we think about the courses we teach, we can usually identify fairly easily those places where students always

- **ask questions** (in week 2, nobody gets the concept of carry-forward accounting right away),
- **get things wrong on tests** (the midterm questions on meiosis stump a lot of students), and
- **ask for different explanations** (I show my students how to dice vegetables properly, but they always want me to show them a different angle or they go find YouTube videos from others who use a different technique).

These three pinch points are great places to start thinking about giving information, assessing skill, and keeping students motivated in just one more way than exists right now. The underlying reasons this works are because (a) it's a manageable scope of work for a faculty member to accomplish, and (b) it reduces the amount of rework, re-teaching, and question answering that faculty members have to do. Who doesn't want to reduce the amount of repetition and reteaching?

2. MAKE TARGETED PLUS-ONE CHANGES

Create at least one more way to have the interactions in the gaps that you identified above. Think especially about where you can help to keep learners engaged and on track, where you can offer alternative ways for them to experience materials and information, and how you can provide them with choices about how they show what they know. This holds true for students' interactions with instructors and service areas across the institution, such as tutoring, financial aid, the registrar, counseling services, and the admissions office.

3. TRACK THE NUMBERS

Once you have a few faculty members who have made some inclusive-design changes, work with them to demonstrate the impact of those changes. Collect comparison data on the number of questions asked, student performance on assessments, and ask the learners to rate their experience by sharing their study habits (and the impact that the changes have on those habits).

The learning management system is also a key source of comparative data for some before-and-after numbers, such as frequency and quality of discussion postings or overall student performance on assessments. This helps to change the mind-set about inclusive design by showing the scope of the impact of design efforts. In a faculty meeting, it's powerful to say "I made one change, and now I don't have 732 student questions about meiosis in week 2." Colleagues will want to know what that one change is. Have the data available to show them the impact.

4. ADOPT A TEAM MODEL

The more we can work with faculty members as part of a team of experts, the less work we have to put on individual faculty members' shoulders. Most of us were never trained in inclusive design or UDL, and that's okay. Way back in 2008, the folks at the University of Vermont got a federal grant to adopt UDL (Wakefield, 2008) by creating design teams with faculty members, media experts, instructional designers, project managers, graphics people, and web designers. The team approach succeeds because it makes UDL part of the everyday work of the institution. No matter where faculty members turn for support, the response contains inclusive methods.

Note, too, that you don't have to have a huge staff of support people for a team approach to work well. By identifying the most pressing or most beneficial areas for applying UDL (back in stage 1 of this process), you create a manageable list of priorities—it's the commitment that matters, and the practice follows from that.

5. GET YOUR LEADERS ON BOARD

All of the strategies above prepare us to be subtle evangelists who argue for making things smoother for our students and for our faculty members. That's how you can talk to your colleagues. But how do you talk to your senior leadership? You know, the people with the budgets? In our workshops and speeches, we often hear variations on the following questions:

- How do I support this new generation? They are so engrossed in their technology.
- What do I do when the support at my college isn't there? When the administrators and staff aren't supportive?
- Faculty members believe that they should be compensated for creating alternative measures. What's up with that? How do I respond to that?

We believe in paying people for work that goes above and beyond what we'd ordinarily expect them to do, and both of these final thoughts get at the question of how much these efforts are going to cost—and we can hear concerns about money, people, and time inside that question too.

Turn this question inside out, though, and we can see an assumption that underlies the lack of support or the desire to get paid to implement UDL work: it's the assumption that UDL is an add-on, that it's extra effort, that it's not part of the everyday work that we do. This is where you can talk to senior leaders in order to start change at your institution.

If you've piloted UDL with your coalition of the willing, so to speak, then you have some solid data about three things that presidents, provosts, and budget directors use as their leading indicators of institutional success: student persistence, retention, and satisfaction.

279

Persistence is the term that institutional research people use for how many students are enrolled on the first day of the semester versus how many are there to take the final exam or turn in the final project. High dropout rates during a course indicate low student persistence. Persistence is a reliable indicator of overall student success (Godfrey and Matos-Elefante, 2010) and students who drop out of courses early enough get full or partial refunds, costing the institution twice: once when we refund their tuition, and again because we used institutional resources to get them into the courses in the first place (not to mention that their professors had to grade their work). UDL works to improve learner persistence (Tobin, 2014) because it offers choices to learners about how they take in information and choices about how they demonstrate their skills. Show your leaders the data from the national studies, as well as from your pilot program.

Retention is measured when students come back and take classes in the next semester or year. Many colleges and universities see a statistical cliff on their retention graphs, where many freshman students don't come back for their sophomore year. This is due to many factors, including financial ones, but time-management concerns always seem to be among the top three reasons for retention concerns. UDL helps with time allocation in two specific and measurable ways. First, by giving learners estimates for how long it will take to accomplish tasks, they can better plan their study time. Second, by offering alternative access to materials and interactions, we expand the number of opportunities for study throughout the day.

Imagine the single mother who puts her kids to bed and still wants to watch the safety procedures video to prep for her next day's lab work. If she can read the transcript or turn off the sound and use the captions, she's just found twenty minutes for study that she wouldn't have had otherwise. Collect the data about student retention after students take your UDL-based courses—it's likely that your UDL students are coming back at greater rates that the average student population.

Talk to your campus leaders about the effect of UDL on student satisfaction too. We want our learners to find value in their experiences with us. This one is easy to measure because we are already asking our learners about their experiences with us via end-of-course ratings instruments. Compare the ratings for the same instructor in course sections where other variables are the same, and see how UDL choices and plus-one design have an impact on learners' impressions of the value they got out of their courses. Share those data with your senior leaders, and share them with the folks in the faculty senate and anyone else who's involved with the process of promotion and asking contingent faculty members to come back and teach again.

All of these strategies at the course, program, and campus level help us to take accessibility—something that can be seen as a numinous, feel-good idea that we just don't have the people or money or time to do—and turn it into a hard-nosed practice—UDL—that has a measurable impact on the budgetary bottom line. Talk numbers, and go get 'em!

The Whole Book on One Page

Figure 11.1 is a print-friendly version of the entire process that we've outlined in this book. In order to make a meaningful change that benefits students, faculty members, staffers, and the entire institution, focus your efforts on changing the mind-set by which you and your colleagues approach the concept of accessibility, primarily by reframing it in terms of how people get access to the interactions they need in order to be more successful.

ONE LAST THOUGHT EXERCISE

If you have followed along with the thought exercises throughout this book, you now have the outline of a comprehensive UDL campus plan. This final thought exercise is a way to bring those plans to fruition. For each of the stages you have outlined in the previous thought exercises, do the following three things.

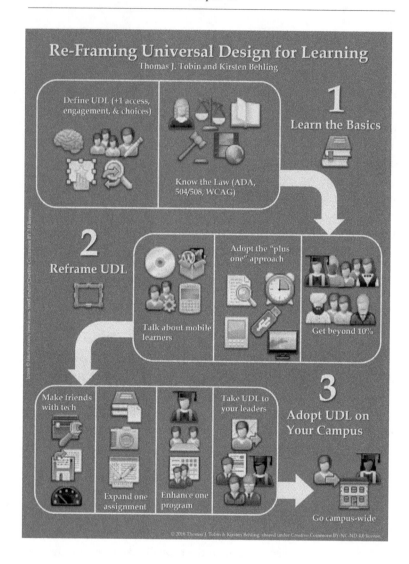

Figure 11.1: The UDL life cycle

1. Note the names of the people involved. Be specific about who would be responsible for each of the stages of the process.
2. Write down who would be able to give that person permission, funding, or resources to accomplish the task or goal. For example, if you want to put together a UDL team that includes an external consultant, for the purpose of developing accessible interactions throughout an entire degree program, which administrator(s) would need to sign off on the allocation of people, money, and time? See table on following page.
3. Sketch a one-page proposal for your project, writing it for the audience of people who can approve the work and resources. In your one-page proposal, talk about
   • the scope of the project (e.g., a pilot with three courses the first semester, followed by evaluation and expansion over the next two years),
   • the resources needed (in terms of people, funds, and time),
   • the work to be accomplished (e.g., creation of alternative interactions in three key areas in each course, and alternative versions of all multimedia),
   • how you plan to communicate (i.e., who gets reports, how often, and about what details), and
   • your plan to turn the UDL process into part of the everyday operations of your department, college, or institution.

Previous Thought Exercise	Who Is Responsible for This?	Who Can Accomplish This?
UDL in Higher Education		
It's the Law		
Meet the Mobile Learners		
Engage Digital Learners		
Adopt the Plus-One Approach		
Coach the Coaches		
Expand One Assignment		
Enhance One Program		
Extend to One Modality		
Embrace One Mind-Set		

CODA

Figure 12.1: Stairs Closed. Use Ramp. (Tobin, 2017)

In 2017, Tom Tobin was in Grand Rapids, Michigan, to give a keynote speech on UDL. Before the event, he went for a morning run and found the situation you see in figure 12.1. The stairs leading to the pedestrian bridge were blocked off for repairs, but everyone could still use the bridge via the ramp—the ramp that had been put in place originally as a disability service alternative. Having the option of the ramp allows everyone to continue to use the bridge. This analogy is powerful when we talk with our colleagues in higher education about reframing UDL: design interactions inclusively to begin with, and everyone benefits when barriers come into the picture (in the case of figure 12.1, quite literally).

Many fields in higher education embrace evidence-based practices, in which we base our practices and predictions on careful observation of what actually happens and what actually works when we make changes to the way we operate in the world. Universal Design for Learning is a mind-set that is grounded in evidence-based practice. UDL has been tested for decades, in physical classrooms and online learning environments, at two-year colleges and research universities, across all kinds of subjects, curricula, and teaching methods. It is starting to get wider attention thanks to recent lawsuits where people and organizations are fighting for equal and timely access to education for everyone, regardless of the individual barriers people may face.

Atul Gawande, in his article on the importance of primary care doctors, makes a distinction between the incrementalists and the rescuers in his profession. In higher education, Gawande's point is a hopeful one because we will always need the rescuers: professionals who can make individual changes to help provide educational access in the face of immediate (and sometimes pressing) challenges. The research about UDL and accessible design over the past three decades suggests that inclusion is a goal that responds to slow, steady work: "There is a lot about the future that remains unpredictable. Nonetheless, the patterns are becoming more susceptible to empiricism—to a science of surveillance, analysis, and iterative correction. The incrementalists are overtaking the rescuers. But the transformation has itself been incremental. So we're only just starting to notice" (Gawande, 2017, 44). We wish you success with your efforts to get your colleagues and your institution to make incremental changes in order to reach out to those people whom you have traditionally served poorly, or perhaps not at all, and we would enjoy hearing your story as well.

REFERENCES

Accessibility at Penn State. 2011. Settlement between Penn State
University and National Federation of the Blind. http://accessibility.
psu.edu/nfbpsusettlement.

Accessibility for Ontarians with Disabilities Act. 2005. S.O. 2005, c. 11.
https://www.ontario.ca/laws/statute/05a11.

Adams, C. J. 2015, September 4. 2015 SAT, ACT scores suggest many students aren't college-ready. *Education Week.* http://www.edweek.org/
ew/articles/2015/09/09/2015-sat-act-scores-suggest-many-students.
html.

Adams, L., Burkholder, E., and Hamilton, K. 2015. Micro-moments: Your
guide to winning the shift to mobile. Mountain View, CA: Google.
https://think.storage.googleapis.com/images/micromoments-guide-
to-winning-shift-to-mobile-download.pdf.

Afriprov.org. 1998, November. African proverbs of the month. African
Proverbs, Sayings, and Stories. http://www.afriprov.org/african-prov-
erb-of-the-month/23–1998proverbs/137-november-1998-proverb.html.

Ahern, A. A. 2010. A case study: Problem-based learning for civil
engineering students in transportation courses. *European Journal of
Engineering Education* 35 (1): 109–16.

Allen, I. E., and Seaman, J. 2013. *Changing Course: Ten Years of Tracking
Online Education in the United States.* Babson Survey Research Group.
https://www.onlinelearningsurvey.com/reports/changingcourse.pdf.

Allen, I. E., and Seaman, J. 2017. *Digital Learning Compass: Distance
Education Enrollment Report 2017.* Babson Survey Research Group.
https://www.onlinelearningsurvey.com/reports/digtiallearningcom-
passenrollment2017.pdf.

Alliance for an Inclusive and Accessible Canada. 2017, August 22.
Disability expert conference live-stream. YouTube. https://youtu.be/
c8_D5M4pvdY.

American Federation of Teachers. 2011, March. Exploring student attitudes, aspirations, and barriers to success. http://www.aft.org/sites/
default/files/studentfocusgrp0311.pdf.

American Institutes for Research. 2015. Concerns-based adoption model (CBAM). http://www.sedl.org/cbam.

Americans with Disabilities Act of 1990, Pub. L. No. 101-336, 104 Stat. 328. 1990. As amended, 2008. https://www.ada.gov/pubs/adastatute08.htm.

Andrews, K., and Pettyjohn, H. 2016, December 2. Telephone interview with Thomas J. Tobin.

Assistive Technology Act. 1998. P.L. 394.105. As amended, 2004 (P.L. 108-364). https://www.section508.gov/assistive-technology-act-1998.

[Basham, J.]. 2017. Instructional planning process. UDL Implementation and Research Network. http://udl-irn.org/instructional-process.

Beach, A., Sorcinelli, M. D., Austin, A., Rivard, J. 2016. *Faculty Development in the Age of Evidence.* Sterling, VA: Stylus.

Behling, K., and Linder, K. 2017. Collaborations between centers for teaching and learning and offices of disability services: Current partnerships and perceived challenges. *Journal of Postsecondary Education and Disability* 30 (1): 5–15.

Benham, N. E. 1997. Faculty members' attitudes and knowledge regarding specific disabilities and the Americans with Disabilities Act. *College Student Journal* 31: 124–29.

Bento, R. F. 1996. Faculty decision-making about "reasonable accommodations" for disabled college students. *College Student Journal* 30 (4): 494.

Bigaj, S. J., Shaw, S. F., and McGuire, J. M. 1999. Community-technical college faculty willingness to use and self-reported use of accommodation strategies for students with learning disabilities. *Journal for Vocational Special Needs Education* 21 (2): 3–14.

Bigatel, P. 2015. 7 Tips and 7 Principles for Accessibility and Universal Design. Penn State World Campus Online Faculty Development. https://web.archive.org/web/20170116143506/https://wcfd.psu.edu/7-tips-and-7-principles-for-accessibility-and-universal-design.

Bongey, S. B. 2011. Making the grade: Standards and promoting achievement through technology. In *Dancing with Digital Natives,* ed. M. Manafy and H. Gautschi, 269–90. Medford, NJ: Information Today.

Braxton, J. M., Doyle, W. R., Hartley III, H. V., Hirschy, A. S., Jones, W. A., and McLendon, M. K. 2013. *Rethinking College Student Retention.* San Francisco: Jossey-Bass.

Brookfield, S. 2007. Diversifying curriculum as the practice of repressive tolerance. *Teaching in Higher Education* 12 (5–6): 557–68.

Brooks, D. C. 2016. ECAR study of undergraduate students and information technology. Louisville, CO: EDUCAUSE Center for Analysis and Research (ECAR). https://library.educause.edu/~/media/files/library/2016/10/ers1605.pdf.

Brown, A. L., and Cocking, R. R. 2000. *How People Learn.* Ed. J. D. Bransford. Washington, DC: National Academy Press.

Burgstahler, S. 2012. Equal access: Universal design of instruction. Seattle: University of Washington DO-IT Center. http://www.washington.edu/doit/equal-access-universal-design-instruction.

Burgstahler, S. 2015a. Promoters and inhibitors of Universal Design for Learning in higher education. In *Universal Design in Higher Education: From Principles to Practice*, 287–96. 2nd ed. Cambridge, MA: Harvard Education Press.

Burgstahler, S. 2015b. Universal Design in higher education. In *Universal Design in Higher Education: From Principles to Practice*, 3–20. 2nd ed. Cambridge, MA: Harvard Education Press.

Bush, V. 1945, July. As we may think. *Atlantic.* http://www.theatlantic.com/magazine/archive/1945/07/as-we-may-think/303881.

Cameron, J., and Cope, J. 2016, June 21. The big four: Teaching faculty members about online accessibility responsibilities. Presentation. Distance Learning Administration conference. Jekyll Island, GA: University of West Georgia. http://www.westga.edu/~distance/dla/concurrentsessions_2016.php#tue4.

The Canadian Press. 2017, October 15. Canada's first national accessibility legislation to be ready by spring: Hehr. https://www.cp24.com/news/canada-s-first-national-accessibility-legislation-to-be-ready-by-spring-hehr-1.3633016.

Carlson, L. L. 2017. Higher ed accessibility lawsuits, complaints, and settlements. University of Minnesota Duluth. http://www.d.umn.edu/~lcarlson/atteam/lawsuits.html.

CAST. 2014a. 5 examples of Universal Design for Learning in the classroom. Understood. https://www.understood.org/en/learning-attention-issues/treatments-approaches/educational-strategies/5-examples-of-universal-design-for-learning-in-the-classroom.

CAST. 2014b. Universal Design for Learning guidelines, Version 2.0. http://www.udlcenter.org/aboutudl/udlguidelines.

CAST. 2015. About Universal Design for Learning. http://www.cast.org/ our-work/about-udl.html#.WoLm4KhKuUk.

CAST. 2016a. UDL and assessment. *UDL on Campus.* http://UDL oncampus.cast.org/page/assessment_UDL.

CAST. 2016b, February 16. UDL in the ESSA. http://www.cast.org/whatsnew/news/2016/udl-in-the-essa.html.

CAST. 2017, April 22. Expectation at @TowsonU. Twitter. @CAST_UDL. https://twitter.com/CAST_UDL/status/855765418023284736.

CAST. 2018. The UDL guidelines. http://udlguidelines.cast.org/?utm_medium=web&utm_campaign=launch&utm_source=cast-news&utm_content=body-text.

Center for Teaching and Scholarly Excellence. 2004. Tips for writing goals and objectives. Boston, MA: Suffolk University. http://www.suffolk.edu/documents/CTSE/tips_for_writing_goals_objectives.pdf.

Center for Teaching Excellence. 2012. Other teaching centers. University of Kansas. https://cte.ku.edu/other-teaching-centers.

Center for Universal Design. 2008. About the center: Ronald L. Mace. https://www.ncsu.edu/ncsu/design/cud/about_us/usronmace.htm.

Center on Postsecondary Education and Disability. 2012. Universal Design for Instruction in postsecondary education. Neag School of Education, University of Connecticut. http://www.udi.uconn.edu.

Chen, B., and Denoyelles, A. 2013. Exploring students' mobile learning practices in higher education. *EDUCAUSE Review* 48 (5). http://www.educause.edu/ero/article/ exploring-students-mobile-learning-practices-higher-education.

Chen, B., Seilhamer, R., Bennett, L., and Bauer, S. 2015, June 22. Students' mobile learning practices in higher education: A multi-year study. *EDUCAUSE Review.* http://er.educause.edu/articles/2015/6/students-mobile-learning-practices-in-higher-education-a-multi-year-study.

College Board. 2015. 2015 College Board program results, expanding access, challenging students, equipping educators. https://www.collegeboard.org/program-results/2015/home.

College STAR (Supporting Transition, Access, and Retention). 2015. About College STAR. https://www.collegestar.org/about.

Connell, B. R., Jones, M., Mace, R., Mueller, J., Mullick, A., and Ostroff, E. 1997. The principles of universal design. North Carolina State University Center for Universal Design. http://www.ncsu.edu/ncsu/design/cud/about_ud/udprinciplestext.htm.

Cook, B., and Hartle, T. 2011. Why graduation rates matter—and why they don't. *The Presidency* (American Council on Education). http://www.acenet.edu/the-presidency/columns-and-features/Pages/Why-Graduation-Rates-Matter%E2%80%94and-Why-They-Don%E2%80%99t.aspx.

Cook, L., Rumrill, P. D., and Tankersley, M. 2009. Priorities and understanding of faculty members regarding college students with disabilities. *International Journal of Teaching and Learning in Higher Education* 21 (1): 84–96.

Cooper, A., and Reimann, R. 2003. *About Face 2.0: The Essentials of Interaction Design.* Hoboken, NJ: John Wiley and Sons.

Council for Exceptional Children. 2011. New guidelines for universal design for learning provide a roadmap for educators and educational publishers. https://web.archive.org/web/20120116035812/http://www.cec.sped.org/AM/Template.cfm?Section=Home&CAT=none&CONTENTID=10573&TEMPLATE=/CM/ContentDisplay.cfm.

Council of Ontario Universities (COU). 2017. Accessibility. http://cou.on.ca/key-issues/education/accessibility.

Credé, M., and Kuncel, N. R. 2008. Study habits, skills, and attitudes: The third pillar supporting collegiate academic performance. *Perspectives on Psychological Science* 3 (6): 425–53.

Culatta, R. 2016, August 10. Technology as a tool to reimagine learning. Keynote address. Distance Teaching and Learning conference. Madison: University of Wisconsin-Madison. https://dtlconference.wisc.edu/2016/featured-speakers/technology-as-a-tool-to-reimagine-learning.

D2L. 2017. Committed to accessibility in education. https://www.d2l.com/accessibility.

Danielsen, C. 2010. National Federation of the Blind files complaint against Penn State. National Federation of the Blind. https://nfb.org/node/1026.

Danielsen, C. 2015. National Federation of the Blind and two blind students resolve complaint against Atlantic Cape Community College. National Federation of the Blind. https://nfb.org/national-federation-blind-and-two-blind-students-resolve-complaint-against-atlantic-cape-community.

Davies, P. L., Schelly, C. L., and Spooner, C. L. 2012. Measuring the effectiveness of Universal Design for Learning intervention in postsecondary education. *Journal of Postsecondary Education and Disability* 26 (3): 195–220. http://files.eric.ed.gov/fulltext/EJ1026883.pdf.

Diamond, R. M. 1998. *Designing and Assessing Courses and Curricula: A Practical Guide.* Jossey-Bass Higher and Adult Education Series. San Francisco: Jossey-Bass.

Drouin, M., Kaiser, D. H., and Miller, D. A. 2013. Phantom vibrations among undergraduates: Prevalence and associated psychological characteristics. *Computers in Human Behavior* 28 (4): 1490–96.

Dukes, L. 2014. Closed-captioning matters: An examination of the use of captioning for all students. Paper presented at the Postsecondary Training Institute conference, Philadelphia.

EDUCAUSE IT Accessibility Constituent Group. 2015. IT accessibility risk statements and evidence. https://library.educause.edu/~/media/files/library/2015/7/accessrisk15-pdf.pdf.

Edyburn, D. L. 2010. Would you recognize Universal Design for Learning if you saw it? Ten propositions for new directions for the second decade of UDL. *Learning Disabilities Quarterly* 33 (1): 33–41.

Fang, B. 2009, December 22. From distraction to engagement: Wireless devices in the classroom. *EDUCAUSE Review.* http://er.educause.edu/articles/2009/12/from-distraction-to-engagement-wireless-devices-in-the-classroom.

Fang, B. 2014, October 13. Creating a fluid learning environment. *EDUCAUSE Review.* http://er.educause.edu/articles/2014/10/creating-a-fluid-learning-environment.

Fichten, C. S. 1986. Self, other, and situation-referent automatic thoughts: Interaction between people who have a physical disability and those who do not. *Cognitive Therapy and Research* 10 (5): 571–87.

Fink, D. L. 2003. *Creating Significant Learning Experiences: An Integrated Approach to Designing College Courses.* San Francisco: Jossey-Bass.

Flaherty, C. 2017, September 15. A hill to retire on? *Inside Higher Ed.* https://www.insidehighered.com/news/2017/09/15/atmospheric-scientist-illinois-leave-after-refusing-provide-lecture-slides-student.

Flanders, V. 2015. *Web Pages that Suck.* http://www.webpagesthatsuck.com/.

Florida Orange Growers Association. 1979. Orange juice: It isn't just for breakfast anymore. Television commercial. YouTube. https://youtu.be/7lhFNAYfxNg.

Fonosch, G., and Schwab, L. O. 1981. Attitudes of selected university faculty members toward disabled students. *Journal of College Student Personnel* 22 (3): 229–35.

Freedom Scientific. 2015. Products and services: WYNN Literacy Software Solution. http://lsg.freedomscientific.com/products/wynn.asp.

Frijda, N. H. 1986. *The Emotions.* Studies in Emotion and Social Interaction series. Cambridge: Cambridge University Press.

Froehle, C. 2016, April 14. The evolution of an accidental meme: How one little graphic became shared and adapted by millions. *Medium* blog. https://medium.com/@CRA1G/the-evolution-of-an-accidental-meme-ddc4e139e0e4.

Fronteer, Ltd. 2016. Ally: Making course content accessible. http://ally.ac.

Galitz, W. O. 2007. *The Essential Guide to User Interface Design: An Introduction to GUI Design Principles and Techniques.* Hoboken, NJ: John Wiley and Sons.

Gardner, H., and Davis, K. 2013. *The App Generation: How Today's Youth Navigate Identity, Intimacy, and Imagination in a Digital World.* New Haven, CT: Yale University Press.

Gawande, A. 2017, January 23. Tell me where it hurts. *New Yorker* 92 (46): 36–45.

Gaylord, V., Johnson, D. R., Lehr, C. A., Bremer, C. D., and Hasazi, S., eds. 2004. *Impact: Feature Issue on Achieving Secondary Education and Transition Results for Students with Disabilities* 16 (3). Minneapolis: University of Minnesota, Institute on Community Integration. http://ici.umn.edu/products/impact/163.

Godfrey, K. E., and Matos-Elefante, H. 2010. Key indicators of college success: Predicting college enrollment, persistence, and graduation. American Educational Research Association (AERA) Annual Conference, Denver. https://research.collegeboard.org/publications/content/2012/05/key-indicators-college-success-predicting-college-enrollment.

Gorman, S. E., and Gorman, J. M. 2017. *Denying to the Grave: Why We Ignore the Facts that Will Save Us*. New York: Oxford University Press.

Government of Canada. 1977. Canadian Human Rights Act. RSC 1985 c. H-6. http://laws-lois.justice.gc.ca/eng/acts/h-6.

Government of Canada. 2016. Consulting with Canadians on accessibility legislation. https://www.canada.ca/en/employment-social-development/programs/disability/consultations/accessibility-legislation.html.

Government of Canada. 2017, May 17. Accessible Canada—Creating new federal accessibility legislation: What we learned from Canadians. https://www.canada.ca/en/employment-social-development/programs/planned-accessibility-legislation/reports/consultations-what-we-learned.html.

Hake, R. R. 1998. Interactive-engagement versus traditional methods: A six-thousand-student survey of mechanics test data for introductory physics courses. *American Journal of Physics* 66 (1): 64.

Harper, S. R., and Quaye, S. J. 2007. Shifting the onus from racial/ethnic minority students to faculty: Accountability for culturally inclusive pedagogy and curricula. *Liberal Education* 92 (3): 19–24.

Harrison, E. 2006. Working with faculty members toward universally designed instruction: The process of dynamic course design. *Journal of Postsecondary Education and Disability* 19 (2): 152–62. Special Issue: Universal Design for Learning in Higher Education.

Harrison, E. 2016, March 11. Telephone interview with Thomas J. Tobin.

Harrison, E. 2017, April 23. E-mail message to Thomas J. Tobin.

Heller, N. 2016, May 30. The big uneasy: What's roiling the liberal-arts campus? *New Yorker*, 48–57. http://www.newyorker.com/magazine/2016/05/30/the-new-activism-of-liberal-arts-colleges.

Henderson, C., Beach, A., and Finkelstein, N. D. 2012. Four categories of change strategies for transforming undergraduate instruction. In

Transitions and Transformations in Learning and Education, ed. P. Tynjälä, M.-L. Stenström, and M. Saarnivaara. Dordrecht: Springer Netherlands. http://homepages.wmich.edu/~chenders/Publications/ HendersonTransitions2011.pdf.

Higher Education Opportunity Act. Public Law 110-315. 2008. https:// www.gpo.gov/fdsys/pkg/PLAW-110publ315/html/PLAW-110publ315. htm.

Houck, C. K., Asselin, S. B., Troutman, G. C., and Arrington, J. M. 1992. Students with learning disabilities in the university environment: A study of faculty members and student perceptions. *Journal of Learning Disabilities* 25 (10): 678–84.

Institute for Human Centered Design. 2016. History of Universal Design. http://www.humancentereddesign.org/universal-design/ history-universal-design.

International Center for Disability Resources on the Internet. 2000. North Carolina State University OCR letter. http://www.icdri.org/legal/north_ carolina_state_university_letter.htm.

Isai, V. 2017, August 23. Liberal minister Carla Qualtrough wants to make history with federal accessibility laws. *Toronto Star*. https://www. thestar.com/news/gta/2017/08/23/qualtrough-wants-to-make-histo- ry-with-federal-accessibility-laws.html.

Jackson, B. W. 2005. The theory and practice of multicultural organiza- tional development in education. In *Teaching Inclusively, Resources for Course, Department, and Institutional Change in Higher Education*, ed. M. Ouellett. Stillwater, OK: New Forums Press. http://sait.uoregon.edu/ Portals/0/MCOD/Theory and Practice of Multicultural Organizational Development in Education.pdf.

Jorgensen, C. 2016, May 5. How to use UDL principles to boost accessibility and student engagement. http://blog.brookespublishing.com/guest- post-how-to-use-udl-principles-to-boost-accessibility-and-student-en- gagement.

Kahneman, D. 2011. *Thinking, Fast and Slow*. New York: Farrar, Straus and Giroux.

Kasnitz, D. 2013. The 2012 biennial AHEAD survey of disability service and resource professionals in higher education. AHEAD. Huntersville, NC.

Kauffmann, N. M. 2014. Universal Design for Learning: Penn State World Campus's approach to course design. *Penn State World Campus* blog. http://blog.worldcampus.psu.edu/2014/06/universal-design-for-learning-penn-state-world-campuss-approach-to-course-design.

Kelley, B., Jackson, A., Los, R., and Jerke, D. 2016. Developers' response to the redefined ADA: Leading from the middle. POD Network annual conference, Louisville, KY. https://podnetwork.org/content/uploads/2016-POD-Program-Final.pdf#page=40.

Kelley, B., Mosterd, E., and Jackson, A. 2016, December 2. Telephone interview with Thomas J. Tobin.

Kennesaw State University. 2016. Microsoft Office Word 2013 Accessibility. Kennesaw, GA: University Information Technology Services. https://apps.kennesaw.edu/files/pr_app_uni_cdoc/doc/Word_2013_Accessability_rev.pdf.

Koshland, C. 2017, March 1. Campus message on course capture video, podcast changes. *Berkeley News.* http://news.berkeley.edu/2017/03/01/course-capture.

Lang, J. 2017, September 27. A welcoming classroom. *Chronicle of Higher Education.* http://www.chronicle.com/article/A-Welcoming-Classroom/241294.

Lawson, D. 2016, November 11. Personal interview with Thomas J. Tobin.

Lessman, A. 2016a, January 13. Legal accessibility. Keynote speech, Alfred State Accessibility Conference. Alfred State University, Alfred, NY. http://mathcs.duq.edu/~tobin/cv/20160113.Alfred.State.Program.pdf.

Lessman, A. 2016b, February 2. Telephone interview with Thomas J. Tobin.

Lewin, T. 2015, February 12. Harvard and MIT are sued over lack of closed captions. *New York Times.* http://www.nytimes.com/2015/02/13/education/harvard-and-mit-sued-over-failing-to-caption-online-courses.html.

Li, D. 2017, August 17. Here's what Chinese takeout menus can teach us about immigration. *Medium* blog. https://medium.com/aj-news/heres-what-chinese-takeout-menus-can-teach-us-about-immigration-4b41fcf5c0f7.

Linder, K., Fountaine-Rainen, D., and Behling, K. 2015. Whose job is it?

Key challenges and future directions for online accessibility in U.S. institutions of higher education. *Open Learning* 30 (1): 21–34.

Lombardi, A. R., and Murray, C. 2011. Measuring university faculty attitudes toward disability: Willingness to accommodate and adopt Universal Design for Learning principles. *Journal of Vocational Rehabilitation* 34 (1): 43–56.

Lombardi, A. R., Murray, C., and Gerdes, H. 2011. College faculty members and inclusive instruction: Self-reported attitudes and actions pertaining to Universal Design for Learning. *Journal of Diversity in Higher Education* 4 (4): 250–61.

Losh, E. 2014, June 14. Education's war on Millennials: Why everyone is failing the "digital generation." *Salon*. http://www.salon.com/2014/06/14/educations_war_on_millennials_why_everyone_is_failing_the_digital_generation/.

Maier, M. 2016. Rotating note taker. *College Teaching* 64 (3): 146.

Mason, K. C. August 25, 2014. Colleges adjust to new reality that more students juggle work, family. *PBS NewsHour*. http://www.pbs.org/newshour/updates/colleges-adjust-to-new-reality-that-students-juggle-work-family-more.

Menand, L. 2010. *The Marketplace of Ideas: Reform and Resistance in the American University*. New York: Norton.

Metz, J. B. 2016. Accessibility is a process, not a project. *Jon Metz* blog. https://medium.com/@jonbmetz/accessibility-is-a-process-not-a-project-ce1c1cdc3aa7.

Meyer, A., Rose, D., and Gordon, D. 2014. *Universal Design for Learning: Theory and Practice*. Wakefield, MA: CAST.

Michigan State University. 2015. MSU web accessibility policy. http://webaccess.msu.edu/Policy_and_Guidelines/web-accessibility-policy.html.

Michigan State University. 2017. Accessible Learning Conference. College of Arts and Letters. http://www.accessiblelearning.org.

Miller, M. D. 2014. *Minds Online: Teaching Effectively with Technology*. Cambridge, MA: Harvard University Press.

Mulgrew, A. D. 2017, November 20. Telephone interview with K. Behling.

Murray, C., Lombardi, A., and Wren, C. 2011. The effects of

disability-focused training on the attitudes and perceptions of university staff. *Remedial and Special Education* 32 (4): 290–300.

Murray, C., Lombardi, A., Wren, C. T., and Keys, C. 2009. Associations between prior disability-focused training and disability-related attitudes and perceptions among university faculty. *Learning Disability Quarterly* 32 (2): 87–100.

National Center for Education Statistics (NCES). 2015. Retention of first-time degree-seeking undergraduates at degree-granting postsecondary institutions, by attendance status, level and control of institution, and percentage of applications accepted: Selected years, 2006 to 2014. Digest of Education Statistics. https://nces.ed.gov/programs/digest/d15/tables/dt15_326.30.asp.

National Center on Universal Design for Learning. 2014. About UDL: What is UDL? Wakefield, MA: CAST. http://www.UDL center.org/aboutUDL /whatisUDL.

Nelson, J., Dodd, J., and Smith, D. 1990. Faculty willingness to accommodate students with learning disabilities. *Journal of Learning Disabilities* 23 (3): 185–89.

Nielsen, J. 1995. 10 usability heuristics for user interface design. https://www.nngroup.com/articles/ten-usability-heuristics.

Office for Students with Disabilities. 2016. *UDL@McGill*. Montreal: McGill University. https://www.mcgill.ca/osd/facultyinfo/universal-design.

Ofiesh, N., Rojas, C., and Ward, R. 2006. Universal Design for Learning and the assessment of student learning in higher education. *Journal of Postsecondary Education and Disability* 19 (2): 173–81.

Ostrowski, C. P., Lock, J., Hill, S. L., da Rosa dos Santos, L., Altowairiki, N. F., and Johnson, C. 2017. A journey through the development of online environments: Putting UDL theory into practice. *Handbook of Research on Innovative Pedagogies and Technologies for Online Learning in Higher Education*, 218–35. Advances in Higher Education and Professional Development (AHEPD) series. Hershey, PA: IGI Global.

Ouellett, M., Longstreet, C. S., and Kacin, S. 2016. Centers as integral partners in building and sustaining accessible campuses. Louisville,

KY: POD Network annual conference. http://podnetwork.org/content/uploads/2016-POD-Program-Draft-21Oct2016.pdf#57.

Palfrey, J., and Gasser, U. 2008. *Born Digital: Understanding the First Generation of Digital Natives*. New York: Basic Books.

Palmer, J. S. 2015. "The Millennials are coming!": Improving self-efficacy in law students through Universal Design for Learning. *Cleveland State Law Review* 63 (3): 675–706.

Patel, S. 2016, May 16. 85 percent of Facebook video is watched without sound. *Digiday*. https://digiday.com/media/silent-world-facebook-video.

PDF Association. 2012. PDF/UA: The ISO standard for universal accessibility. https://www.pdfa.org/pdfua-the-iso-standard-for-universal-accessibility.

Rapp, W. H., and Arndt, K. 2012. *Teaching Everyone: An Introduction to Inclusive Education*. Baltimore: Brookes Publishing.

Reavis, G., and Sitton, R. 2017, April 14. *15 Years after an OCR Suit: NC State's Accessibility Refresh*. Webinar. 3Play Media. https://www.3playmedia.com/resources/recorded-webinars/15-years-after-an-ocr-suit-nc-states-accessibility-refresh.

Rehabilitation Act of 1973, Section 508. Electronic and information technology. 29 U.S. Code 16 §794d. Government Publishing Office. https://www.gpo.gov/fdsys/pkg/USCODE-2011-title29/html/USCODE-2011-title29-chap16-subchapV-sec794d.htm.

Rehabilitation Act of 1973, Section 504. Nondiscrimination under federal grants and programs. 29 U.S. Code §794. Legal Information Institute. https://www.law.cornell.edu/uscode/text/29/794.

Reitman, I., dir. 1984. *Ghostbusters*. Film. Columbia Pictures. http://www.imdb.com/title/tt0087332/quotes.

Roberts, K. D., Park, H. J., Brown, S., and Cook, B. 2011. Universal Design for Instruction in postsecondary education: A systematic review of empirically based articles. *Journal of Postsecondary Education and Disability* 24 (1): 5–15.

Rose, D. H., Meyer, A., Strangman, N., and Rappolt, G. 2002. *Teaching Every Student in the Digital Age: Universal Design for Learning*.

Alexandria, VA: Association for Supervision and Curriculum Development.

Sabino v. Ohio State University. 2010. Consent decree 2:09-cv-544. U.S. District Court, Southern District of Ohio, Eastern Division, Columbus. http://ia600300.us.archive.org/5/items/gov.uscourts.ohsd.131247/gov.uscourts.ohsd.131247.26.0.pdf.

Schneider, W. J. 2014. Misunderstanding regression to the mean. YouTube. https://youtu.be/aLv5cerjV0c?t=34m0s.

Schwab, C. 2015, October 9. The innovator of Universal Design, Mr. Ron Mace explained differences between Universal Design and barrier free in 1989. *Universal Design Home and Accessible Design* blog. http://www.accessiblehealthhome.com/2015/10/09/the-father-of-universal-design-mr-ron-mace-explained-differences-between-universal-design-and-barrier-free-in-1989.

Sensus ApS. 2017. SensusAccess: Alternate media made easy. http://www.sensusaccess.com.

Singleton, K. S. 2014. Improving faculty adoption of Universal Design for Learning for instruction in the higher education classroom. White paper. George Mason University. http://eportfolio.kjsingle.com/wp-content/uploads/2014/08/EDIT-803-DBR-Plan__Singleton_Spr14_Final.pdf.

Smith, A. 2015. U.S. smartphone use in 2015. Pew Research Center. http://www.pewinternet.org/2015/04/01/us-smartphone-use-in-2015.

Sonka, K. 2017, February 21. Telephone interview with Thomas J. Tobin.

Sousa, T. 2015, September 9. Student retention is more important than ever. *Higher Ed Live* blog. http://higheredlive.com/3-reasons-student-retention-is-more-important-than-ever.

Spector, A. 2016, December 6. Telephone interview with Kirsten T. Behling.

StatCounter Global Stats. 2017. Desktop vs. mobile vs. tablet market share worldwide: Mar. 2009 to Mar. 2017. http://gs.statcounter.com/platform-market-share/desktop-mobile-tablet#monthly-200903-201703.

Straumsheim, C. 2017a, March 6. Berkeley will delete online content. *Inside Higher Ed.* https://www.insidehighered.com/news/2017/03/06/u-california-berkeley-delete-publicly-available-educational-content.

Straumsheim, C. 2017b, March 14. "No plans" to delete free content. *Inside Higher Ed.* https://www.insidehighered.com/news/2017/03/14/after-uc-berkeley-announcement-universities-say-they-will-continue-offer-free.

Su, J., Truong, M., Detivaux, G., Zell, D., Bansavich, J., and Yates, N. 2016, May 13. Leveraging mobile devices to further teaching and learning. Webinar panel discussion. POD Network Teaching with Technology Special Interest Group. https://sigtwt.wordpress.com/2016/05/13/172/.

Teach Access. 2017. *Teach Access.* http://teachaccess.org.

Tobin, T. J. 2014. Increase online student retention with Universal Design for Learning. *Quarterly Review of Distance Education* 15 (3): 13–24. http://www.engl.duq.edu/servus/cv/QRDE.UDL.Article.pdf.

Trammell, J., and Hathaway, M. 2007. Help-seeking patterns in college students with disabilities. *Journal of Postsecondary Education and Disability* 20 (1): 4–15.

United States Access Board. 2016. Architectural Barriers Act (ABA) of 1968. https://www.access-board.gov/the-board/laws/architectural-barriers-act-aba.

United States Access Board. 2017a. About the ICT Refresh. https://www.access-board.gov/guidelines-and-standards/communications-and-it/about-the-ict-refresh.

United States Access Board. 2017b. Final Rule: Information and Communication Technology (ICT) final standards and guidelines. https://www.access-board.gov/guidelines-and-standards/communications-and-it/about-the-ict-refresh/final-rule.

United States Department of Education. 2004. *IDEA—Reauthorized Statute.* Pub. L. No. 108-446, 118 Stat. 2647. National Instructional Materials Accessibility Standard (NIMAS). https://www2.ed.gov/policy/speced/guid/idea/tb-accessibility.doc.

United States Department of Education. 2015, September. Demographic and enrollment characteristics of nontraditional undergraduates: 2011–12. https://nces.ed.gov/pubs2015/2015025.pdf.

United States Department of Justice, Civil Rights Division. 2010. ADA standards for accessible design. https://www.ada.gov/2010ADAstandards_index.htm.

United States Department of Justice, Civil Rights Division. 2016.

Information and technical assistance on the Americans with Disabilities Act. http://www.ada.gov.

United States Department of Labor. 2015. Employment and Training Administration (ETA). WIOA overview. https://www.doleta.gov/wioa/overview.cfm.

United States Department of Labor. 2016. Employment and Training Administration (ETA). Trade Adjustment Assistance Community College and Career Training (TAACCCT) grant program summary. https://doleta.gov/taaccct.

University of Massachusetts System Board of Trustees. 2006, February 14. Minutes of the meeting of the committee as a whole. https://www.umassp.edu/sites/umassp.edu/files/content/board-meetings/2006/COTW-Minutes-02-14-06.pdf.

User Experience Professionals' Association. 2005. Usability body of knowledge: Principles for usable design. http://www.usabilitybok.org/principles-for-usable-design.

Vanderbilt, T. 2016. *You May Also Like: Taste in an Age of Endless Choice.* New York: Knopf.

Venable, M. 2011, September 16. The 7 C's of effective communication in your online course. http://www.onlinecollege.org/. Retrieved July 15, 2017 (article has been removed from site as of October 12, 2017).

Vogler, C., Anderson, R. M., Burke, T., Boudreault, P., Center, C., Chen, M. Y., Chua, M., Clegg, G., Cohen, L., Constable, M., Cureton, A., Gotanda, P. K., Iles, A., Kerschbaum, S. L., Kushalnagar, R., Langan, C., Mayerson, A., Nakamura, N., Nowak, S., Rosenbaum, S. A., Salzinger, L., Schweik, S., Sherwood, K., Smith, C., Waldo, J. F., Wymore, L., American Council of the Blind (Bridges, E.), Association of Late-Deafened Adults (Roberts, S.), Communication Service for the Deaf (Bahar, D.), Faculty Coalition for Disability Rights at the University of California, Berkeley (Kleege, G.), Hearing Loss Association of America (Kelley, B.), Telecommunications for the Deaf and Hard of Hearing, Inc. (Stout, C.). 2017, April 18. Access denied. *Views* blog. *Inside Higher Ed.* https://www.insidehighered.com/views/2017/04/18/scholars-and-others-strongly-object-berkeleys-response-justice-department.

Voorhees, P. 2015, October 14. Accessibility audit and review process. East Tennessee State University. YouTube. https://youtu.be/G59R6v18wpM.

W3C Web Accessibility Initiative. 2013. Web Content Accessibility Guidelines (WCAG) overview. https://www.w3.0rg/WAI/intro/wcag.

Wakefield, J. 2008. Learning by (universal) design: $1 million grant aids accessible learning program at UVM. University of Vermont. http://www.uvm.edu/~cdci/universaldesign/udlpdf/learning.pdf.

Wang, M., and Shen, R. 2011. Message design for mobile learning: Learning theories, human cognition and design principles. *British Journal of Educational Technology* 43 (4): 561–75.

Watson, L. 2005, November. What is a screen reader? *NoMENSA* blog. http://www.nomensa.com/blog/2005/what-is-a-screen-reader.

Wilson, M. 2004. Teaching, learning, and millennial students. *New Directions for Student Services* 2004 (26): 59–71.

Wine, J., Janson, N., Wheeless, S., and Hunt-White, T. 2011. 2004/09 beginning postsecondary students longitudinal study: Full-scale methodology report. U.S. Department of Education, Institute of Education Sciences. http://nces.ed.gov/pubs2012/2012246_1.pdf.

World Health Organization (WHO). 2007. *International Classification of Functioning, Disability, and Health (ICF)*. Geneva, Switzerland: WHO Press.

Yager, S. 2015. Small victories: Faculty development and Universal Design for Learning. In *Universal Design in Higher Education: From Principles to Practice*, 2nd ed., ed. S. E. Burgstahler, 307–14. Cambridge, MA: Harvard Education Press.

Young, J. R. 2017, March 21. Why students living on campus take online courses. *EdSurge*. https://www.edsurge.com/news/2017-03-21-why-students-living-on-campus-take-online-courses.

Zhang, D., Landmark, L., Reber, A., Hsu, H., Kwok, O., and Benz, M. 2010. University faculty knowledge, beliefs, and practices in providing reasonable accommodations to students with disabilities. *Remedial and Special Education* 31 (4): 276–86.

Zou, J. J. 2011. Blind Florida State U. students sue over e-learning systems. *Chronicle of Higher Education. Wired Campus*. http://www.chronicle.com/blogs/wiredcampus/blind-florida-state-u-students-sue-over-e-learning-systems/32028.

INDEX

ABA, 2, 21, 301
ability, 1, 7, 10, 23, 24, 30, 53, 81, 87, 95, 96, 131, 160, 162, 163, 175, 176, 179, 186–88, 197, 216, 225, 240, 262
ACCC, 60, 61, 292
access, 1–3, 8–10, 13, 20, 22–24, 27–30, 35, 42, 45, 48–50, 52, 53, 55–58, 63, 66, 67, 69, 76–78, 82, 87, 88, 90, 91, 94, 95, 103, 107, 108, 110, 112, 119, 124, 130, 131, 134, 137–39, 142, 143, 146–48, 159, 170, 171, 186, 198, 203, 204, 206, 212, 219, 220, 225, 227, 229, 236–39, 241, 244, 247, 249–58, 260, 261, 265, 267, 268, 271, 280, 281, 286, 289–91, 301, 302
   ease of, 160, 210, 256
accessibility, 1, 3, 9, 13, 14, 19–22, 28–30, 41, 44–50, 52–63, 66–69, 74, 78, 87, 94, 95, 98, 102, 103, 107, 108, 124, 126, 128, 129, 134, 137, 138, 141–44, 167, 195, 203–8, 210, 211, 213, 216, 217, 219–23, 226–31, 234–38, 240, 242–46, 251–60, 262–67, 270–73, 275, 276, 281, 283, 286–89, 291–303
   access-as-a-civil-right program, 10
   access-expanding techniques, 106–7
   accessibility-review process, 245
   provincial (Canada) law and requirements for, 34, 48, 49, 63, 102, 137 (*see also* laws)

accommodation, 1, 3–5, 12, 19, 23, 25, 32, 36, 37, 39, 44–46, 50–52, 54, 56, 57, 60–62, 64, 65, 74, 75, 95, 98–101, 104, 108, 125–27, 134, 136, 138, 139, 141–43, 145, 167, 170, 184–86, 202, 206, 207, 213, 219, 231, 239, 244, 250, 264, 275–77, 288, 297, 298, 303
   note-takers as, 61, 138, 139
   just-in-time, 39, 273
   written request for, 62
accountability, 146, 236, 294
accuracy, 68, 84, 85, 179, 194
Acevedo, Melba, 213, 216
Acey, Zakiya, 125
Adams, C. J., 6, 77, 79, 287
adaptation, 21, 78, 93, 99, 121, 186, 217, 293
ADHD (Attention Deficit Hyperactivity Disorder), 65, 142
administration, 2, 4, 8, 10–13, 19, 36, 39, 53, 63, 67, 69, 74, 82, 130, 143, 144, 147, 148, 150, 159–61, 172, 175, 197, 203–6, 210, 237, 259, 265, 266, 268, 270, 271, 279, 283, 289, 302
advocates, 14, 22, 31, 46, 88, 90, 148, 150, 203, 206, 255
Ahern, A. A., 139, 287
Alfred State University, 44, 296
Allen, I. E., 223, 224, 287
allies, 3, 172, 216, 220, 255, 263, 293
alternatives, 1, 9, 25, 43, 63, 92, 98, 107, 115, 117, 118, 120, 124, 125, 129, 132–34, 136, 177, 178, 216, 228, 229, 232–34, 254, 278–80, 283, 285

ALT-text, 56, 107, 233–35
Americans with Disabilities Act
   (ADA), 3, 51, 52, 63, 143, 195,
   288
ADA, 3, 22, 41, 44, 51, 52, 141,
   195, 203, 244, 245, 288, 296,
   301, 302
Anderson, R. M., 302
announcements, 61, 62, 113
anxiety, 79, 186, 221
AODA (Accessibility for
   Ontarians with Disabilities
   Act), 53
Architectural Barriers Act, 2, 21,
   301
architecture, 2, 21, 28, 29, 42, 50,
   89, 247, 301
Arndt, K., 7, 299
Arrington, J. M., 295
Asselin, S. B., 295
assessment, 20, 28, 29, 34, 35, 42,
   43, 48, 54, 58, 96, 114, 115, 117,
   135, 136, 140, 177–80, 182,
   183, 186–92, 194–201, 210, 217,
   222, 225, 226, 238, 240, 241,
   243, 277, 278, 290, 292, 298
assignment, 12, 15, 26, 43, 105,
   111, 113–18, 123, 125, 134–36,
   152, 154, 156, 164–66, 171,
   175, 177, 178, 180, 182–84, 186,
   189–93, 195, 196, 199–202,
   211, 213, 226, 240, 241, 250,
   251, 260, 284
assistance, 4, 22, 47, 49, 58, 81, 85,
   142, 212, 230, 242, 249, 302
assistive technology, 52, 79, 81,
   82, 98, 176, 252, 288
Association on Higher Education
   and Disability (AHEAD), 39,
   143
Atlantic Cape Community
   College, 60, 61, 292
at-risk students, 82

attention, 2, 6, 9, 21, 24, 36, 83,
   100, 106, 119, 121, 136, 167,
   171, 179, 203, 236, 237, 244,
   249, 255, 269, 286
audio, 21, 22, 26, 27, 40, 43, 58,
   61, 67, 73, 74, 95, 107, 112–15,
   117, 120, 123–25, 133, 135, 183,
   195, 196, 204, 216, 217, 222,
   229, 235, 241
audit, 13, 45, 59, 60, 245, 265,
   270–72, 302
augmentation, 81, 100, 251
awareness, 13, 22, 28, 52, 55, 99,
   130–32, 171, 176, 207, 222,
   236, 245, 252, 263, 264, 271,
   273

bachelor's degree, 176, 177
bandwidth, 38, 39, 79, 91, 112
barriers, 1, 2, 9, 21, 22, 24, 25, 31,
   34, 38, 46, 48, 50, 53–55, 59,
   62–65, 74, 81, 82, 95, 99–101,
   106, 107, 111, 121, 126, 130,
   131, 142, 145, 148, 160, 168,
   170, 176, 178, 182, 204, 206,
   207, 212, 220, 225–27, 230, 237,
   239, 249, 250, 254, 258, 266,
   270, 285–87, 300, 301
baseline, 91, 140
Basham, James, 47, 48, 288
behavior change, 206
Behling, Kirsten, 26, 31, 138, 149,
   170, 183, 220, 224, 227, 231,
   236, 237, 249, 260, 288, 296,
   297, 300, 313
Bellmore, Eileen, 141, 142, 151,
   170
Bento, R. F., 3, 104, 288
biases, 168–69
Bibeau, Lisa, 176–78, 199
Bigaj, S. J., 3, 104, 288
Bigatel, P., 59, 288
Blackboard, 171, 219, 220, 240

blind persons, 253, 287, 303
and forced reliance on sighted
persons, 58, 60
National Federation of the
Blind, advocating for, 45,
58–60, 227, 265, 287, 292
tactile graphics for, 60
See also disabilities
blogs, 303
Bluetooth, 81
Bongey, Sarah, 85, 86, 288
Braille, 204
broadband, 82
broadcasts, 62
budgets, 33, 66, 148, 153, 161,
170, 245, 251, 274, 279, 281
Burgstahler, Sheryl, 137, 145,
186, 289, 303
Burkholder, E., 77, 79, 287
buy-in, 149, 160, 208, 237, 242

Cameron, Jordan, 106–8, 289
Canada, 1, 14, 27, 32, 34, 48–51,
53–56, 63, 102, 137, 167, 287,
289, 294
Canvas, 59
capabilities, 52
captioning, 4, 30, 46, 62, 66–68,
73, 74, 95, 98, 100, 104, 107,
112, 118, 128, 130, 132–35,
137, 138, 142, 143, 171, 178,
196, 204, 229, 235, 241, 245,
254, 267, 280, 292, 296
as cultural shift, 39–41
in-house solutions for, 40–41,
68, 205
hybrid model for, 205
See also closed-captioning
Carlson, L. L., 256, 265, 289
case studies, 165, 177, 237, 287
CAST. *See* Center for Applied
Special Technology
CBAM, 64, 65, 288

Center for Applied Special
Technology (CAST), 2, 5, 24,
25, 28, 29, 34, 42, 105, 129,
175, 179, 180, 187, 197, 211,
289, 290, 297, 298
champions, 36, 147, 205, 218, 273
chancellors, 2, 15, 66, 206
charts, 109, 229, 234, 235
checklists, 41, 116, 243
checkpoints, 48
Chen, B., 6, 84, 86, 87, 290, 302
choices, 12, 14, 25, 27, 35, 36,
42, 68, 77, 90–92, 97, 101,
105, 108, 113, 116–20, 123,
125, 135–37, 139, 178, 182,
183, 186, 187, 189–91, 193,
200, 220, 229, 250, 251, 253,
256–58, 272, 278, 280, 281
Cioffi, Andrew, 249, 250, 252
classrooms, 1, 6, 10, 25, 26, 29,
32, 38, 44, 58, 61, 84, 86, 90,
92, 94, 102, 104, 105, 110, 112,
114, 116, 148, 167–69, 195,
222, 223, 225, 226, 240, 241,
250, 251, 259, 263, 276, 286,
289, 292, 296, 300
closed-captioning, 22, 47, 179,
285, 292, 296
CMS, 272
coaches, 15, 108, 141, 284
cognition, 303
collaborations, 26, 31, 36, 41, 64,
91, 171, 192, 257, 266, 288
college star, 8, 9, 291
college students, 6, 32, 35, 75, 79,
83, 84, 86, 87, 125, 198, 224,
288, 291, 293, 301
committees, 30, 35, 162, 180,
205, 208, 216, 221, 254, 261,
265, 277, 302
communication, 5, 21–23, 45, 50,
53, 56, 59, 66, 76, 80, 88, 89,
121, 124, 135, 142, 216, 240,

communication (*continued*)
244–46, 254–56, 259, 270,
273, 274, 301, 302
community, 8, 20, 26, 37–39, 49,
60, 73, 75, 170, 199, 209, 210,
213, 246, 253, 254, 272, 273,
292, 293, 302
competence, 179
compliance, 10, 13, 41, 44,
46–48, 50, 56, 59, 63, 64, 66,
69, 119, 141, 143, 207, 210,
211, 246, 253, 261, 263, 265,
270–72, 277
computers, 24, 76, 78, 82, 93, 94,
171, 292
concepts, 24, 31, 33, 36, 37, 61,
64, 91, 92, 105, 111–13, 115,
117, 121, 124, 131, 132, 135,
140, 153, 179, 180, 204, 210,
229
Concerns-Based Adoption
Model (CBAM), 64, 65, 288
conferences, 19, 20, 31, 36, 39, 41,
42, 44, 126, 143, 151, 206, 211,
216, 219, 239, 244, 245, 248,
266, 273, 287, 289, 291, 292,
294, 296, 297, 299
connections, 82, 90, 130, 210,
226, 250
Connell, B. R., 23, 291
constraints, 96, 130–32, 183, 186,
190
construct relevance, 133, 179,
182, 189
consultants, 55, 56, 98, 126, 142,
144, 151–53, 156–58, 283, 294
content-management system,
272
coordinators, 20, 41, 170, 206
copyright, 114–17
counseling, 2, 15, 143, 278
course assessments, 182, 187, 195
course components, 236

course concepts, 113, 121, 210,
229
course content, 8, 100, 116, 134,
196, 210, 226, 293
course delivery, 221
course design, 5, 28, 37, 119, 218,
221, 223, 245, 246, 271, 276,
294, 296
course designers, 34, 47, 99, 126,
131, 187, 191, 194, 196, 225
course designs, 28, 99
course development, 48, 242
course environments, 44, 103,
110
course goals, 188, 196, 240
course interactions, 32, 46, 90,
99, 103, 110, 111, 117, 118, 188,
196, 225, 231, 247
course materials, 39, 60, 85, 112,
129, 132, 133, 170, 177, 183,
213, 221, 222, 225, 231, 236,
237, 243
course objectives, 189, 191, 199,
200
course projects, 86, 115, 117, 189,
254
courts, 102, 220
creativity, 11, 149, 196, 197
Culatta, Rich, 103, 116, 291
cultural appropriation, 198
cultural diversity, 256
cultural norms, 207
cultural practices, 12, 78
curricula, 8, 12, 24, 28, 29, 34,
41, 48, 54, 95, 148, 154, 203,
206–9, 212, 217–20, 242, 247,
272, 286, 289, 292, 294, 300

Danielsen, C., 58, 59, 61, 292
Davies, P. L., 84, 292
Davis, K., 75, 76, 79, 293
DCMP, 107
deaf persons, 142–43, 302

National Association of the
Deaf, advocating for, 46, 137
See also disabilities
deans, 2, 8, 15, 69, 131, 163, 167,
176, 206, 251, 262–64
decisions, 27, 61, 67, 77, 102, 107,
193, 209, 237, 239, 288
deliverables, 211
demographics, 24, 38, 39, 154,
156, 157, 160, 254, 301
demonstration, 35, 89, 118, 135,
138, 182, 188, 193, 194, 199,
202, 207, 211, 217, 218, 220,
228, 259, 261, 272
Denoyelles, A., 84, 87, 290
department chairs, 2, 15, 40, 69,
131, 144, 167, 238, 239, 261
dependence, 76, 79
Described and Captioned Media
Program (DCMP), 107
Desire2Learn, 267
developers, 14, 31, 33, 35, 75, 107,
111, 126, 197, 220, 236, 237,
244, 296
diagnosis, of disability, 32, 65,
168
differentiated instruction, 25
digital divide, 82, 84
digital generation, 75, 78, 79, 94,
96, 297
digital learners, 15, 98, 284, 287
digital natives, 75, 78, 83, 85, 86,
95, 288, 299
directions for assignments, 114,
116, 123–25, 190, 213, 258
directors, 39, 40, 44, 69, 141,
170, 206, 213, 219–21, 245,
247, 249, 251, 256, 259, 260,
264–67, 279
disabilities, 1–7, 9–15, 19, 20, 22,
23, 25, 27–32, 36, 39–44, 46,
49–54, 57–65, 67, 68, 74, 75,
80, 81, 89, 90, 95, 96, 98, 100,

101, 103, 104, 113, 126, 130,
132, 134, 138, 141–45, 147,
151, 160, 167–71, 175–77, 183,
184, 186, 195, 198, 199, 203,
204, 208, 210, 216, 219, 220,
222, 225–29, 231, 236, 238,
239, 242, 244, 249–54, 257,
260, 264–67, 270, 272, 276,
285, 287, 288, 290–95, 297–99,
301–3
Disabilities, Opportunities,
Internetworking, and
Technology (DO-IT) Center,
29, 186, 187, 289
discrimination, 45, 49–51, 57,
61, 250
discussions, 26, 109, 110, 118,
121, 175, 180, 240, 245, 272
dissonance, 121
distance education, 44, 73, 245,
267, 287, 301
diversity, 1, 14, 24–26, 28, 30, 65,
155, 160, 169, 205, 207, 216,
223, 225, 241, 247, 256, 263,
273, 297
DO-IT Center. *See*
Disabilities, Opportunities,
Internetworking, and
Technology (DO-IT) Center
Dropbox, 195
Drouin, M., 93, 292
dyslexia, 254

e-books, 87, 204
ECAR, 84, 87, 289
edX, 46, 137
education, 1–3, 6–9, 13, 15,
19–21, 24–37, 39, 42, 44, 45,
49, 50, 52–56, 64–66, 68, 74,
80, 82–84, 91, 100, 103, 104,
106, 115, 117, 119, 126, 130,
141, 143, 145, 146, 159, 171,
178, 180, 186, 190, 193, 198,

education (*continued*)
203, 209, 211, 219, 220, 223–
25, 228, 229, 236, 244–47, 252,
253, 257, 261, 262, 264, 266,
267, 272, 284–301, 303
educators, 10, 14, 53, 77, 94, 153,
180, 247, 290, 291
EDUCAUSE, 6, 45, 84, 86, 90,
211, 289, 290, 292
EDUCAUSE Center for Analysis
and Research (ECAR), 84,
87, 289
Edyburn, Dave, 33, 133, 137, 292
e-learning, 8, 205, 219, 220, 271,
272, 303
elementary schools, 24–28, 34,
42, 229
e-mail, 33, 93, 109, 116, 135, 142,
212, 226, 243, 262, 265, 294
emotions, 3–6, 65, 74, 75, 82,
253, 257, 293
employment, 51, 53, 83, 302
engagement, 2, 8, 15, 20, 25–27,
29, 36, 42, 54, 78, 83–88, 91,
92, 94, 98, 99, 108, 110, 112,
113, 119, 121, 125, 126, 129,
131, 134–36, 138, 142, 145,
148, 151, 162, 169, 175–78,
183, 188, 189, 191–93, 197,
198, 210, 216–18, 220, 222,
223, 228, 230, 237, 241, 242,
255, 256, 259, 266, 267, 270,
272–74, 277, 278, 284, 292,
295
enrollments, 224, 225, 250, 253,
280, 287, 294, 301
e-portfolio, 300
equality, 22, 100, 101
equity, 100, 101
evaluation, 31, 83, 188, 193, 199,
201, 210, 216, 223, 252, 283
evangelists, 74, 90, 102, 126, 273,
279
Evernote, 94

evidence-based practices, 188,
271, 285
examinations, 32, 35, 43, 46, 100,
109, 110, 133, 136, 179, 180,
186–89, 193, 194, 198–200,
262, 280, 292
expectations, 54, 65, 157, 162,
186, 188, 189, 211, 241, 242,
290
experiments, 20, 80, 87, 92, 109,
123, 132, 192, 200, 261

Facebook, 95, 299
face-to-face courses, 100–101,
103, 114, 116, 120–21, 148,
176–77, 267
transition from, to online
courses, 217, 220–23, 230,
240–42
face-to-face environment, 89,
110, 121, 123
face-to-face interactions, 12, 88,
111, 230
face-to-face-services, 104, 212
facilitations, 26, 43, 64, 97, 128,
152, 153, 155, 157, 159, 207,
216, 226, 260
facilities, 21, 50–52, 250, 251
faculty attitudes, 297
faculty champions, 147
faculty consultations, 208
faculty developers, 14, 31, 33, 197
faculty development, 31–34, 36,
59, 102, 128, 145, 147, 151,
163, 169–71, 208, 210, 211,
222, 226, 230, 237, 240, 242,
247, 288, 303
faculty evaluation, 210
See also student evaluation of
teaching
Faculty Four. *See* Kennesaw
State University
faculty groups, 64
faculty interactions, 66, 206

faculty leaders, 69
faculty learning, 209, 210, 272
faculty meeting, 278
faculty meetings, 216
faculty members, 1, 3–5, 7–13,
   15, 19, 20, 28–42, 46, 47, 58,
   59, 63–65, 68, 74, 75, 79, 84,
   85, 98, 99, 101–4, 106–11, 123,
   127–31, 139, 141, 142, 145–50,
   152, 153, 158–72, 178, 180,
   186, 187, 190–200, 203–7,
   210–12, 216, 218, 221–31,
   236, 237, 239, 242, 247, 248,
   250, 251, 253, 265, 267, 268,
   271–79, 281, 288, 289, 291,
   293–95, 297
faculty orientation, 31, 210, 267
faculty resources, 66
faculty responsibilities, 167
faculty senate, 270, 281
faculty services, 15
faculty volunteers, 248
faculty workload, 210
Fang, Bailin, 90, 91, 93, 94, 292
features, 66, 107, 195, 227, 229,
   233, 249, 259, 293
federal agencies, 51
federal aid, 33
federal funds, 2, 22, 49, 52, 57
federal grants, 28, 49, 299
federal law, 49, 63
federal regulations, 44
feedback, 4, 20, 26, 31, 55, 105,
   110, 114, 116, 120, 128, 187,
   192, 195, 196, 201, 218, 220,
   242, 260
Fichten, C. S., 3, 292
final assessment, 186, 189–91,
   200, 280
final examinations, 32, 133, 136,
   186, 194, 262, 280
Finkelstein, N. D., 208, 294
504. *See* Section 504
508. *See* Section 508

Flaherty, C., 4, 293
Flanders, V., 99, 293
Flash (*software*), 235, 238
flexibility, 23, 29, 38, 54, 93, 101,
   105, 158, 161, 171, 187, 188,
   190, 191, 194, 196, 199, 204,
   222, 246, 256
flipped classrooms, 223
Fonosch, G., 3, 104, 293
fonts, 144, 182, 233, 234, 254
formats, 1, 43, 98, 103, 113,
   115, 117, 122, 125, 133, 135,
   136, 140, 162, 178, 182, 184,
   186, 187, 189–91, 193, 195,
   198, 201, 204, 211, 223, 229,
   232–35, 238, 254
Fountaine-Rainen, D., 227, 236,
   296
four-square model, 208–9, 218
frameworks, 2, 6, 19, 20, 23, 25,
   28–30, 33–35, 39, 42, 47, 49,
   54–56, 58, 61, 62, 64–66, 68,
   74, 85, 86, 94, 148, 162, 167,
   171, 182, 188, 197, 206, 212,
   225, 229, 241, 242, 246, 249,
   255, 257, 267, 275
Frijda, N. H., 3, 293
Froehle, C., 101, 293
Fronteer Software, 220
full-text alterative versions, 117
functions, 9, 50, 52, 74, 148, 169,
   204, 235, 239, 250, 252, 303
funding, 2, 8, 19, 22, 37, 39, 49,
   52, 57, 59, 61, 63, 137, 140, 152,
   153, 216, 219, 245, 246, 252,
   265, 283

gains, 2, 13, 30, 37, 74, 94, 108,
   154–57, 165, 171, 179
Galitz, W. O., 99, 293
games, 4, 21, 62, 186
gaps, 13, 58, 63, 94, 114, 116, 118,
   270, 271, 277
Gardner, Howard, 75, 76, 79, 293

Gasser, Urs, 75, 78, 83, 299
Gawande, Atul, 274, 275, 286, 293
Gaylord, V., 21, 293
Gerdes, H., 99, 297
Ghostbusters, 168, 299
ghosts, 168
goal-oriented courses, 129, 193
Godfrey, K. E., 118, 280, 294
Gordon, David, 8, 24, 297
governance, 277
governments, 47, 49–51, 53–56, 67, 69, 105, 175, 270, 294, 299
grades, 4, 7, 26, 31, 54, 113, 118, 122, 177–80, 182, 183, 187, 190, 192, 194, 196, 197, 238, 280, 288
graduation, 209, 291, 294
grants, 27–29, 49, 54, 146, 209, 299
Graphical User Interface (GUI), 293
graphics, 60, 135, 213, 216, 278, 293
graphs, 229, 233–35, 280
grievances, 60, 185
group behavior, 78
group brainstorming, 165, 166
group instruction, 105
group members, 248, 255
group study, 133
group work, 105, 186, 241
growth, 88, 216, 271
guidelines, 45, 56, 158, 196, 235, 245, 260, 290, 291, 297, 301, 303

Hamilton, K., 77, 80, 287
handouts, 43, 84, 106, 121, 122, 128, 195
Harrison, Beth, 182, 203–5, 216, 294
Harvard University, 46, 137, 139, 256, 289, 296, 297, 303

Heller, N., 126, 294
Henderson, C., 208, 294
heuristics, 298
Hidy, Lance, 213–16
homework, 86, 100, 154–58, 193, 237, 238
Houck, C. K., 3, 104, 295
hurdles, 38, 225
hybrid courses, 211, 221–23, 231
hyperlinks, 233, 235, 254

IEPs, 26
images, 56, 78, 85, 107, 233–35, 262, 287
impairments, 22, 81, 213, 251, 275
inaccessibility, 30, 58, 102, 110, 127, 144, 227, 228, 239, 253, 261, 266, 268
inclusion, 7, 10–14, 19, 22, 28–30, 33, 34, 36, 37, 39, 45, 47, 53, 55, 64–66, 69, 74, 102, 126, 160, 169, 171, 172, 203, 205, 206, 208, 212, 216, 226, 228, 246, 247, 251–53, 256, 258, 259, 265–67, 271, 272, 278, 286, 287, 294, 297, 299
Individualized Education Programs (IEPs), 26
inequalities, 63, 82
information and communication technology (ICT), 45, 50, 54, 56, 59, 244, 256–58, 262, 270, 301
in-house expertise, 28, 146, 151–52, 154, 248, 266
initiatives, 22, 31, 36, 42, 131, 145, 146, 150, 153, 158, 159, 161, 171, 204, 221, 222, 246–48, 250, 251, 261, 262, 265, 267, 268, 273, 303
innovation, 52, 103, 133, 298, 300
instruction, 8, 24, 25, 28–30, 54, 86, 105, 116, 152, 223, 225,

247, 261, 289, 290, 294, 297, 299, 300
instructional activities, 94
instructional design, 35, 133, 152, 204, 242, 247
instructional designers, 8, 65, 122, 129, 148, 228, 236, 240–42, 278
instructional materials, 60, 61, 228, 301
instructional methods, 24, 186, 187
instructional planning, 47, 288
instructional strategies, 33
instructional technologists, 87, 141, 148, 236, 237
instructional technology, 37, 38, 170, 213, 265
instructors, 13, 15, 25, 26, 29–31, 34, 36, 38, 42, 67, 85, 87, 96, 110–12, 114–17, 119, 121–25, 129, 131, 137, 141, 148, 171, 178, 180, 188–90, 192, 194–96, 199, 200, 204, 206, 222, 223, 226, 227, 231, 238, 240, 242, 254, 261, 271, 276, 278, 281
interactions, 1, 2, 8–10, 12–14, 20, 24, 25, 27, 29, 32–35, 42, 43, 46, 48–51, 55–58, 61, 63, 66, 68, 69, 74, 77, 83–94, 96, 97, 99, 100, 102–8, 110, 111, 113–21, 124–27, 129–35, 137, 139, 140, 148, 159–62, 169, 171, 188, 193, 196, 198, 200, 206, 210–12, 217, 220, 223, 225, 230, 231, 236, 240–43, 247, 249, 251–53, 255, 257, 259, 260, 262, 265, 267, 268, 271, 275, 277, 278, 280, 281, 283, 285, 291–93
Internet, 10, 22, 50, 56, 75, 76, 78, 79, 82, 89, 90, 226, 250, 295

interviews, 4, 13, 46, 64, 65, 69, 105, 120, 121, 125, 135, 245, 253, 254, 270, 288, 294, 296, 297, 300
invisible disabilities, 142, 168
iPads, 267
Isai, V., 56, 295
iterative process, 111, 134, 266, 274, 286
iTunes, 66, 235

Jackson, Angela, 207, 244, 245, 266, 267, 295, 296
Jerke, Darin, 244, 296
Johnston, Sam, 5
Journal of College Student Personnel, 293
Journal of Diversity in Higher Education, 297
Journal of Educational Technology, 303
Journal of Engineering Education, 287
Journal of Learning Disabilities, 295, 298
Journal of Postsecondary Education and Disability, 288, 292, 294, 298, 299, 301
Journal of Teaching and Learning, 291
Journal of Vocational Rehabilitation, 297

Kacin, Sara, 206, 298
Kahneman, Daniel, 168, 295
Kaiser, D. H., 93, 292
Kasnitz, D., 36, 295
Kauffmann, N. M., 59, 296
Kelley, Bruce, 244, 245, 266, 267, 296, 302
Kennesaw State University, 106–8, 296
knowledge, 2, 23, 27, 42, 54, 64, 79, 85, 90, 91, 95, 97, 109, 113,

knowledge (*continued*)
118, 131, 137, 140, 147, 151, 152, 155, 164, 167, 178–80, 183, 186–89, 192, 195–201, 203, 217, 218, 237, 273, 288, 302, 303
Koshland, C., 66, 67, 296

lab, 43, 60, 123, 124, 135, 138, 280
labels, 37, 65, 75, 78, 83, 225, 233, 241
Labouré College, 143, 144
Lang, James, 275, 276, 296
languages, 22–24, 55, 62, 78, 107, 138, 142, 175, 193, 206, 212, 225, 244, 258, 264
laptops, 78, 84, 87, 91, 106, 133, 194, 267
laws, 4, 9, 14, 15, 22, 27, 30, 33, 44–50, 52–57, 59, 63, 66, 68, 69, 88, 96, 119, 128, 130, 137, 138, 207, 239, 244, 253, 255, 257, 264, 265, 284, 287, 295, 299, 301
See also legislation
Lawson, Doug, 61, 296
lawsuits, 10, 36, 42, 46, 48, 56–58, 60, 61, 63, 206, 207, 211, 244, 249, 257, 262, 266, 277, 286, 289
leadership, 2, 8–11, 13, 15, 19, 20, 27, 37, 59, 67, 69, 82, 83, 104, 106, 130, 143, 144, 205–9, 212, 213, 219, 223, 242, 245, 249, 252, 255, 256, 259, 264–67, 270, 271, 274, 275, 279–81
learners, 1, 4–15, 24–27, 29–31, 33–35, 37, 41–43, 46–48, 56, 57, 65, 68, 69, 73–75, 78, 79, 82–86, 89–92, 94, 96, 98–101, 103, 104, 106–14, 116–26, 129–41, 144–46, 148, 150, 154, 160, 167, 169, 170, 176,

178–83, 186, 187, 189, 191–94, 196, 197, 200, 201, 204, 206, 207, 210–12, 217, 220, 223–26, 228–30, 237, 239, 242, 247–50, 252, 259, 266, 267, 270–72, 275, 276, 278, 280, 281, 284
learning, 1–3, 6–10, 19, 20, 22, 24–29, 33, 36, 37, 41, 43, 45, 47, 48, 54, 57–59, 61, 64, 65, 68, 69, 74–76, 79, 80, 83–87, 89–94, 96–99, 104–6, 108, 110, 112, 114, 118, 120, 121, 129, 133, 136, 138, 141–43, 151, 158, 159, 161, 170, 178, 180, 182, 183, 186, 188–90, 193–96, 200, 203–7, 209–11, 213, 216, 217, 219, 223, 224, 226, 227, 230–32, 236, 237, 240–42, 244, 259, 262, 271–73, 276, 278, 285–301, 303
hands-on approach to, 140, 175–76
learning management system (LMS), 8, 59, 84–86, 103, 110, 115, 117, 120–23, 132, 195, 197, 203, 216, 219–21, 226–28, 230, 232, 236, 240, 242, 265
lectures, 4, 24, 30, 43, 66, 74, 84, 90, 91, 93, 100, 103, 110, 114, 123–25, 128–30, 132, 133, 135, 140, 163, 175–77, 194, 218, 230, 240
legislation, 49, 53–55, 289, 294
See also laws
Lessman, Andrew, 44–48, 67, 296
Lewin, T., 102, 137, 296
liability, 63
librarians, 22, 46, 57–60, 75, 90, 117, 133, 148, 152, 171, 204, 216, 237, 245, 247, 257, 258, 289, 292
Linder, Kathryn, 31, 149, 224, 227, 236, 288, 296

Lombardi, A., 3, 7, 99, 104, 297, 298
Losh, Elizabeth, 78, 88, 95, 297

Mace, Ron, 21, 23, 25, 28, 290, 291, 300
Maier, M., 139, 297
managers, 8, 278
mapping, 25, 116, 192, 208, 249
Marquette University, 206
Mason, K. C., 6, 297
Massachusetts Institute of Technology (MIT), 46, 296
mastery, 91, 177, 181, 210
mathematics, 30, 136, 234, 235
Matos-Elefante, H., 118, 280, 294
McGill University, 55, 63–66, 298
McGuire, J. M., 104, 288
MCOD, 207, 295
measurements, 13, 34, 48, 56, 59, 66, 74, 113, 119, 122, 133, 179–82, 188, 189, 199, 200, 210, 259, 261, 268, 275, 279–81, 292, 297
media, 1, 2, 7, 8, 15, 46, 67, 77, 88, 100, 102, 105, 107, 113–18, 125, 131, 178, 195, 213, 216, 218, 231, 243, 254, 255, 278, 289, 292, 299, 300
Menand, Louis, 297
metadata, 107
Metz, Jon, 126, 297
Meyer, Anne, 8, 297, 299
Michigan State University (MSU), 19, 20, 297
millennials, 76, 88, 96, 297, 299, 303
Miller, D. A., 93, 292, 297
mind-set, 1, 6, 14, 15, 24, 35, 41, 47, 48, 75, 79, 80, 89, 101, 102, 119, 129, 130, 134, 136, 195, 198, 206, 207, 212, 230, 244,
255, 257, 264, 278, 281, 284, 285
mobile devices, 7, 56, 76, 77, 79, 80, 83, 84, 86–94, 96, 97, 108, 121, 132, 170, 226, 230, 250–52, 260, 270, 301
See also phones
mobile learners, 6, 9, 15, 73, 75, 78, 79, 84, 86, 93, 94, 101, 112, 150, 187, 284, 290, 303
Morrison, Jessica Dyzak, 143–45, 151, 170
Mosterd, Eric, 245, 246, 266, 267, 296
motivators, 22, 108, 113, 119, 125, 129, 131, 135–37, 178, 191, 198, 277
Mulgrew, Anne de Laire, 192, 297
Multicultural Organizational Development (MCOD), 207, 295
multimedia, 8, 19, 30, 40, 56, 85, 93, 125, 129, 180, 229, 231, 267, 283
multimodal learning, 96, 117, 118
Murray, C., 3, 7, 99, 104, 297, 298

narration, 84, 230, 235
narratives, 6, 39, 57, 58, 106, 133, 207, 211, 250, 252
National Federation of the Blind (NFB), 227, 265, 292
National Instructional Materials Accessibility Standard (NIMAS), 228, 229, 301
Neag School of Education, 186, 290
NECC, 213, 216
NEIU. *See* Northeastern Illinois University
Nelson, J., 3, 104, 298

networks, 20, 25, 47, 94, 129, 130, 134, 164, 206, 208, 210, 211, 271, 273, 288, 296, 299, 301
neuroscience, 2, 11, 24, 42, 92, 129, 198
Nielsen, J., 99, 298
nondiscrimination, 51, 207, 299
nontraditional learners, 37, 160, 224, 225, 246
Northeastern Illinois University, 61, 93, 197, 211, 216
Northern Essex Community College, 213, 216

Oberlin College, 125
objectives, 27, 34, 65, 108, 113, 117, 180–85, 188–91, 196, 199, 200, 202, 240, 243, 290
observations, 6, 38, 119, 184, 285
OCR. *See* Office of Civil Rights
ODA, 53, 287
Office of Accessibility Services, 275
Office of Civil Rights, 56–58, 219, 256, 270, 271, 295, 299
Office of Disability Resources, 132
Office of Diversity Services, 7, 58, 219–22, 231, 247, 249, 252
Office of Educational Technology, 103
Office of Learning Resources, 203–5
Office of Postsecondary Education (OPE), 27–29, 37, 190
Ofiesh, N., 136, 298
OLC, 211, 219, 223
online access, 82, 90, 257, 265–67
online content, 30, 62, 66, 106, 177, 187

online courses, 30, 45, 46, 73, 85, 100–1, 103, 114–17, 119–21, 211–13, 217, 249, 273
online environment, 148, 219–28, 230–32, 236–38, 240–43, 273, 286
online habits, 76, 78
Online Learning Consortium, 211, 219, 223
online tools/technology, 12, 64, 259, 262
Ontarians with Disabilities Act, 53, 287
OPE. *See* Office of Postsecondary Education
open access, 148
open-captioning, 95
operations, 13, 59, 73, 75, 87, 124, 150, 206, 248, 249, 259, 260, 283
options, 24, 37, 82, 96, 105, 106, 112, 113, 130, 136, 178, 183, 184, 188–91, 195, 197, 205, 211, 238, 251
Oregon State University, 240, 242
organizations, 10, 51, 55, 68, 74, 179, 206, 207, 226, 255, 286, 295, 303
orientations, 29, 31, 210, 232, 264, 267
Ostrowski, C. P., 55, 298
Ouellett, Mathew, 206–8, 295, 298
outcomes, 34, 43, 47, 48, 61, 90, 109, 161, 163, 170, 180, 196, 199, 206, 208, 212, 222, 239
ownership, 76, 83, 84, 86, 196, 268, 272, 273

Palfrey, John, 75, 78, 83, 299
Palmer, Jason, 88, 89, 96, 299
Parliament (Canada), 53, 55

participants, 12, 78, 102, 126, 138, 147, 151, 161, 163, 167, 169, 170, 178, 184, 211, 217, 241, 248

Patel, S., 95, 299

paths, 14, 108, 113, 114, 116–22, 137, 172, 203, 206, 213, 223

patterns, 77, 80, 99, 119, 120, 189, 240, 250, 286, 301

PBS (Public Broadcasting Service), 142, 297

PDF (Portable Document Format), 73, 103, 115, 117, 121, 204, 219, 230, 234–36, 244, 287, 290, 295, 296, 299–301, 303

pedagogy, 64, 87, 88, 209, 218, 294, 298

peers, 24, 97, 142, 188, 192, 196, 201, 209, 238, 249

pen-casts, 112, 122

Pennsylvania State University, 45, 58, 59, 234, 265, 287, 288, 292, 296

personnel, 60, 147, 293

Pettyjohn, Heidi, 13, 270–73, 288

Pew Research Center, 82, 83, 300

phones, 10, 22, 33, 43, 56, 267
  mobile, 68, 75–83, 91, 95, 97, 193–95, 241
  smartphones, 6, 75, 76, 79, 82–87, 93–95, 104, 110, 169, 300
  See also mobile devices

Photoshop, 213

Picard, Jean Luc (*fictional character*), 273

pilot program, 37, 61, 147, 149, 279, 280, 283

pinch points, 109–11, 113, 118, 119, 134, 136, 140, 277

plus-one approach, 11, 15, 85, 102, 128, 130, 132, 134–37,

139, 140, 147, 150, 177, 178, 183, 187–91, 193, 195, 198, 199, 206, 211–13, 217, 218, 220, 229, 230, 239–41, 243, 249, 257, 258, 261, 262, 268, 275, 277, 281, 284

PNC Bank, 58, 59

podcasts, 66, 73, 91, 105, 123, 135, 183, 189, 236, 241, 296

POD Network. *See* Professional and Organizational Development (POD) Network

point-of-need alternatives, 118

policies, 1, 19, 20, 29, 36, 41, 45, 51, 57, 59, 60, 64, 67, 205, 207–9, 218, 244, 246, 252, 257, 262, 263, 266, 267, 297, 301

politics, 79, 171, 175, 206

portfolios, 167

postsecondary education, 27, 37, 143, 186, 190, 288, 290, 292, 294, 298, 299, 301, 303

PowerPoint, 85, 87, 110, 132, 133, 177, 200, 222, 230, 234, 235, 240, 241

preferences, 23, 36, 96, 113, 175, 178, 183, 196, 211

principles, 5, 8, 9, 11–13, 20, 22–25, 27–30, 34, 43, 46, 49, 54, 55, 59, 61, 63, 74, 92, 96, 101, 106, 109, 116, 119, 120, 124, 126, 139, 145, 147, 152, 158, 175, 177, 178, 180, 203, 205, 210–12, 217, 220, 223, 227, 242, 245, 246, 249, 252, 263, 267, 271–73, 276, 288, 289, 291, 293, 295, 297, 302, 303

proctoring, 32

Professional and Organizational Development (POD) Network, 206, 208, 211, 296, 299, 301

professors, 1, 15, 65, 69, 73, 74, 87, 92, 93, 100, 126, 132, 137, 139, 142, 159, 187, 190, 199, 238, 246, 247, 275, 280
projects, 8, 11, 13, 19, 29, 37–39, 54, 64, 86, 115, 117, 123, 126, 146, 159, 162, 183, 189–93, 195, 196, 200, 208, 213, 222, 241, 247, 248, 254, 261, 278, 280, 283, 297
provosts, 2, 15, 19, 20, 69, 163, 167, 205, 206, 208, 222, 247, 251, 252, 261, 266, 270, 271, 279
psychology, 68, 132–35, 139
Punnett squares, 109
purchasing processes, 20, 59, 107, 208

Qualtrough, Carla, 295
Quarterly Review of Distance Education, 301
questions, 10, 12, 20, 21, 25, 27, 29, 43, 67, 69, 78, 85, 86, 108, 109, 113, 118, 120, 122, 124, 134, 135, 139, 151, 153, 156, 164, 172, 178, 180–83, 186, 188–91, 222, 226, 229, 236, 238, 239, 244, 245, 249, 250, 253, 263, 264, 268, 277–79
QuickTime, 235
quizzes, 61, 87, 109, 113, 187, 194, 195, 200, 201, 226, 229, 232

Rapp, Whitney, 7, 299
ratings, 12, 33, 61, 150, 210, 222, 247, 281
RealPlayer, 235
real-time communication technologies, 124, 255
real-time interactions, 89, 212
reasonable accommodations, 45, 288, 303
Reavis, G., 57, 299

recognition networks, 129
recording course materials, 111–13, 128, 194
redesign, 116, 126, 138, 143, 151, 154, 200, 208, 213, 253
referrals, 8, 27, 33, 39, 45, 50, 156, 170, 252, 261, 270
reflection, 11, 26, 159, 171, 196, 200, 208–10, 218, 255
reframing, 5, 6, 9–11, 56, 65, 66, 68, 71, 90, 95, 134, 148, 150, 169, 170, 194, 230, 239, 250, 252, 257, 259, 265, 267, 281, 285
registrar, 2, 8, 15, 69, 106, 118–20, 250–52, 278
Rehabilitation Act, 22, 44, 49, 50, 52, 56, 203, 244, 299
See also Section 504, Section 508
Reitman, I., 168, 299
repetition, 38, 64, 108, 134, 147, 165, 166, 192, 195, 240, 275, 277
representation, 29, 94, 129
requirements, 1, 10, 25, 34, 37, 44, 45, 48–50, 54, 56, 57, 63, 66, 68, 102, 111, 124, 132, 133, 135–38, 163, 167, 196, 208, 220, 231, 241, 250, 253, 256, 257, 263, 270
research studies, 3, 11, 146, 254, 261
re-teaching, 61, 109, 124, 132, 277
retention, 2, 8, 9, 11, 20, 33, 37, 82, 109, 125, 138, 159, 162, 206, 209, 210, 224, 246, 247, 249, 253, 268, 279, 280, 288, 291, 298, 300, 301
retrofitting, 64, 65, 102, 109, 133
rigor, 35, 178, 182, 199
risks, 45, 137, 150, 192, 292
Roberts, K. D., 37, 299, 302
Rojas, C., 136, 298

rubrics, 183, 184, 186, 190, 199,
201, 241, 245
Rumrill, P.D., 104, 291
Rutgers University, 267

Saarnivaara, M., 295
Sabino v. Ohio State University,
62, 300
Salem State University, 176
Salzinger, L., 302
satisfaction, 2, 9, 11, 20, 33, 37,
47, 86, 109, 125, 137, 138, 206,
207, 246, 253, 279, 280
scaffolding, 41, 186, 191–93, 213
Schelly, C. L., 84, 292
Schlesinger, Michael, 4
Schneider, W. J., 136, 300
Schwab, C., 300
Schwab, L. O., 293
Schweik, S., 302
screencasts, 93, 111, 112, 123
screen readers, 67, 103, 126, 170,
219, 229, 234, 236–38, 249,
251, 303
Seaman, J., 224, 287
secondary schools, 24–27, 34, 42,
65, 229, 293
Section 504, 22, 44, 49, 50, 141,
203, 299
See also Rehabilitation Act
Section 508, 22, 44, 50, 54, 56,
203, 244–46, 288, 299
See also Rehabilitation Act
Seilhamer, R., 290
self-assessment, 243
self-efficacy, 88, 96, 299
self-motivation, 222
self-paced tutorials, 33, 171, 238,
239
self-regulation, 112, 225, 241
senior leaders, 9, 20, 82, 150, 176,
205–8, 245, 266, 267, 270, 271,
279, 281
Sensus, 204, 300

settlements, 45, 46, 256, 257, 262,
289
Sherwood, K., 302
simulations, 92, 193, 194, 229
single-stream content, 110, 111,
140, 199, 260
Sitton, R., 57, 299
skills, 2, 6, 20, 23, 24, 35, 54, 79,
86, 92–95, 107, 108, 113, 117,
119, 123, 125, 134, 135, 137,
138, 140, 146, 148, 157, 169,
176, 178–80, 187, 189, 191–93,
197–99, 210, 211, 217, 220,
222, 225, 228, 277, 280, 291
Skype, 243
smartphones. *See under* phones
Snapchat, 89
social interactions, 24, 91
social justice, 207, 216, 255
social media, 88, 195, 254, 255
sociology, 78
software, 40, 45, 56, 58, 95, 107,
126, 170, 171, 194, 204, 220,
226, 235, 239, 245, 249, 250,
252, 258, 259, 293
Sonka, Kate, 19, 20, 41, 42, 300
Sorcinelli, M. D., 288
SoundCloud, 113
Sousa, T., 300
speaking, 26, 85, 97, 130, 182,
254
spectrum, 7, 30, 53, 65, 96, 131,
138, 160, 247
spreadsheets, 93, 233
staff development, 167, 208, 211
staff engagement, 218
staff meetings, 74
staff members, 2–4, 10, 11, 19,
20, 29–31, 33, 42, 46, 66, 68,
98, 102, 107, 118, 131, 148,
159, 161, 168, 171, 178, 198,
205, 206, 212, 217, 223, 229,
230, 249, 255, 258, 264, 266,
277, 281

stakeholders, 146, 151, 205
standards, 19, 34, 45, 47, 50, 53, 56, 59, 121, 176, 179, 228, 229, 233, 244, 245, 253, 270, 288, 299, 301
statistics, 74, 83, 88, 119, 120, 123, 169, 182, 280, 298, 300
stipends, 8
Strangman, N., 299
strategic goals, 216
strategic partnerships, 249–53
strategic plan, 155–57, 159, 160, 172, 206, 207
Straumsheim, C., 66, 67, 300, 301
streaming, 79
student activists, 264
student affairs, 8, 132, 148, 263, 264, 270
student athletics, 69
student body, 33, 37, 158, 160
student captioners, 205
student clubs, 255, 256
student engagement, 87, 131, 162, 295
student evaluation of courses, 12, 30–31, 61, 150, 210, 222, 281
student government, 69
student interactions, 29, 96, 139, 212
student life, 91, 148
student organizations, 255
student ratings, 12, 33, 61, 150, 210, 222, 247, 268
surveys, 26, 30, 84, 86, 87, 122–24, 187, 190, 191, 222, 236, 254, 287, 294, 295
syllabi, 7, 97, 111, 116, 120, 123, 157, 186, 195, 208, 231, 232, 272
system administrator, 197
systems, 2, 25, 56, 59, 87, 121, 125, 216, 219, 220, 226–28, 249, 252, 255, 262, 265, 303

tablets, 81, 87, 88, 92, 104, 106, 300
Tankersley, M., 104, 291
targets, 27, 56, 112, 119, 145, 171, 185, 205, 223, 261, 264, 277
tasks, 9, 35, 42, 63, 76, 97, 118, 134, 136, 155, 156, 180, 182, 187, 189, 207, 227, 280, 283
teachers, 24–27, 33, 34, 48, 54, 74, 86, 94, 105, 153, 168, 180, 208, 209, 287
teacher-training programs, 54
teaching, 1, 2, 10, 15, 20, 32, 33, 35, 39, 40, 42, 47, 54, 66, 74, 87, 90, 91, 93, 102, 106, 107, 128, 131, 132, 137, 139, 142, 148, 155, 162, 163, 167, 169, 170, 176, 183, 188, 190, 195, 197, 199, 206, 207, 209–11, 216–18, 231, 237, 240, 242, 244, 247, 248, 253, 261, 263, 268, 271, 272, 275, 276, 286, 288–91, 295, 297, 299, 301, 303
teams, 8, 12, 19, 20, 28, 37–39, 41, 64, 65, 68, 76, 98, 100, 106, 109, 123, 126, 130, 141, 143, 145–67, 170–72, 199, 204, 208, 211, 213, 216, 219, 220, 223, 237, 245, 247, 251, 253, 260, 261, 264, 266, 267, 269, 271, 272, 278, 279, 283
team-based approaches, 242
technologies, 2, 6–10, 12, 15, 19, 22, 24, 28, 29, 34, 36–38, 45, 46, 50, 52, 56, 59, 60, 75, 78–83, 85–88, 92, 94–98, 102–4, 106, 111, 112, 124, 129, 131, 140–42, 144, 148, 152, 170, 171, 176, 186, 194, 195, 210, 211, 213, 217, 219–23, 226, 230, 236, 240, 243–46, 250–52, 254, 256, 257, 259, 260, 262, 265, 270, 275, 279,

288, 289, 291, 296–99, 301, 303
telecommunications, 22, 302
teletype machines, 81
television, 14, 22, 62, 273, 293
templates, 107, 163, 208, 217, 257, 291
tenure, 1, 15, 69, 150, 162
tests, 3, 48, 56, 61, 95, 99, 103, 107, 109, 113, 122, 126, 134, 170, 177, 179, 183, 186, 199, 216, 226, 228, 241, 259, 260, 262, 277, 286
text-based materials, 106, 107, 110, 111, 113, 114, 116, 117, 122, 125, 129, 135, 136, 254
textbooks, 30, 43, 57, 60, 85, 131, 193, 194, 229, 231, 232, 236, 238, 261, 262
text-only materials, 110, 112, 116, 120, 123, 234, 240, 250
text-to-speech tools, 143, 144, 170, 204
therapists, 31, 193, 194, 261, 292
third-party tools, 20, 45, 68, 107, 205
timeline, 49, 59, 114, 146, 154, 155, 157, 221
Tobin, Thomas J., 7, 26, 114, 128, 135, 136, 138, 197, 211, 226, 253, 280, 285, 288, 294, 296, 300, 301, 312
touchpoints, 8, 256, 258
Trade Adjustment Assistance Community College and Career Training (TAACCCT), 49, 302
training, 5, 7–9, 13, 28, 29, 33, 34, 38, 40, 49, 52, 54, 60, 103, 143, 151, 167, 175, 176, 180, 203, 208, 211, 220–22, 230, 245, 247, 255, 256, 267, 271, 273, 292, 298, 302
Trammell, J., 32, 301

transcripts, 105, 107, 112, 128, 132–35, 137, 138, 196, 204, 229, 235, 250, 280
transformations, 75, 76, 220, 221, 286, 294, 295
Troutman, G. C., 295
Truong, M., 301
tutorials, 19, 41, 107, 171, 267
tutoring, 2, 8, 15, 44, 69, 106, 124, 152, 212, 222, 278
Tynjälä, M.-L., 295

UCD (Universal Course Design), 28, 29, 37–39
UDE (Universal Design in Education), 29
UDI (Universal Design for Instruction), 29, 290
UDL-IRN (Universal Design for Learning Implementation and Research Network), 47, 288
undergraduate courses, 110, 175, 294
undergraduate students, 19, 32, 42, 68, 84, 86, 87, 125, 220, 289, 292, 298, 301
Universal Design for Learning (UDL), 2, 3, 5–15, 19–22, 24–43, 45–49, 54–56, 58, 59, 61–69, 71, 74, 75, 79, 80, 82–86, 88–96, 98, 100–106, 108–16, 118–21, 123–26, 128–67, 169–73, 176–80, 182, 183, 186–90, 193–201, 203, 205–13, 216, 217, 219, 220, 223–25, 227–31, 236, 237, 239–42, 244–49, 251–53, 255–76, 278–86, 288–90, 292, 294–99, 301
action-choices in, 117
agenda for, 116, 152–57, 163, 256
attitudes about, 30, 74, 104, 287, 288, 291, 293, 297, 298

Universal Design for Learning
(*continued*)
empowering faculty and
institutions to adopt, 236,
264, 273
empowering students through
use of, 42, 199
faculty adoption of, 300
faculty advocacy for, 228
faculty attitudes about, 104
faculty expectations for, 242
framing UDL as value neutral
or positive, 6, 41, 65, 210
hands-on approach to, 33, 102,
147
implementation of, 8, 11, 28,
30–33, 35–37, 42, 44, 47, 50,
52, 54, 55, 57, 59, 63, 64, 69,
75, 99, 102, 107–9, 113, 116,
119, 127, 129, 131, 133, 140,
145, 146, 149, 152, 170, 172,
189, 196, 201, 211, 219, 245,
258, 262, 268, 272, 279, 288
low-tech strategies for, 84, 106,
114, 116
medical model of, 142, 176
methods of, 24, 25, 28, 43, 74,
85, 88, 92, 105, 107, 111, 113,
114, 130, 131, 134–37, 139,
141, 153, 159, 161, 163, 171,
178, 180, 182–84, 186, 187,
190, 191, 195, 198, 199, 202,
204, 212, 218, 221, 223, 237,
239, 241, 243, 250, 261, 262,
264, 278, 286, 294, 303
misperceptions of, 5, 34, 300
multiple means and, 2, 14, 25,
29, 33, 35, 62, 90, 105, 129,
137, 138, 176, 178, 181, 186,
187, 191, 194, 195, 197, 198,
211, 213, 216, 217, 220, 222,
228, 229

University of Arizona, 203
University of Calgary, 55
University of California,
Berkeley, 66, 67
University of Central Florida,
100
University of Cincinnati, 12, 13,
245, 270–73
University of Colorado Boulder,
139
University of Connecticut, 29,
186, 290
University of Dayton, 203–5
University of Hawaii, 29
University of Illinois, 4, 114
University of Iowa, 29
University of Massachusetts, 37,
169, 246, 247, 302
University of Massachusetts
Boston, 37, 169, 246, 247
University of Minnesota, 67,
289, 293
University of Montana, 45, 266
University of Nevada, Las
Vegas, 98
University of New Hampshire,
28, 31, 261, 262
University of Ohio, 256
University of South Dakota,
244, 245, 266, 267
University of South Florida, 30
University of Vermont, 303
University of Washington, 29,
186, 289
University of West Georgia, 289
University of Wisconsin, 28, 291
uploads, 112, 128, 296, 299, 300
usability, 28, 99, 126, 230, 236,
239, 254, 255, 258–62, 298,
302
user experience, 23, 119, 126,
254, 259, 293, 298, 302

valence, 3, 5, 65, 74, 75, 82
validity, 35, 257
Vanderbilt, T., 302
variability, 24, 25, 30, 33, 35, 42,
    56, 58, 65, 67, 79, 125, 131,
    141, 145, 146, 176, 178, 182,
    187–89, 197, 213, 223, 225,
    228, 229, 239, 242, 247, 252,
    259, 279
vendors, 68, 208, 257, 258, 262,
    263, 266
versions, 27, 73, 74, 112, 117, 128,
    129, 198, 213, 232, 234, 240,
    281, 283, 290
videos, 4, 7, 30, 31, 40, 43, 56, 66,
    68, 73, 74, 79, 91, 93, 95, 98,
    100, 104–7, 110–12, 114, 115,
    117, 118, 122–25, 128–35, 137,
    138, 141, 142, 164–66, 177,
    178, 182–84, 186, 189–96, 199,
    200, 202, 204, 205, 217, 229,
    235, 240, 241, 254, 257, 261,
    262, 270, 277, 280, 296, 299
videographer, 261
video-only path, 120
video-proctored exams, 187

W3C, 56, 303
Wakefield, J., 278, 297, 298, 303
Wang, M., 224, 303
Watson, L., 303
Wayne State University, 206, 207

WCAG (Web Content
    Accessibility Group), 45, 56,
    59, 244, 253, 270, 303
web content, 13, 45, 56, 58, 59,
    99, 102, 137, 235, 236, 237,
    244, 253–55, 270–71
WebAIM, 203
webinar, 91, 299, 301
WebPagesThatSuck.com, 99, 293
What You See Is All There Is
    (WYSIATI) bias, 168, 169
wheelchairs, 1, 3, 21, 264
Wikipedia, 75, 196
Wilson, M., 225, 303
workarounds, 258
workflows, 20, 205
workforce, 52, 54
workload, 35, 149, 206, 210, 237
workplaces, 55, 86
worksheets, 105, 122, 123, 127,
    139, 200, 201, 231, 233, 269
workshops, 33, 38, 66, 128, 153,
    163, 168–71, 178, 189, 203,
    208–11, 216, 245, 255, 264,
    266, 267, 272, 277, 279
Wren, C., 7, 104, 297, 298

Yager, Susan, 130–32, 303
Yates, N., 301

Zhang, D., 3, 104, 303
Zou, J. J., 228, 303

ABOUT THE AUTHORS

THOMAS J. TOBIN is a faculty associate on the Learning Design, Development, & Innovation (LDDI) team at the University of Wisconsin–Madison. Before joining UW–Madison, Tobin spent seven years in the learning and development arm of Blue Cross and Blue Shield of Illinois, and then served for five years as the coordinator of learning technologies in the Center for Teaching and Learning (CTL) at Northeastern Illinois University in Chicago. He earned his Ph.D. in English literature from Duquesne University in 2000, a second master's degree in library science in 2002, the Project Management Professional certification in 2010, the Master Online Teacher certification from the University of Illinois in 2016, and the Quality Matters Peer Reviewer certification in 2017. He was proud to represent the United States on a Spring 2018 Fulbright core grant to help Eötvös Loránd University in Budapest create its first faculty development center. He tells his nieces and nephews that (as of press time) he is in the fortieth grade.

Tom is an internationally recognized speaker and author on topics related to quality in distance education, especially copyright, evaluation of teaching practice, academic integrity, accessibility, and Universal Design for Learning. Since the advent of online courses in higher education in the late 1990s, Tom's work has focused on using technology to extend the reach of higher education beyond its traditional audience. He advocates for the educational rights of people with disabilities and people from disadvantaged backgrounds.

Tom serves on the editorial boards of *eLearn Magazine*, *InSight: A Journal of Scholarly Teaching*, the *Journal of Interactive Online Learning*, and the *Online Journal of Distance Learning Administration*. His most recent book is *Evaluating Online Teaching: Implementing Best Practices* (2015) with Jean Mandernach and Ann H. Taylor. *The Copyright Ninja* comic book (2017) teaches college and university faculty members, support staff, and campus leaders about copyright, fair use, licensing, and permissions. Plus, it has ninjas.

About the Authors

KIRSTEN BEHLING is the director of student accessibility services at Tufts University and an adjunct professor at Suffolk University, teaching in the disability services certificate program. Kirsten earned her master's degree in sociology with a focus on inclusive education from Boston University in 2002. Kirsten began her work in higher education at the University of New Hampshire's Institute on Disability, a University Center for Excellence on Disability. While at UNH, Kirsten co-directed a U.S. Department of Education Office of Postsecondary Education (OPE) grant focused on bringing reflective practice to faculty members teaching students with disabilities. Kirsten then relocated to the Institute for Community Inclusion at the University of Massachusetts Boston, where she wrote and received two federal grants aimed at bringing the concept of Universal Design for Learning into higher education.

After spending nearly seven years traveling throughout New England supporting colleges and universities in their efforts to implement UDL, Kirsten assumed the role of director of the Office of Disability Services, a newly developed office, at Suffolk University. Her goal was to increase her awareness of how to implement best practices around inclusive education while studying the programmatic make-up of an institution. Kirsten spent eight years at Suffolk developing the Office of Disability Services and initiating a change across the university in how students with disabilities are supported.

Kirsten taught for three years at the University of Connecticut in the Neag School of Education's online certificate program in postsecondary disability services. Recently, Kirsten co-developed a new graduate certificate in disability services in higher education at Suffolk University. Kirsten currently develops courses for this program and teaches online.

Kirsten is also heavily involved in New England AHEAD, a regional affiliate of the Association on Higher Education and Disability (AHEAD). She spent six years as the president of the organization and currently serves on the board of directors. Her research interests, publications, and speaking engagements center on campuswide buy-in around access needs, access in online learning, teaching the diverse learner, and educating current and future disability service professionals.

325

CPSIA information can be obtained
at www.ICGtesting.com
Printed in the USA
FFHW010303200519
52513741-57963FF